London
2013

WHAT'S NEW | WHAT'S ON | WHAT'S BEST

www.timeout.com/london

Contents

Published by Time Out Guides Ltd
Universal House
251 Tottenham Court Road
London W1T 7AB
Tel: + 44 (0)20 7813 3000
Fax: + 44 (0)20 7813 6001
Email: guides@timeout.com
www.timeout.com

Editorial Director Sarah Guy
Management Accountants Clare Turner, Margaret Wright

Time Out Guides is a wholly owned subsidiary of Time Out Group Ltd.

© Time Out Group Ltd
Director & Founder Tony Elliott
Chief Executive Officer David King
Chief Operating Officer Aksel Van der Wal
Editor in Chief Tim Arthur
Group Financial Director Paul Rakkar
UK Chief Commercial Officer David Pepper
Time Out International Ltd MD Cathy Runciman

Time Out and the Time Out logo are trademarks of Time Out Group Ltd.

This edition first published in Great Britain in 2012 by Ebury Publishing
A Random House Group Company
Company information can be found on www.randomhouse.co.uk
Random House UK Limited Reg. No. 954009
10 9 8 7 6 5 4 3 2 1

Distributed in the US and Latin America by Publishers Group West (1-510-809-3700)

For further distribution details, see www.timeout.com

ISBN: 978-1-84670-272-3

A CIP catalogue record for this book is available from the British Library.

Printed and bound in Germany by Appl.

The Random House Group Limited supports The Forest Stewardship Council (FSC®), the leading international forest certification organisation. Our books carrying the FSC label are printed on FSC® certified paper. FSC is the only forest certification scheme endorsed by the leading environmental organisations, including Greenpeace. Our paper procurement policy can be found on www.randomhouse.co.uk/environment .

Time Out carbon-offsets all its flights with Trees for Cities (www.treesforcities.org).

MIX
Paper from
responsible sources
FSC™ C004592

London Shortlist

The **Time Out London Shortlist 2013** is one of a series of annual guides that draws on Time Out's background as a magazine publisher to keep you current with everything that's going on in town. As well as London's key sights and the best of its eating, drinking and leisure options, it picks out the most exciting venues to have opened in the last year and gives a full calendar of events running from September 2012 to December 2013. It also includes features on the important news, trends and openings, all compiled by locally based editors and writers. Whether you're visiting for the first time in your life or the first time this year, you'll find the *Time Out London Shortlist* contains all you need to know, in a portable, easy-to-use format.

The guide divides central London into six areas, each containing listings for Sights & Museums, Eating & Drinking, Shopping, Nightlife and Arts & Leisure, and maps pinpointing their locations. At the front of the book are chapters rounding up these scenes city-wide, and giving a shortlist of our overall picks. We also include itineraries for days out, plus essentials such as transport information and hotels.

Our listings give phone numbers as dialled in London. To dial them from elsewhere in the UK, preface them with 020. From abroad, use your country's exit code followed by 44 (the country code for the UK), 20 and the number given.

We have noted price categories by using one to four pound signs (**£-££££**), representing budget, moderate, expensive and luxury. Major credit cards are accepted unless otherwise stated. We also indicate when a venue is NEW, and give **Event highlights**.

All our listings are double-checked, but places do sometimes close or change their hours or prices, so it's a good idea to call a venue before visiting. While every effort has been made to ensure accuracy, the publishers cannot accept responsibility for any errors that this guide may contain.

Venues are marked on the maps using symbols numbered according to their order within the chapter and colour-coded as follows:

❶ Sights & Museums
❶ Eating & Drinking
❶ Shopping
❶ Nightlife
❶ Arts & Leisure

Map key	
Major sight or landmark	
Railway or coach station	
Underground station	⊖
Park	
Hospital	
Casualty unit	✚
Church	✚
Synagogue	✡
District . . . . MAYFAIR	
Theatre	●

Time Out **London** Shortlist 2013

EDITORIAL
Editor Ros Sales
Researcher Christian Kingston
Proofreader Anna Norman

DESIGN
Senior Designer Kei Ishimaru
Guides Commercial Senior Designer
Jason Tansley

Picture Editor Jael Marschner
Picture Researcher Ben Rowe

ADVERTISING
Sales Director St John Betteridge

Account Manager Bobbie Kelsall-Freeman,
The Media Sales House

MARKETING
Senior Publishing Brand Manager
Luthfa Begum
Group Commercial Art Director
Anthony Huggins
Circulation & Distribution Manager
Dan Collins

PRODUCTION
Group Production Manager
Brendan McKeown
Production Controller
Katie Mulhern-Bhudia

CONTRIBUTORS
This guide was researched and written by Ros Sales, Simon Coppock, Guy Dimond,
Anna Norman, Sara O'Reilly, Kate Hutchinson and the writers of *Time Out London*
and *Time Out* magazine.

PHOTOGRAPHY
pages 7, 89 (top), 170, 173, 177 Jonathan Perugia; 8/9 Andrew Chambers/
Shutterstock.com; 11, 16, 45 (bottom), 89 (bottom), 145 Scott Wishart; 13 (top)
Rama Knight/Wellcome Images; 13 (bottom) Julie Cockburn 2005/Wellcome Images;
15, 18, 19, 24, 25, 93, 153, 164, 166 Rob Greig; 21, 55, 102 Ed Marshall; 26
Marc de Groot; 29, 54, 57, 90, 98, 117, 156, 181 Ben Rowe; 31 Manuel Harlan/
RSC; 34, 125, 137, 142, 163 (right and bottom) Michelle Grant; 36 Jon Enoch; 37
James O Jenkins; 41 (left), 82 Heloise Bergman; 41 (right) Martyn J Brooks; 42 Alison
Henley/Shutterstock.com; 43 Doug Douthall; 44 Benjamin Eagle; 45 (top) Nick Ballon;
47 QQ7/Shutterstock.com; 48 Len Green/Shutterstock.com; 49 Paolo Gianti;
51 Lee Mawdsley; 52 Dan Breckwoldt; 58 Cris Tapper; 63 Richard Bowden; 66
www.jasonhawkes.com; 71 Michael Franke; 74, 84, 110, 120, 126 Britta Jaschinski;
77 R Nagy; 78 Thomas Riggs; 107 Olivia Rutherford; 131 Eva Barton; 134 David Parry;
149 Justin Black; 160 Ralph Hodgson; 163 Tove K Breitstein; 184 Cutty Sark Trust;
190 aislin; 192 Elisabeth Blanchet; 193 Emma Wood; 194 W London; 200 Niall
Clutton; 203 The Dorchester; 205 St Pancras Renaissance; 208 Chris Tubbs.

Cover photograph: Tower Bridge by Gavin Hellier.

MAPS
JS Graphics (john@jsgraphics.co.uk).

About **Time Out**

Founded in 1968, Time Out has expanded from humble London beginnings into the
leading resource for those wanting to know what's happening in the world's greatest
cities. As well as our influential what's-on weeklies in London, New York and Chicago,
we publish nearly 30 other listings magazines in cities as varied as Beijing and
Mumbai. The magazines established Time Out's trademark style: sharp writing,
informed reviewing and bang up-to-date inside knowledge of every scene.

Time Out made the natural leap into travel guides in the 1980s with the City Guide
series, which now extends to over 50 destinations around the world. Written and
researched by expert local writers and generously illustrated with original photography,
the full-size guides cover a larger area than our Shortlist guides and include many more
venue reviews, along with additional background features and a full set of maps.

Throughout this rapid growth, the company has remained proudly independent, still
owned by Tony Elliott four decades after he started Time Out London as a single fold-
out sheet of A5 paper. This independence extends to the editorial content of all our
publications, this Shortlist included. No establishment has been featured because it
has advertised, and no payment has influenced any of our reviews. And, for our critics,
there's definitely no such thing as a free lunch: all bars and restaurants are visited and
reviewed anonymously, and Time Out always picks up the bill.

For more about the company, see www.timeout.com.

Don't Miss 2013

London Eye

Sights & Museums

London has some amazing sights. We're blessed with no fewer than four UNESCO World Heritage Sites: the **Tower of London** (p162), the cluster of fine buildings round Parliament Square in **Westminster** (pp74-80), soothing **Kew Gardens** (p191) and, above all, the numerous attractions in **Greenwich** (pp185-187). **Discover Greenwich** has been doing a superb job of pulling the disparate Greenwich sites together since it opened in 2010, and the opening of the renovated **Cutty Sark** tea clipper (see box p184) and new Sammy Ofer Wing of the **National Maritime Museum** (p186) were perfectly timed to entertain spectators after the London 2012 Equestrian events in Greenwich Park. An ambitious plan to link the Greenwich Peninsula

to the Royal Docks business hub with a cross-river **cable car** (p185), to go into service after the 2012 Games, is likely to help shift the sightseeing map of London eastwards, while the reopening as London Overground of train lines that will form an orbital route round the city has been immensely useful.

In addition to the reopening of the *Cutty Sark*, other recently completed projects include **Kensington Palace** (see box p93), the first stage of the restoration and expansion of the **Sir John Soane's Museum** (see box p160) and the pod-by pod refurbishment of the **London Eye** (p62). Other projects – the expansion of the **British Museum** (p119) and **Tate Modern** (p67), interior redevelopment of **Tate Britain** (p79) and the Triforium Galleries

SHORTLIST

Best new
- The Emirates Air Line cable car (p185)
- Kensington Palace transformed (p93)
- Expansion at the Sir John Soane Museum (p160)

Most welcome returns
- Cutty Sark (p184)
- Grant Museum of Zoology (p121)

Best views
- London Eye (p2)
- Monument (p161)
- Top deck of a Heritage Routemaster bus (p78)

Finest free attractions
- British Museum (p119)
- Museum of London (p161)
- National Gallery (p76)
- Victoria & Albert Museum (p85)

Unsung museums
- Old Operating Theatre, Museum & Herb Garret (p65)
- Petrie Museum (p121)
- Wellcome Collection (p124)

Best late events
- Science Museum (p85)
- Sir John Soane's Museum by candlelight (p160)
- Tate Britain (p79)
- Victoria & Albert Museum (p85)

Best outdoor
- Swimming in the ponds on Hampstead Heath (p190)
- Royal Botanic Gardens, Kew (p91)
- Watching the pelicans in St James's Park (p81)

at **Westminster Abbey** (p79) – were still in progress at the time of writing. The **Imperial War Museum** (p62) is closing its doors for the first half of 2013 for a major refurbishment, reopening in July. After the £35-million redesign, the entire lower ground floor will be devoted to the Great War, in time for the centenary of its outbreak.

The **South Bank** remains London's key tourist destination. The principal attractions are well established: Tate Modern, **Shakespeare's Globe** (p65) and **Borough Market** (p70), the lively **Southbank Centre** (p73), the **Sea Life London Aquarium** (p65) and the newly refurbished London Eye. Do take the time also to explore minor highlights such as the **Garden Museum** (p59) and **Topolski Century** mural (p67).

Across the river, the **City** authorities have been making a concerted effort to alter the reputation of the most ancient part of London as a place for bank workers rather than

Before your book your **London hotel,** check out the **LondonHotelMap™** at LondonTown.com

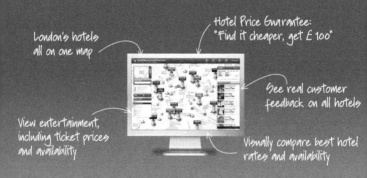

Hotel Price Guarantee:
"Find it cheaper, get £ 100"

London's hotels
all on one map

See real customer
feedback on all hotels

View entertainment,
including ticket prices
and availability

Visually compare best hotel
rates and availability

www.londontown.com/hotels

pleasure-seekers. It's been a pretty easy sell, given the number of historic attractions – the Tower of London and **St Paul's** (p162) are only the best known – and easy access from the South Bank over the Millennium Bridge. St Paul's and the **Monument** (p161) have been vividly refurbished, and the **Museum of London** (p161) is approaching its rightful place in locals' affections with four amazing new galleries, inviting street-level windows (through which you can see the Lord Mayor's golden coach) and a revitalised events programme.

The other London essentials are South Kensington and Bloomsbury. In **South Kensington**, the Medieval & Renaissance Galleries at the lovely **V&A** (p85) have been a huge hit, propelling this superb Victorian mansion up the visitors' lists. The **Natural History Museum** (p85) has an ultra-modern white Cocoon, and the neighbouring **Science Museum** (p85) has been following a steady programme of new openings, with the up-to-the-minute, all-bells-and-whistles Atmosphere gallery for climate change and an old-fashioned reconstruction of James Watt's attic workshop. In **Bloomsbury**, half a dozen new rooms had been completed at the world-class **British Museum** (p119) before work on the north-west extension even began. To the north, the ancient Egyptiana at the **Petrie** (p121) and the ghoulish animal remains at the **Grant Museum of Zoology** (p121) are tiny but atmospheric treats, while the **Wellcome Collection** (p124) by Euston station has carved itself a special niche for arresting themed exhibitions, often drawing together cutting-edge science and unusual or underground art.

North-east of Bloomsbury, **King's Cross** is becoming a major European transport hub.

St Paul's

The restored **St Pancras International** (p123) was the key arrival, but neighbouring King's Cross now has a stunning new western concourse and is to lose its unattractive 1970s frontage, creating a new public square. The gaping badlands to the north are being transformed into a mixed-use nucleus called **King's Cross Central**, with the University of Arts London now in residence. Other places to explore here are the new **King's Place** arts complex (see box p125) and the **London Canal Museum** (p123).

The other 'new' area of London worth exploring is the **Olympic Park** (p183). Following the Games, the first section of the Park will reopen in July 2013. It will retain some features from the Games, including the Olympic Stadium, but landscaping and rebuilding is set to create a new residential, cultural and leisure hub for east London.

Fans of art are especially well catered for in London these days. It isn't just the superstars – Tate Modern, Tate Britain, the **National Gallery** (p76) – that keep our visual culture vibrant: visitors can check out unabashedly modern work at east London's **Whitechapel** (p182), and the constellation of private galleries that cluster in Shoreditch and north into Hackney, as well as at the **Saatchi** (p95) in Chelsea. Not at all contemporary is the **Courtauld** (p149), which enjoyed a gentle rehang in summer 2011.

The key problem with a visit to London remains what it's always been: how do you do it all? The answer is simple: you can't… not in a single trip, not in a single lifetime. So relax, do whatever you fancy and – if you've only a couple of days of holiday – consider following our two-day **itinerary** (pp52-53).

Wellcome Collection p12

Doing the geography

This book is divided by area. The **South Bank** primarily covers riverside Bankside, home of Tate Modern, and the revamped Southbank Centre. Over the river, **Westminster & St James's** cover the centre of UK politics, while the impressive Victorian museums of **South Kensington**, the Knightsbridge department stores, and the boutiques and eateries of **Chelsea** lie to the west.

The **West End** includes most of what is now central London. We start north of unlovely Oxford Street, in the elegant, slightly raffish shopping district of **Marylebone**. South, between Marylebone and St James's, is **Mayfair**, as expensive as its reputation but less daunting, with fine mews and pubs. Eastward are **Fitzrovia**, its elegant streets speckled with inviting shops and restaurants; the squares and Georgian terraces of literary **Bloomsbury**, home of academia and the British Museum; and up-and-coming **King's Cross**. Head south for **Covent Garden**, so popular with tourists that locals often forget about the charms of its boutique shopping, and **Soho**, formerly notorious centre of fun.

The **City** comprises the once-walled Square Mile of the original city, now adjoined by the focal area for bars and clubs, **Shoreditch**; **Holborn & Clerkenwell** have wonderful food.

Around these central districts neighbourhood London has clusters of fine restaurants, bars and clubs, servicing mainly residential zones, while further London must-sees are worth a day-trip: among them, gorgeous **Kew Gardens** (p191) and grand **Hampton Court Palace** (p190).

Making the most of it

Don't be scared of London's public transport: it's by far the best way of getting around town. Invest in an **Oyster travel smartcard** (p213) and roam cashless through the city by bus, tube (underground trains) and train. The excellent London Overground – considered part of the underground network when it comes to ticketing – is developing into a handy rail orbital and already a neat north–south link across the river on the east of town, running right through Shoreditch.

The tube is the easiest mode of transport for newbies, but buses are best to get a handle on the city's topography. Some good sightseeing routes are RV1 (riverside), 7, 8 and 12, but hop on a **Routemaster Heritage bus** (p76) to enjoy a ride on a classic red double-decker.

Crime in central London is low, so walk whenever you can to get a feel for the character of different areas of the city. No one thinks any the less of someone consulting a map – so long as they dive out of the stream of pedestrian traffic while doing so. And, despite Londoners' not entirely undeserved reputation for being sullen and unhelpful, most of us are quietly delighted to show off the breadth of our local knowledge by assisting with directions.

To avoid the worst of the crowds, avoid big attractions at weekends and on late-opening nights, and aim to hit blockbuster exhibitions in the middle of a run; January to March are the quietest months for visiting attractions, July to September the busiest. Last entry can be up to an hour before closing time (we specify when it is more than an hour before), so don't turn up at the last minute and expect to get in. Some sights close at Christmas and Easter – ring ahead to confirm opening hours.

10 Greek Street

Eating & Drinking

The last few years have been hard for London's restaurateurs, with the country's fragile economy ensuring there's been no shortage of restaurant closures. Even so, new openings continue apace.

Notable newcomers at the high end include **Dabbous** (p116), serving outstanding food that's best described as 'Modernist', from chef-proprietor Ollie Dabbous. **Dinner by Heston Blumenthal** (p92) successfully takes inspiration from British cultural history. And Jason Atherton has won plaudits for his pretty, daring and tiny dishes (you'll need to order a few) at **Pollen Street Social** (p109).

No bookings taken

There's a growing trend for quality dining at the lower end of the scale, demonstrated by the recent flurry of openings of places that don't take bookings: diners have shown themselves willing to eschew this luxury and instead queue to enjoy good food at good prices at new restaurants like **Burger & Lobster** (p106), **Pitt Cue Co** (p135) and **10 Greek Street** (p130).

Eats & attractions

Over the last decade, London's museums and galleries have begun to look beyond the sandwich to provide visitors with quality food. The **National Dining Rooms** (p80) has long led the field (and the pricing if you stray from the set lunch), but **Gallery Mess** (p95) at the Saatchi Gallery and **Restaurant at St Paul's** (p165) are both also fine eateries in their own right.

Dabbous p15

Hot zones

These days you can eat well all over London, but our favourite restaurants still seem to cluster around Soho and Clerkenwell.

In the heart of Soho, **Hix** (p132), **Polpo** (p135) and **Arbutus** (p130) are reliably excellent (and, in the case of Arbutus, competitively priced), but among numerous appealing new arrivals are New York diner **Spuntino** (p135), American restaurant **Pitt Cue Co**, and the buzzy **10 Greek Street**.

In Clerkenwell, Anna Hansen – one of the original co-owners of Marylebone's Providores & Tapa Room – has quietly jolted the tired concept of 'fusion food' out of its torpor at **Modern Pantry** (p157), and Exmouth Market has been rediscovering that foodie is fun with long-term Moorish favourite **Moro** opening a nicely relaxed new version next door: 'little Moro' or **Morito** (p157). **St John** (p157) is just down the road: this restaurant was the game-changer in modern British cooking in the 1990s and continues to serve brilliantly simple, classic combinations of gutsy, carefully sourced ingredients. A third outpost, this with bedrooms too, opened in early 2011 in the West End (p135).

Towards Covent Garden, we're still loving Paul Merrony's **Giaconda Dining Room** (p143), amid the guitar shops of London's 'Tin Pan Alley', and **Great Queen Street** (p143), but the area has had a real restaurant revival over the last year: steakhouse **Hawksmoor Seven Dials** (p143), classy Indian café **Dishoom** (p141) and tapas venue **Opera Tavern** (p144) have become instant favourites. In Aldwych, new opening **Delaunay** (p155) is a brasserie in the European grand café tradition.

SHORTLIST

Best new restaurants
- 10 Greek Street (see p130)
- Dabbous (p116)
- Delaunay (p155)

Best no-bookings restaurants
- 10 Greek Street (p130)
- Burger & Lobster (p106)
- Pitt Cue Co (p135)

Best of British
- Albion (p176)
- Hereford Road (p188)
- St John (p157)

Best food in galleries
- National Gallery Dining Rooms (p80)
- Gallery Mess (p95)

Best drop-in nosh
- Hummus Bros (p122)
- Princi (p135)

Best coffee
- Espresso Room (p121)
- Prufrock Coffee (p157)

Best ice-cream
- Icecreamists (p143)
- Scoop (p144)

Best gastropubs
- Anchor & Hope (p68)
- Eagle (p155)

Best pubs
- Euston Tap (p124)
- Ye Olde Mitre (p158)

Best for wine
- Terroirs (p146)
- Vinoteca (p158)

Best cocktails
- Book Club (p167)
- Experimental Cocktail Club (p132)

Burger & Lobster p15

Brit bites

Following the lead set by St John, Brit bites continue to be very much in vogue. **Hereford Road** (p188) is a great exponent at the upper end of the scale, while **Clerkenwell Kitchen** (p155) is a leader in terms of support for traditional farming. The British nostalgia trend is exemplified at Sir Terence Conran's Boundary Project by **Albion** (p176), a casual ground-floor café that serves unpretentious, nostalgic dishes, from kedgeree to welsh rarebit. Not far away, by Spitalfields Market, **Poppies** (p176) is a fun new retro setting for fish and chips, produced by a fryer who learnt his trade in the 1950s on the Roman Road – proper East End, in other words.

Ethnic eats

Against the backdrop of all this Britishness, it's pleasing that ethnic eateries flourish. Everyone says it – and we really believe it's true: the whole world's food can be found here. Recent years have seen more sophisticated takes on Chinese cuisine, such as at **Barshu** (p130). Indian food is still strong – ranging from the haute cuisine of **Cinnamon Club** (p80) through Dishoom's take on the Irani café to cheap-and-cheerful chains such as **Masala Zone** (p171) – but you'll also find Koya's Japanese noodles in Soho, Middle Eastern just off Oxford Street at **Comptoir Libanais** (p101), brilliant Vietnamese at Shoreditch's **Song Que** (p176), authentic burritos at **Benito's Hat** (p113) and great tapas all over the place.

Drinking it all in

London's top-end cocktail venues are drawing the capital's drinking scene ever closer to the quality of New York or Sydney – **Mark's Bar** (p132) has been joined by the **Experimental Cocktail Club** (p132) in Soho, for example – but variety is the key. Shoreditch is home to both the events-driven **Book Club** (p167) and the crazy back room of **Callooh Callay** (p168). Covent Garden has the 'natural' wines of **Terroirs** (p146). **69 Colebrooke Row** (p174) and **Zetter Townhouse** (p158) serve inventive cocktails. There's also a notable revival in venues for great beer: **Euston Tap** (p124) is just one.

Gastropubs have contributed hugely to the revolution in modern

British dining, their ambition to turn out top nosh in relaxed surroundings becoming an enduring part of the city's culinary repertoire, despite pale imitations. Old favourites include the **Anchor & Hope** (p68) and, widely accepted as the pioneer of the genre, the **Eagle** (p155).

Neighbourhood watch

The **South Bank**, close to foodie-magnet Borough Market (p70), offers plenty of quality chain options on the riverside – you should also check out Skylon (p73) for a drink with fantastic views – but **Soho**, in the West End just across the river, is probably the best place in London for eats, both cheap and chic: canteen-style Busaba Eathai (p101), Hummus Bros (p122) and Princi (p135) do a brisk trade near upmarket neighbours such as Bocca di Lupo (p130), Arbutus and Dehesa (p132). Also in the West End, **Covent Garden** remains a busy tourist trap, but some very decent options have emerged, from Mexican at Wahaca (p146) to tapas at the Opera Tavern. Expense-account eats are concentrated in **Mayfair**: top-name chefs here include Claude Bosi at Hibiscus (p108), while celebrity executive chefs populate

the posh hotel dining rooms. Further west, **Marylebone** is another foodie enclave, replete with top-notch delis, cafés and – on Sundays – a farmers' market. Superb options here include the formidable L'Autre Pied (p101) and café-style La Fromagerie (p103). Both **South Kensington** and **Chelsea** do expensive, special-occasion destinations, such as **Zuma** (p92) and **Nahm** (p94), though more affordable fare is available at **Haché** (p96). The **City** remains relatively poor for evening and weekend eats, but **Clerkenwell**, next door, is famously a culinary hotspot: from the Modern Pantry to the Eagle, St John and Moro, most London restaurant trends have been kicked off here. Shoreditch, just north-east of the City, is still the place for a top night out – the edgy bars have been joined by interesting restaurants, and are themselves beginning to head upmarket.

Hix p17

Apple Store p146

WHAT'S BEST
Shopping

In its celebration of both tradition and cutting-edge style, the recent revamp of **Liberty** (p136), captures just what's great about London's shopping scene. For each fashion-forward new opening and pop-up store – east London's **Redchurch Street** (p179) has been particularly lively over the last couple of years – you'll find a classic independent that's still going strong after centuries in operation (like umbrella specialists **James Smith & Sons**, p147).

Londoners are unstoppable shoppers. They've been battered by the recession, but the economic downturn underlined their tenacity: they're still out there trawling the city's markets and superluxe department stores, sniffing out the snips in London's flagship fashion outlets, tradition-soaked arcades and world-class boutiques.

We're even learning to love the shopping centre: at least when they combine good eating, quirky events and a mix of chains and higher-end fashion. The biggest of the bunch is the new **Westfield Stratford City** (p185), gateway to Olympic Park and Europe's largest urban mall. Other key players are **St Martin's Courtyard** (p147), **One New Change** (p167).

In the past couple of years, London's shopkeepers have fallen back on their creative instincts, thinking up increasingly wily ways to tempt in the customers. High-concept pop-up shops, packed with limited-edition products, appear and disappear across the capital each month; high-street outlets stock young design talent at budget prices; and department stores are refreshed and renewed.

Style city

London's design strength has long been its young upstarts: recent graduates firmly entrenched in the youth scene they create for. Most young Londoners mix vintage with high street, shopping in chain stores full of high-profile design collaborations at rock-bottom prices (Japanese chain **Uniqlo**, p112; the indefatigable **Topshop**, p105). For the vintage side of the equation, Shoreditch still does the maths. The likes of **Vintage Emporium** (p179) are exemplary but certainly not without local challengers. And Dalston, to the north, has headed into the fray with a new branch of **Beyond Retro** (p178). Heading elsewhere might take you upmarket (**Lucy in Disguise**, p136) or cheerfully downmarket (**Camden Market**, p172, still rewards rummaging).

To find something a little more unusual, get the lowdown on sample sales, pop-up shops and one-off events in *Time Out* magazine's weekly Shopping & Style section, or indulge Londoners' obsession with the concept store – try newcomers **Wolf & Badger** (p189) on Ledbury Road or edgy Dalston's **LN-CC** (p179). When money is no object, Mayfair's hallowed **Dover Street Market** (p111) is the city's most revered example.

It's worth checking out the well-established department stores: **Selfridges** (p105) and the newly revitalised **Liberty** are our long-term favourites, but even **Harrods** (p94) and **Harvey Nichols** (p94) are no longer bywords among locals for 'more money than sense'.

Luxury labels continue to open on **Mount Street** (p112), the historic pink-brick Mayfair road that is fast replacing Sloane Street as the 'in' place to shop: we would

SHORTLIST

Best new
- Westfield Stratford City (p185)

Best shopping streets
- Broadway Market (p178)
- Carnaby Street (p136)
- Lamb's Conduit Street (p122)
- Marylebone High Street (p105)
- Redchuch Street (p179)

Best department stores
- Harrods (p94)
- Liberty (p136)
- Selfridges (p105)

Best for technology
- Apple Store Covent Garden (p146)

Best books & music
- Foyles (p136)
- London Review Bookshop (p122)
- Rough Trade East (p179)

Best vintage
- Beyond Retro (p178)
- Lucy in Disguise (p136)
- Vintage Emporium (p179)

Cutting-edge concepts
- Dover Street Market (p111)
- LN-CC (p179)
- Wolf & Badger (p189)

Best markets
- Borough Market (p70)
- Camden Market p172)
- Columbia Road Market (p178)
- Portobello Road Market (p189)

Best London souvenirs
- London Transport Museum shop (p140)

Best old-style British
- Burlington Arcade (p111)
- James Smith & Sons (p147)

DON'T MISS: 2013

have loved to have been a fly on the wall at the gunsmith, antique galleries and traditional butcher when they first clapped eyes on goth-rock designer Rick Owens or the five-floor Lanvin flagship. At the other side of the blade, Redchurch Street is a primer in why Shoreditch remains the fashionista's first port of call.

Get cultural

In a city bursting with history, the steady closure of London's independent bookshops is sad, even incongruous. Still, you can browse travel literature in the Edwardian conservatory of Daunt Books on **Marylebone High Street** (p105) or the never-ending selection of new titles at **Foyles** (p136), which also has a fine café. Persephone Books on **Lamb's Conduit Street** (p122) and the **London Review Bookshop** (p122) are new London classics, while **Cecil Court** (p146) is an irrepressible old stager – long may the landlord stay benevolent.

Selfridges p23

Don't neglect the museum stores, either: the **London Transport Museum** (p140) and **Southbank Centre** (p73) led the way with strikingly designed gifts, but the renewed **Museum of London** (p161) and the **V&A** (p85) are also terrific for original items.

Record and CD shops have also taken a beating, but second-hand vinyl and CDs linger on **Berwick Street** (p136). Indie temple **Rough Trade East** (p179) now feels like it's been on Brick Lane forever, but **HMV** (p116) – last of the big beasts roaring on Oxford Street – seems rather isolated.

Markets valued

Neighbourhood markets remain the lifeblood of London shopping, but few are the domain of Cockney costermongers. Instead, you'll find fashion kids flashing new vintage sunglasses over a soy latte. **Borough Market** (p70) is superb for foodies (the more adventurous might prefer Maltby Street), but **Broadway Market** (p178) is well worth the trek into Hackney. Also in Hackney, flower market **Columbia Road** (p178) is a classic Sunday morning outing; try to get there before 11am, then follow Brick Lane down to **Old Spitalfields Market** (p179) and the nearby Sunday (Up)Market, which is great for fashion, crafts and vintage clobber. You'll be an expert in East End street-style by early afternoon.

London's most famous markets are also both going strong: despite ongoing major redevelopment, Camden's markets remain a major tourist attraction, and – if you can stomach the crowds – **Portobello Road Market** (p189) is terrific for antiques, bric-a-brac and, not to mention star-spotting.

Borough Market

Neighbourhood watch

Shopping in London can be exhausting, so limit the territory you cover in each outing, sticking to one or two earmarked areas at a time. **Regent Street** is home to the flagships of many mid-range high-street clothing ranges. For a taste of retail past, the area around **St James's Street** is full of anachronistic specialists, including London's oldest hatter and the royal shoemaker; **Savile Row** has been given a shake-up in recent years by a handful of tailoring upstarts. **Mayfair** – especially Conduit Street, Bond Streets Old and New, and now Mount Street – remains the domain of catwalk names.

To the north, it's best to hurry across heaving **Oxford Street** with its department stores and budget fashion. Duck instead into

pedestrianised Gees Court and St Christopher's Place – interconnecting alleyways lined with cafés and shops. Curving **Marylebone High Street** has excellent fashion, perfumeries, gourmet shops and chic design stores.

A couple of London's most celebrated streets have recently been lifted out of chain-dominated doldrums. **Carnaby Street** has been salvaged by an influx of quality youth-clothing brands and Kingly Court; the decline of the **King's Road** has been arrested with some hip new stores, taking cues from the Shop at Bluebird.

Similarly, **Covent Garden** can no longer be written off as a tourist trap. The area has been revitalised (see box p145). New flagships have opened up in the piazza, while, to the north-west, cobbled Floral Street and the offshoots from Seven Dials remain fertile boutique-browsing ground. Don't miss sweet little Neal's Yard, with its wholefood cafés and herbalist. A little further north, **Lamb's Conduit Street** crams in appealing indie shops.

Unless you're working the plastic in the designer salons of Sloane Street or plan to marvel at the art nouveau food halls of Harrods, there's little reason to linger in **Knightsbridge**. Instead, for deluxe designer labels without the crush of people, try **Notting Hill**, especially where Westbourne Grove meets Ledbury Road.

On the other side of town, **Brick Lane** (mostly around the Old Truman Brewery and, at its northern end, Redchurch Street) has a dynamic collection of offbeat clothing and homeware shops.

The boutiques of **Islington** are also worth having a nose around, along Upper Street and on former antiques haven Camden Passage.

XOYO

WHAT'S BEST
Nightlife

Years ago, many of London's most popular venues were large and centrally located. You could rely on them for a memorable, cutting-edge clubbing experience. But recent times have seen the closure of many of the capital's historic nightlife venues – the likes of Turnmills, the Cross and Matter. That wasn't the end of London nightlife – it's very much alive and kicking – but finding the clubs takes a little effort these days. Not least because the merry-go-round of parties sees no need to stick to one club. You can often stumble across the greatest nights bubbling out of pub clubs such as the **Lock Tavern** (p172), car parks and warehouse spaces such as **Corsica Studios** (p72), or makeshift clubs in restaurant basements and former shops in

Dalston, along Kingsland Road and Stoke Newington High Street.

Some big clubs have continued to thrive. In the railway arches behind the major tourist draws along the South Bank is **Cable** (p70). **Fabric** (p158) is still doing a roaring trade in leftfield electronic wiggery, while the **Ministry of Sound** (p72) has kept right on hauling in big-name DJs for marquee-sign nights… now beyond its 20th birthday.

Dalston

If recession forced some promoters out of business, it made the survivors get creative: hence the birth of Dalston (easily accessible on the new Overground) as London's centre of edgy nights out, a land where surreal bars used to open every week under Turkish cafés and in not massively altered former video shops. Even here licensing and opening hours have begun to become more formalised, with the much-loved but barely organised Bardens Boudoir, for example, reopening as **Nest** (p180). A hit ever since it opened, the **Dalston Superstore** (p180) is already a clubbing reference point in the area, as is the underground labyrinth of the **Alibi** (see box p177) and the divey **Shacklewell Arms** (see box p177), but there are still plenty of smaller dive bars – on Stoke Newington Road, you can try **Vogue Fabrics** (no.66) or the **Waiting Room** (no.175) – that keep the scene from ossifying.

Shoreditch

It's many years since Shoreditch was the watchword for clubbing cool, but it has seen a revival of sorts. Venues such as the **Book Club** (p167) continue to make a virtue of diverse programming, but the appearance of **XOYO** (p169) has seemed a bit more like the good old days: great music in an old-fashioned loft setting. One of the remaining fixtures from way back when, **Plastic People** (p169), has had a brush-up too.

Cabaret

Burlesque continues to bring out the kitsch and feathers, with many a regular club night adding a stripper, some twisted magic or a bit of surreal cabaret. The best nights are at the sweet supper club **Volupté** (p159), **RVT** (p187) and the **Bethnal Green Working Men's Club** (p180). The basement at the **Leicester Square Theatre** (p138) divides opinion (our cabaret critic likes it, one of our theatre critics doesn't), while the **Soho Theatre** (p139) attracts a young,

SHORTLIST

Best basements
- Alibi (p177)
- Dalston Superstore (p180)
- Nest (p180)

Best superclub
- Fabric (p158)

Best stadium gigs
- O2 Arena (p186)

Rockin' pub-clubs
- Nest (p180)
- Old Blue Last (p169)
- Paradise (p189)
- Proud (p172)
- Shacklewell Arms (p177)

Best for bands
- Koko (p172)
- Scala (p127)

Best leftfield dance action
- Plastic People (p169)
- XOYO (p169)

Best for jazz
- 100 Club (p118)
- Ronnie Scott's (p138)
- Vortex Jazz Club (p180)

For the outer limits
- Café Oto (p180)

Best comedy
- Comedy Store (p138)
- Soho Theatre (p139)

Best gay clubbing
- Dalston Superstore (p180)
- Fire (p187)

Best cabaret
- Bethnal Green Working Men's Club (p180)
- RVT (p187)
- Soho Theare (p139)
- Volupté (p159)

hip crowd and very effectively to the theatre/comedy/cabaret crossover scene.

Small stage, big music

London's music scene is defined by rampant diversity. On any night, you'll find death metal, folk whimsy and plangent griots on one or other of the city's many stages.

At the top of the tree, and the most popular concert venue for four successive years (in 2010 it sold 1.7m tickets), is the **O2 Arena** (p186). This enormodome has pretty much cornered the market for classic rock and retro gigs (from Led Zeppelin to Duran Duran), as well as booking pop stars (Britney to Barry Manilow).

Although club/gig mash-ups have taken up some of the slack, London's mid-size venues have suffered carnage over the last several years: **Koko** (p172) and the **Scala** (p127) are the pick of the survivors, and the roster at upmarket jazz classic **Ronnie Scott's** (p138) is much improved over the last couple of years, after a brief period of bland rebranding.

There's also plenty of microscene life. Camden and Shoreditch are thriving with guitar-heavy music bars like **Proud** (p172) and the **Old Blue Last** (p169), and Dalston shines bright on the cutting edge: the **Vortex Jazz Club** (p180) and **Café Oto** (p180) both have ridiculously diverse programmes. Even Oxford Street's redoubtable **100 Club** (p118) has managed to stay afloat.

Gay disco

Despite the influx of straight ravers to some club nights, 'Vauxhall Village' remains the hub for all folks gay and out who want to party hard. **RVT** is the key venue,

Old Blue Last

a friendly, historic gay tavern that hosts comedy nights, arty performance parties and discos. **Fire** (p187) and its rave-tastic Lightbox room remains the key party place, opening through to very, very late. The closure of numerous West End venues has also encouraged plenty of club nights to up sticks to Shoreditch and Dalston, creating a third gay scene to add to Vauxhall and, of course, Soho. **Dalston Superstore** is the stand-out venue for the new breed of young, gay hipster.

Just for laughs

Stand-up comedy has gone stadium-sized: Michael McIntyre followed the likes of Peter Kay in playing the **O2** in 2012. It's not all supernova shows, though: on an extremely boisterous scene, check out the **Comedy Store** (p138), still the one that all the comedians want to play, and **Soho Theatre** great for interesting solo shows from breaking comics, for starters.

While London's nightlife is lively all year, anyone who's come here to see some comedy in late July or August is likely to be disappointed. Most of the city's performers head to Scotland for the Edinburgh Festival and consequently many venues are dark. Come in June or October instead: comedians are either trying out fresh shows or touring their Edinburgh triumph.

Making the most of it

Whatever you're doing, check the transport before you go: festivals, repairs and engineering tinkerage throw spanners in the works all year, notably on public holidays, but also many weekends. Regularly updated information can be found at **www.tfl.gov.uk**. Public transport isn't as daunting as

you might think. The tube is self-evident, even to newcomers, but it doesn't run much after midnight (New Year's Eve is the exception). Black cabs are pricey and hard to find at night, but safe. There are also licensed minicabs; on no account take an illegal minicab, even though they're touted outside every club. Far better to research the slow but comprehensive **night bus** system (p214) before leaving your hotel (see www.tfl.gov.uk's Journey Planner). A few minutes working out which bus gets you safe to bed can save hours of blurry-visioned confusion later.

You'll also kick yourself if you came all this way to see an event, only to arrive the one weekend it isn't on – or to find dates have changed. We've done our best to ensure the information in this guide is correct, but things change with little warning: www.timeout.com has the latest details or, if you're already here, buy *Time Out* magazine for weekly listings. Record shops are invaluable for flyers and advice – try the friendly folk at **Rough Trade East** (p179) for starters.

If the dates won't quite work out, don't despair. There's something going on here, no matter the day, no matter the hour. So if a useless mate forgets to get tickets, it isn't the end of the world. Even long-in-the-tooth Londoners fall across brand new happenings just by taking the wrong street, and the best way to get a taste of 'real London' – instead of the city every postcard-collecting tourist sees – is to go with the flow. Someone tells you about a party? Check it out. Read about a new band? Get a ticket. Sure, you've some 'essentials' in mind, but if you miss them this time… hell, come back next year.

Matilda the Musical

WHAT'S BEST
Arts & Leisure

London isn't just the political hub of Britain. It's the country's cultural and sporting capital too. Classical music of all types is studied and performed here, ambitious and inventive actors, directors and dancers learn their chops, and films are premièred and shot. The city also has two of the nation's top three football teams, national stadiums for football and rugby, and international centres of tennis and cricket.

Theatre & musicals

London's theatreland is looking oddly healthy and wealthy. It seems economic hard times have sent people to the theatre in search of distraction, rather than chasing them away – the *Lion King* beat its own record for highest annual West End takings. Nonetheless, producers remain cautious: for 2012/13 you can expect the usual crop of celebrity-led revivals and musicals piggy-backed on nostalgia for hit movies. The excellent *Billy Elliot* (Victoria Palace Theatre, p80), *Jersey Boys* (Prince Edward Theatre, p139) and *Shrek the Musical* (Theatre Royal Drury Lane, p148) have been joined by the Olivier-award-winning *Matilda the Musical* (Cambridge Theatre, Earlham Street, WC2, 0870 830 0200), *Ghost the Musical* (Piccadilly Theatre, 4 Denman Street, W1, 0844 871 7618), with its smoke, mirrors, full-throttle heartache and beguiling special effects, and a stunningly staged *Wizard of Oz* (London Palladium, p138).

The blockbuster musical's dominance in London is certainly under no immediate threat – the

PAST THE DEGAS AND CÉZANNE,
TAKE IN THE VAN GOGH ON
YOUR RIGHT, TURN LEFT
AND BE SURPRISED!
FIND YOURSELF AT THE
NATIONAL GALLERY

25th anniversary of *Les Misérables* (Queen's Theatre, p139) saw two versions playing simultaneously in central London – but straight plays have been making a comeback. The success of new plays like Richard Bean's uproarious update of *A Servant to Two Masters, One Man, Two Guvnors* (Haymarket Theatre Royal, 18 Suffolk Street, SW1, 0845 481, 1870) and *Warhorse*, which moved from the National Theatre to the New London Theatre (Drury Lane, WC2, 0844 412 2708), along with revivals like *Posh* (Duke of York's Theatre, St Martin's Lane, WC2, 0844 871 7623) and *Abigail's Party* (Wyndham Theatre, Charing Cross Road, WC2, 0844 482 5120) have shown there is appetite for drama without a score.

Despite decreasing theatrical subsidies, the **National Theatre** (p72) has had a terrific couple of years. Its programme includes *People*, by Alan Bennett, directed by Nicholas Hytner (Nov 2012-Jan 2013) and *Othello*, with Adrian Lester as Othello and Rory Kinnear as Iago (Apr-June 2013).

Meanwhile, the **Donmar Warehouse** (p148) continues to show great resourcefulness: in addition to bringing real star power to its tiny space (Nicole Kidman, Ewan McGregor), it has made blockbuster successes of serious plays in the West End and, as 'Donmar Trafalgar', runs a showcase for coming directors.

Shakespeare's Globe (p65) makes a wonderfully authentic setting for works by the Bard, but also check out the annual London season of the **Royal Shakespeare Company** (www.rsc.org.uk), usually at the **Roundhouse** (p172).

At the younger, cultier end of the scale, watch out for the masters of immersive theatre, **Punchdrunk** (www.punchdrunk.org.uk), whose masked revels have been sending

SHORTLIST

Best of the West End
- *Matilda the Musical* at the Cambridge Theatre (p31)
- *Warhorse* at the New London Theatre (left)

Best classical venues
- Kings Place (p125)
- Royal Opera House (p148)
- Wigmore Hall (p105)

Best cinemas
- BFI Southbank (p72)
- Curzon Soho (p138)

Best for theatre
- Donmar Warehouse (see box p148)
- National Theatre (p72)
- Royal Court Theatre (p97)

Best for contemporary dance
- Place (p125)
- Sadler's Wells (p175)

Most innovative work
- London Sinfonietta at Kings Place (p125)
- Punchdrunk (p34)
- Royal Court Theatre (p97)

Best festivals
- Greenwich & Docklands International Festival (p43)
- London Film Festival (p36)
- The Proms (p45)

Best bargains
- Half-price West End shows from tkts (p139)
- Prince Charles Cinema (p139)
- Standing tickets at Shakespeare's Globe (p65)
- £10 Monday at the Royal Court Theatre (p97)
- £12 Travelex tickets at the National Theatre (p72)

ecstatically spooked audiences through many-roomed venues in search of spectacular action for several years now. Their success was rewarded by an impressive increase in Arts Council funding. Other theatre companies in favour include **Ockham's Razor** (www.ockhamsrazor.co.uk), who specialise in circus aerialist stunts. Some of the more acrobatic local and international theatre groups get to show off their skills at the always popular annual **Greenwich & Docklands International Festival** and revived **LIFT** (for both, p43).

Classical music & opera

The completion of office block-cum-auditorium **Kings Place** (p125) has been the biggest news in classical music over the last few years. It provides headquarters for the very different Orchestra of the Age of Enlightenment (www.oae.co.uk) and London Sinfonietta (www.londonsinfonietta.org.uk), as well as sculpture galleries and two concert halls with extremely good acoustics.

At the **Barbican** (p167), the London Symphony Orchestra (http://lso.co.uk) continues to play 90 concerts a year. Watch out for the LSO Discovery Family Concert: Music for the Big Screen (14 October 2012); you can bring your own instrument and join in.

The Royal Festival Hall at the **Southbank Centre** (p73) regularly hosts Esa-Pekka Salonen's Philharmonia Orchestra (www.philharmonia.co.uk), whose roster this year includes Salonen conducting *The Rite of Spring* in its centenary performance.

London also has a pair of fine opera houses: Covent Garden's **Royal Opera House** (p148) combines assured crowd-pleasers – Wagner's Ring Cycle, Verdi's *Otello* – with a developing penchant for rarities: the world première of *Anna Nicole*, Mark-Anthony Turnage's opera about Playmate and celebrity widow Anna Nicole Smith, was an unlikely triumph in 2011, selling out its entire run. At the **Coliseum** (p148), the English National Opera performs classics (always in English), but also more experimental projects – increasingly film/music collaborations – with variable success.

Much of the city's classical music action happens in superb venues on an intimate scale. The exemplary **Wigmore Hall** (p105), **Cadogan**

King's Place

DON'T MISS: 2013

Hall (p97) and **LSO St Luke's** (p167) are all very atmospheric, and a number of churches host fine concerts: try **St Martin-in-the-Fields** (p76) and **St John's, Smith Square** (p80).

Film

In the death-struggle against increasingly sophisticated home entertainment systems, many London cinemas try to make film-going an event: witness the luxury seats and auditorium alcohol licences. **Secret Cinema** (www.secretcinema.org) has even pioneered film-watching as immersive theatrical experience – strange locations, dressing up and lots of collateral entertainment. For more on watching films in non-cinema venues, see box p134.

It's been good to see new cinemas open (among them Curzon Millbank, just north of Tate Britain, in spring 2011), but less pleasing is the way mainstream titles creep on to the playbills of even arthouse cinemas, as the likes of the **Curzon Soho** (p138) and Everyman's revamped **Screen on the Green** (175) struggle to keep audiences. Smaller films are finding it hard to breathe in the capital these days. The only cinema committed to foreign and alternative films is the **BFI Southbank** (p72).

But as the multiplexes stuff their screens with bloated blockbusters, smaller, less formal venues have begun to pick up the slack, and

major attractions such as **Tate Modern** (p67) and even **St Paul's Cathedral** (p162) include film screenings on their events rosters. Keep an eye on *Time Out* magazine or www.timeout.com for these various venues, and for details of the city's frequent film festivals.

Dance

Two companies provide the full blocks-and-tutus experience. The **English National Ballet** (at the Coliseum) and the **Royal Ballet** (at the Royal Opera House) oblige with Tchaikovsky's *The Nutcracker* over Christmas. The Royal Ballet's programme includes classics (*La Sylphide*), but increasingly throws in more adventurous fare like George Ballanchine's joyful *Ballo della Regina* and Kenneth MacMillan's *The Prince of the Pagodas*.

London offers an unmatched range of performers and styles, way beyond the usual choice of classical or contemporary, and – apart from the quieter summer months – there's something worth seeing every night. **Sadler's Wells** (p175) offers a packed programme of top-quality work and hosts must-see festivals. Autumn sees **Dance Umbrella** (p39) unfold with cutting-edge work from around the world. Keep an eye also on the **Barbican** and **Southbank Centre**, both of which programme fine dance-theatre hybrids.

What's on

We've included long-running musicals we think are likely to survive through 2013. However, a new crop will inevitably open through the year, along with seasons at individual venues. *Time Out* magazine and www.timeout.com have the city's most informed and up-to-date listings.

WHAT'S ON
Calendar

Chelsea Flower Show p42

This is our pick of annual and one-off events in London. Buy *Time Out* magazine and check www.timeout.com/london for weekly updates, and confirm dates before making plans. Public holidays are given in bold.

September 2012

8-9 **Mayor's Thames Festival**
Westminster & Tower Bridges
www.thamesfestival.org

from 12 **Pre-Raphaelites: the Victorian Avant-Garde**
Tate Britain, p79
www.tate.org.uk

15 **Great River Race**
Thames, Richmond to Greenwich
www.greatriverrace.co.uk
With 300 exotic rowing craft.

22 **Great Gorilla Run**
Mincing Lane, the City
www.greatgorillas.org/london
Fundraising run in gorilla suits.

22-23 **Open-City London**
www.open-city.org.uk
For one weekend only, there's access to 600 amazing buildings normally closed to the public.

30 **Pearly Kings & Queens Harvest Festival**
Guildhall Yard, the City
www.pearlysociety.co.uk

October 2012

Ongoing Pre-Raphaelites: the Victorian Avant-Garde (see Sept).

10-25 **BFI London Film Festival**
BFI Southbank, p72
www.bfi.org.uk/lff

11-14 **Frieze Art Fair**
Regent's Park, p98
www.friezeartfair.com

from 18 Oct **The Lost Prince: The Life & Death of Henry Stuart**
National Portrait Galley, p76
www.npg.org.uk

Festive Fun

How to get the best out of Christmas and New Year.

London never used to be much fun at the turn of the year. With no public transport on Christmas Day, the centre of the capital feels eerily deserted – a magical transformation for a city usually teeming with people, but not one that's easy to enjoy unless you've got a designated driver happy to forgo the egg nog. And New Year's Eve seemed to involve cramming as many idiots as possible into Trafalgar Square (p79), without so much as a drink to warm them.

Things have changed. There's been an explosion of middle European-style Christmas markets across town. Each has its own approach – from the traditional version in Covent Garden (p140) to the annual fairground of Winter Wonderland in Hyde Park (p91) – but mulled wine, spiced German cake and ice rinks are constants.

For pretty Christmas lights, skip the commercialised ones on Oxford and Regent Streets and try St Christopher's Place, Marylebone High Street and Covent Garden.

The best window displays are usually at old-fashioned Fortnum & Mason (p83) and style-palace Liberty (p136). Oxford Street and Regent Street usually close to traffic one weekend early in December in addition to the now traditional Boxing Day closure that facilitates pedestrian access to the sales.

More interested in partying than purchasing? The week after Christmas is when the locals go nuts, and the best advice is to do as they do: forget paying inflated prices for a disappointing New Year's Eve bash and go out instead on New Year's Day. Parties kick off from 5am and attract a cooler crowd, happy in the knowledge they're paying a third of the price for exactly the same DJs as were playing at midnight – check *Time Out* magazine for details. If you do want to join the mob for the trad New Year's Eve bash, head to the South Bank, where a full-on fireworks display is launched from the London Eye and Thames rafts.

New Year's Eve fireworks.

Blues Bourbon & Good Times

The BLUES KITCHEN

The first exhibition to look at the life of Henry, Prince of Wales (1594-1612).

late Oct-late Apr 2013 **Veolia Environnement Wildlife Photographer of the Year**
Natural History Museum, p85
www.nhm.ac.uk/wildphoto

Oct **Dance Umbrella**
www.danceumbrella.co.uk
The city's headline dance festival.

31 Oct-20 Jan 2013 **Seduced by Art: Photography Past & Present**
National Gallery, p76
www.nationalgallery.org.uk

November 2012

Ongoing Seduced by Art: Photography Past & Present (see Oct); Wildlife Photographer of the Year (see Oct); The Lost Prince: The Life & Death of Henry Stuart (see Oct); Pre-Raphaelites: the Victorian Avant-Garde (see Sept).

from 8 Nov **Taylor Wessing Photographic Portrait Prize**
National Portrait Gallery, p76.
www.npg.org.uk

13 **Diwali**
Trafalgar Square, p79
www.london.gov.uk

from 14 Nov **A Bigger Splash: Painting After Performance**
Tate Modern, p67
www.tate.org.uk
Exhibition looking at the relationship between performance and painting since 1950.

5 **Bonfire Night**
Firework displays all over town, marking the arrest of Guy Fawkes, and the thwarting of the attempt to blow up Parliament on 5 November 1604.

4 **London to Brighton Veteran Car Run**
Serpentine Road in Hyde Park, p91
www.lbvcr.com

9-18 **London Jazz Festival**
www.londonjazzfestival.org.uk

10 **Lord Mayor's Show**
The City
www.lordmayorsshow.org
A grand inauguration procession for the Lord Mayor of the City of London.

11 **Remembrance Sunday Ceremony**
Cenotaph, Whitehall

Nov-Dec **Christmas Tree & Lights**
Trafalgar Square, p79
www.london.gov.uk
An impressive Norwegian spruce is mounted and lit in the centre of the city.

December 2012

Ongoing Seduced by Art: Photography Past & Present (see Oct); Wildlife Photographer of the Year (see Oct); Christmas Tree & Lights (see Nov); Taylor Wessing Photographic Portrait Prize (see Nov); The Lost Prince: The Life & Death of Henry Stuart (see Oct); Pre-Raphaelites: the Victorian Avant-Garde (see Sept); A Bigger Splash: Painting After Performance (see Nov).

mid Dec **Spitalfields Festival**
www.spitalfieldsfestival.org.uk
Biannual festival of classical music.

26 **Christmas Day Bank Holiday**

28 **Boxing Day Bank Holiday**

31 **New Year's Eve Celebrations**

January 2013

Ongoing Seduced by Art: Photography Past & Present (see Oct); Wildlife Photographer of the Year (see Oct); Taylor Wessing Photographic Portrait Prize (see Nov); The Lost Prince: The Life & Death of Henry Stuart (see Oct); Pre-Raphaelites: the Victorian Avant-Garde (see Sept); A Bigger Splash: Painting After Performance (see Nov).

DON'T MISS: 2013

Chinese New Year Festival

12-27 **London International Mime Festival**
www.mimefest.co.uk

February 2013

Ongoing Wildlife Photographer of the Year (see Oct); Taylor Wessing Photographic Portrait Prize (see Nov); A Bigger Splash: Painting After Performance (see Nov).

10 **Chinese New Year Festival**
Chinatown, p130
www.londonchinatown.org

12 **Poulters Pancake Day Race**
Guildhall Yard, the City
www.poulters.org.uk
Livery companies race while tossing pancakes; a Shrove Tuesday tradition.

15 Feb-16 Mar **Medea**
ENO, Coliseum, p148
www.eno.org

from 21 Feb **Roy Lichtenstein**
Tate Modern, p67
www.tate.org.uk

The first full-scale retrospective of Lichtenstein's work for over 20 years.

March 2013

Ongoing Wildlife Photographer of the Year (see Oct); Medea (see Feb); Roy Lichtenstein (see Feb); A Bigger Splash: Painting After Performance (see Nov).

11-17 **Maslenitsa Russian Festival**
Trafalgar Square, p79
www.maslenitsa.co.uk

29 **Good Friday**

31 **Oxford & Cambridge Boat Race**
On the Thames, Putney to Mortlake
www.theboatrace.org
The 159th outing for rowers from Oxford and Cambridge universities.

late Mar-early Apr **London Lesbian & Gay Film Festival**
BFI Southbank, p72
www.llgff.org.uk

April 2013

Ongoing Wildlife Photographer of the Year (see Oct); Lesbian & Gay Film Festival (see Mar); Roy Lichtenstein (see Feb).

1 Easter Monday

mid Apr-mid June **Spring Loaded**
Place, p127
www.theplace.org.uk
Contemporary dance festival.

21 London Marathon
Greenwich Park to the Mall.
www.virginlondonmarathon.com

late Apr **Sundance London**
O2 Arena, p186
www.sundance-london.com
Robert Redford's film festival features the best of independent cinema.

late Apr **Breakin' Convention**
Sadler's Wells, p175
www.breakinconvention.com
Jonzi D's street dance festival provides spectacular entertainment.

May 2013

Ongoing Spring Loaded (see Apr); Roy Lichtenstein (see Feb).

early May **Land of Kings**
Dalston, p175
www.landofkings.co.uk
Trendy music and art mash-up.

early May **Camden Crawl**
Camden, p170
www.thecamdencrawl.com
Fun multi-pub music 'microfestival'.

6 Early May Bank Holiday

late May **Chelsea Flower Show**
Royal Hospital Chelsea
www.rhs.org.uk

27 Late May Bank Holiday

June 2013

early June **Beating Retreat**
Horse Guards Parade, Whitehall
www.army.mod.uk

Wimbledon Lawn Tennis Championships

A pageant of military music and precision marching, beginning at 7pm.

early June-mid Aug
Opera Holland Park
www.operahollandpark.com

mid-late **June Spitalfields Festival**
www.spitalfieldsfestival.org.uk
See above Dec 2012.

mid June **Open Garden Squares Weekend**
www.opensquares.org
For one weekend, private gardens are open to the public.

mid June **Meltdown**
Southbank Centre, p58
www.southbank.co.uk
Music and culture festival, curated by a different musician every year.

mid June **Trooping the Colour**
Horse Guards Parade, St James's
www.trooping-the-colour.co.uk
The Queen's official birthday parade, with the Household Cavalry.

24 June-7 July **Wimbledon Lawn Tennis Championships**
www.wimbledon.org

25 June-20 Oct **Lowry & the Painting of Modern Life**
Tate Britain
www.tate.org.uk

late June-mid Aug **LIFT (London International Festival of Theatre)**
www.liftfest.org.uk

late June-mid Aug
City of London Festival
The City
www.colf.org
A festival of mostly free music and art, often in historic City venues.

late June-early July
Greenwich & Docklands International Festival
www.festival.org
Outdoor theatricals, usually on an impressively large scale.

Greenwich & Docklands International Festival

Sounds in the City

The capital's best open-air music festivals.

Lovebox

The summer festival season kicks off in east London's Victoria Park with the leftfield **Field Day** (www.fileddayfestivals.com) in early June. Vicky Park is a key venue for open-air events, also hosting the family-friendly **Apple Cart** festival (www.theapplecart festival.com). Groove Armada's **Lovebox** (right) and the under-18s-only **Underage Festival** (www.underagefestivals.com).

As well as one off mega gigs by big stars, Hyde Park is the setting for the pop/dance-oriented **Wireless Festival** (www.wireless festival.co.uk) and the heritage rock weekender **Hard Rock Calling** (www.hardrockcalling.co.uk). Rihanna, Drake and Deadmau5 played the 2012 Wireless Festival, with Bruce Springsteen headlining at Hard Rock Calling. And Clapham Common lords it over the August bank holiday weekend with its **SW4** rave-up (www.southwestfour.com). If you're after something more salubrious, **Somerset House Summer Series** (right) welcomes an array of big and generally pretty mainstream acts for roughly ten days of open-air shows in July. Previous acts have included Basement Jaxx, Amy Winehouse and Pendulum.

The Southbank Centre (p73) invites a guest artist to curate **Meltdown**, a fortnight of gigs, films and other events. David Bowie Ornette Coleman, Patti Smith and Richard Thompson are among the previous curators.

Other events cover single genres. They include the Southbank Centre's **London African Music Festival** (www.londonafricanmusic festival.com), in September, and **La Linea** (www.comono.co.uk), a fortnight of contemporary Latin American music.

July 2013

Ongoing Opera Holland Park
(see June), Wimbledon (see June),
LIFT (see June), City of London
Festival, Greenwich & Docklands
International Festival (see June);
Lowry & the Painting of Modern
LIfe (see June).

early July **Wireless Festival**
Hyde Park, p91
www.wirelessfestival.co.uk
Three nights of rock and dance acts in
the lovely Royal Park.

early July **Pride London**
Oxford Street to Victoria
Embankment
www.pridelondon.org
Huge annual gay and lesbian parade.

early July-mid Sept **National
Theatre Inside Out**
National Theatre, p72
http://insideout.nationaltheatre.org.uk
Alfresco theatre beside the Thames.

mid July **Lovebox Weekender**
Victoria Park, Hackney
www.lovebox.net
Top-quality weekend music festival.

mid July **Somerset House Series**
Somerset House, p154
www.somersethouse.org.uk/music
A dozen concerts in the fountain court.

mid July-mid Sept **The Proms
(BBC Sir Henry Wood
Promenade Concerts)**
Royal Albert Hall, p91
www.bbc.co.uk/proms
London's best classical music festival,
packed with top-class performers –
tickets are at bargain prices if you're
happy to stand.

August 2013

Ongoing Opera Holland Park
(see June); LIFT (see June); City
of London Festival (see June);
The Proms (see July); Lowry &
the Painting of Modern LIfe (see June)

Notting Hill Carnival

early Aug **Great British Beer Festival**
Earls Court Exhibition Centre
http://gbbf.camra.org.uk

mid Aug **London Mela**
Gunnersbury Park, Ealing
www.londonmela.com
South Asian music and street arts.

25-26 **Notting Hill Carnival**
Notting Hill, p188
www.nottinghillcarnival.biz
Europe's biggest street party bring's a taste of the Caribbean to Notting Hill.

26 **Summer Bank Holiday**

September 2013

Ongoing The Proms (see July); Lowry & the Painting of Modern LIfe (see June).

mid Sept **Mayor's Thames Festival**
See above Sept 2012.

mid Sept **Open-City London**
See above Sept 2012.

late Sept **Great River Race**
See above Sept 2012.

late Sept **Great Gorilla Run**
See above Sept 2012.

October 2013

Ongoing Lowry & the Painting of Modern LIfe (see June).

early Oct **Pearly Kings & Queens Harvest Festival**
See above Oct 2012.

Oct **Dance Umbrella**
See above Oct 2012.

from 15 Oct **Paul Klee**
Tate Modern, see p67
www.tate.org.uk

Oct **London Film Festival**
See above Oct 2012.

mid Oct **Frieze Art Fair**
See above Oct 2012.

from late Oct **Veolia Environnement Wildlife Photographer of the Year**
See above Oct 2012.

November 2013

Ongoing Dance Umbrella (see Sept); London Film Festival, Wildlife Photographer of the Year (see Oct); Paul Klee (see Oct).

3 **Diwali**
See above Oct 2012.

3 **Diwali**
See above Oct 2012.

5 **Bonfire Night**

10 **Remembrance Sunday**
See above Nov 2012.

early Nov **London to Brighton Veteran Car Run**
See above Nov 2011.

early Nov **Lord Mayor's Show**
See above Nov 2011.

mid Nov **London Jazz Festival**
See above Nov 2011.

Nov-Dec **Christmas Tree & Lights**
See above Nov 2011.

December 2013

Ongoing Wildlife Photographer of the Year (see Oct); Christmas Tree & Lights (see Nov); Paul Klee (see Oct).

mid Dec **Spitalfields Festival**
See above Dec 2012.

25 **Christmas Day**

26 **Boxing Day**

31 **New Year's Eve Celebrations**

Itineraries

Liverpool Street Station

London Locations

Although Britain's most celebrated film studios – Pinewood, Elstree and Ealing – were in or near London, many directors have been content to recreate the city on a sound stage rather than face the vagaries of location shooting. However, London has richly rewarded those filmmakers who have ventured out on location: either in terms of establishing an authentic sense of place, or by having the city masquerade as settings as diverse as New York or war-torn Vietnam.

Locations for two of London's most iconic cinematic scenes are in outlying and obscure corners, likely to be sought out by only the most dedicated fans. The park where David Hemmings unwittingly photographs a murder in *Blow Up* (1966) is **Maryon Park**, near Charlton in south-east London; director Michelangelo Antonioni ordered the leaves and grass to be painted a darker shade of green to achieve the precise effect he wanted. Also in the far reaches of south-east London, the bucolically named but unappealing and concrete-heavy housing development of **Thamesmead** has made its contribution to celluloid history. In *A Clockwork Orange* (1971), Stanley Kubrick filmed the notorious scene where Alex and his Droogs attack a tramp in the subway behind Tavy Bridge shopping centre.

For our itinerary, though, we will stay within central London, before heading east to Docklands. We'll be taking the tube and DLR, so you'll need an Oyster card (p212). We begin our tour at **King's Cross** station (p132), starting point of the Hogwarts Express. As aficionados of the Harry Potter books and films will know, the school train leaves from a secret platform – platform 9¾, located by passing through the brick wall barrier between platforms 9 and 10. Following the films' succcess, a 'platform 9¾' sign was put up as a focus for fans, with part of a luggage trolley underneath – giving the effect of the trolley disappearing into the wall, just as the books describe. The sign and the trolley are now located in the newly opened and magnificent western concourse – it's worth a visit to the station to see this alone.

The exterior shot of 'King's Cross' in *Harry Potter and the Chamber of Secrets* (2002) was actually the imposing Victorian Gothic façade of the next door **St Pancras** station, now the **Renaissance Hotel** (p204). If you're already feeling in need of refreshment, or would simply like to explore the glories of the hotel interior, pop into the **Booking Office** bar (p124).

Other directors have been more interested in the seamy reputation of the King's Cross area. Today, little remains of the prostitution for which it was once notorious. Even before the new developments of King's Place and St Pancras station it had been largely swept clean, and although drug dealing and prostitution were rife in the 1980s, when *Mona Lisa* (1986) was made, the area's hellishness was exaggerated in the film. The bridge where the street walkers plied their trade, where high-class call girl Simone goes in search of her friend Cathy, wasn't near King's Cross at all, but on Pindar Street near Liverpool Street, on a road bridge that once spanned the railway line, now lost to development. Of course, Simone's more usual haunts, where she meets wealthy clients, were big central London hotels like the Ritz and Park Lane. And her home, while geographically near the fictionalised King's Cross, was very different in spirit: a striking blue and white art deco apartment block, **Trinity Court**, a ten-minute walk down **Gray's Inn Road**, adjacent to the station.

To reach our next destination, take the Circle, Metropolitan or Hammersmith & City line four

ITINERARIES

Westminster Abbey

stops east from King's Cross to another London terminal – **Liverpool Street**. The CIA safe house where spy Ethan Hunt (Tom Cruise) holed up in *Mission Impossible* (1996) is above the Old Broad Street entrance to the tube station. Hunt heads on to the station concourse to meet up with his handler, Phelps, at a bank of payphones, which has now been replaced by a row of cashpoints.

From Liverpool Street, head west on the Central Line to Chancery Lane. From the station, turn left along Holborn to Holborn Circus, and left again into **Hatton Garden**, centre of the London diamond trade. Stanley Kubrick's *Eyes Wide Shut* (1999) is set in New York City, but Kubrick lived in England and preferred filming here. The real New York appears only briefly. Instead, London is dressed as New York. The Sonata Café, where Dr Bill Harford (Tom Cruise again) meets his friend Nick, is actually Madame Jojo's in Soho (p138). Hatton Garden, meanwhile, had New York-style payphones installed between nos 32 and 38 before filming to help disguise it as the New York street Bill walks along after leaving the apartment of prostitute Domino, and where he is followed by a sinister man. Kubrick's creativity with locations extended beyond having London double as New York. He even managed to make London look like Vietnam: war scenes from *Full Metal Jacket* (1987) were filmed in Beckton, east London.

By now, it will probably be time for a break, and perhaps lunch. There's posh café food in **Le Comptoir Gascon** (p155) on Charterhouse Street, off Holborn Circus. Or, for excellent coffee and snacks, try **Prufrock Coffee** (p157) on Leather Lane, the next street parallel to Hatton Garden.

Refreshed, it's time to follow in the footsteps of the intrepid puzzle-solvers of *The Da Vinci Code* (2006), the film based on Dan Brown's much-maligned 2003 novel. The film has a plot strongly rooted in real locations, many of which appear in the film. To find our next location, head south from Hatton Garden down New Fetter Lane, turn right on Fleet Street, then left down Inner Temple Lane. Here is **Temple Church** (p154), built for the crusader order of the Knights Templars, and consecrated in 1185. The economically powerful order was suddenly disbanded in 1312 under pressure from the Pope. Its abrupt disappearance encouraged speculation and conspiracy theories, and kept the order's name alive. The church is unusual in that, like all Templar churches, its nave follows the circular design of the Holy Sepulchre church in Jerusalem. Our hero and heroine, Robert Langdon and Sophie Neveu, are looking for 'a knight interred by a pope'. To this end, they search among the knights' effigies in the church. They're on the wrong track, though. The effigies in Temple Church are just that, not tombs. The answer to the riddle actually lies in the tomb of Sir Isaac Newton at **Westminster Abbey** (p79), two stops east on the District or Circle line from Temple station for the truly dedicated.

Our next location is another church. **St George in the East** is a handsome Hawksmoor church, built between 1714 and 1729. To reach it from Temple Church, take the District or Circle Line east from Temple station to Tower Hill. From here, swap to Tower Gateway, and travel one stop along the Docklands

King's Cross

Light Railway to Shadwell. Turn right outside the station along Cable Street and walk until you hit Cannon Street Road, then turn left.

St George featured in *The Long Good Friday* (1979), as the church where the mother of old-style gangster Harold Shand (Bob Hoskins) attends a Good Friday service. There follows the first in a series of bombs and murders by an unknown foe that leaves Shand in no doubt that someone is out to get him. His Rolls Royce is blown up in the car park; he escapes but his chauffeur is killed. Shand had been hoping to go straight with a lucrative scheme to redevelop the then-abandoned Docklands area into – guess what – a venue for a future Olympic Games. **Canary Wharf** was the proposed site of a new marina; the future location of One Canada Square (p182) is clearly visible as his yacht tours the site. Check it out by travelling a few more stops on the DLR to Canary Wharf station. Admire the scale of the development around you, and then imagine what the place was like when it was a post-industrial wasteland.

Our itinerary concludes here. You can then head all the way back into the City (Bank station) on the DLR, enjoying some great views of Docklands on the way.

Millenium Bridge/St Paul's

The Sights in a Trice

Got a couple of free days? Fancy ticking off the major sights in double-quick time? This two-day itinerary uses the Thames as its axis. It's mostly on foot, but uses some public transport, so slip on comfy trainers, grab your Oyster travelcard (p213) and get set… go!

Day 1

The **Tower of London** (p162) gets mobbed as the day progresses, so it's a good place to start. Get there for 9am (10am Mon, Sun) and take the travelator past the Crown Jewels before the queue builds up. Then join one of the Yeoman Warder ('Beefeater') tours for an entertaining overview of the place, before checking out the armaments and garderobes in the White Tower and the prisoner graffiti in Beauchamp Tower.

Next, take in the brilliant views as you stroll across **Tower Bridge** (p162; www.towerbridge.org.uk

gives bridge lift times. Turn right, down to the Queen's Walk, and head east along the South Bank, passing **City Hall** (p58) and **HMS Belfast** (p59). On Thursday, Friday or Saturday have a gourmet refuel at **Borough Market** (p70): perhaps a chocolate brownie from Flour Power City Bakery, seared scallops from Shellseekers Fish & Game, or Kappacasein's toasted cheese sandwiches. If the market's closed, **Roast** (p69) can supply slow-roast Wicks Manor pork belly and grilled calf's liver. Then pep yourself up for the next stint with a latte from Monmouth Coffee.

Continue along the Thames until you hit **Tate Modern** (p67), the world's most-visited modern art gallery. The displayed works are superb, of course, but so is the river vista from the Espresso Bar or Tate Modern Restaurant.

Cross the Millennium Bridge and walk up the broad, snaking staircase to **St Paul's Cathedral** (p162), Wren's masterwork. You then have two choices. You could take a nostalgic ride on a red double-decker bus to Aldwych. The old-style Routemaster had been phased out of use (a new version came into service in 2012 on route 38), but a few of the old buses continue to run on Heritage Route 15. Board at Stop SJ, outside St Paul's, for a ride west along Fleet Street, past the Royal Courts of Justice (look right after the griffin statue in the middle of the road) and along the Strand. Get off at Savoy Street (Stop U) for the deco entranceway to the **Savoy Hotel** (p206), then nip across the busy road into Covent Garden for supper – try the **Opera Tavern** (p144), opposite the Drury Lane Theatre – before checking out the buzz and buskers of Covent Garden Market (see p145).

Otherwise, head north from St Paul's through Paternoster Square, along Little Britain, past Smithfield Market and up St John Street, where you'll find a cluster of London's finest restaurants, including modern British classic **St John** (p157). If you've got more energy, superclub **Fabric** (p158) is open at weekends.

Day 2

Feeling the effects from last night's party? Grab a hot perk-me-up and sandwiches for lunch at Green Park tube (Caffè Nero and Pret A Manger, ubiquitous London chains, are both here), then walk across the lawns to **Buckingham Palace** (p81). The Changing of the Guard happens here at 11.30am daily from May to July (alternate days August to April), lasting about half an hour. In summer, you can tour the palace's State Rooms, or the Royal Mews can be visited year-round.

When you're done with the palace, head into lovely **St James's Park** (p81) for your picnic or take the second left at the Queen Victoria

Memorial roundabout on to Spur Road, then along Birdcage Walk, to see Westminster's finest structures. Admire the twin towers and flying buttresses of **Westminster Abbey** (p79), pop into the **Houses of Parliament** (p76) to watch a peppery debate, or just listen to the familiar tune of the tallest four-faced chiming clock in the world – the clocktower of Big Ben. Parliament Square is another, usually traffic-disturbed, picnic possibility.

Wander north up Whitehall, with its war memorials and blank-faced government buildings. On your left, you pass Downing Street – home of the Prime Minister (at no.10) and his Chancellor (at no.11), but with no public access – and, at Horse Guards, sword-bearing cavalrymen in sentryboxes. **Trafalgar Square** (p79) opens out at the end of Whitehall; behind the black statue of a mounted Charles I, a plaque marks the official centre of London. After a look at the Fourth Plinth – now a site for contemporary sculpture commissions – climb the steps on to the pedestrianised northern side of the square.

You're now in front of the **National Gallery** (p76), one of the world's greatest repositories for art. Admission is free, as are ace guided tours that might steer you to masterpieces by Raphael, Rembrandt or Monet. For dinner, the gallery has two options: the **National Dining Rooms** (p80), with a bakery-cafe (open to 5.30pm, or 8.30pm on Fridays) and rather more expensive restaurant, and the darkly handsome National Café, open until 11pm (6pm on Sunday).

Head due north. You'll not want to linger in Leicester Square (see box p131), despite recent improvements, but instead push past Chinatown and into Soho – for great traditional pubs and hip bars (pp127-139).

ITINERARIES

Old Royal Naval College p56

The Wren Route

St Paul's Cathedral is a City landmark with real staying power: in 2010 it was 300 years since Sir Christopher Wren's masterpiece was opened as the centrepiece of the post-Great Fire rebuilding of London. Like some 17th-century Rogers or Foster, Wren and his associates peppered the skyline with spires and towers. Even though many disappeared through demolition or as a result of brutal carpet-bombing during the Blitz, many can still be visited.

Do the route on a weekday – at weekends most churches only open for services – and try to start by about 9am, since this route involves a lot of walking. Opening times and days for the individual churches vary wildly, so don't expect to see inside all of them on any one day.

Jump off the tube at dingy Farringdon station, turn right out of the exit, then immediately left down Farringdon Road until you reach Ludgate Circus. Stand on the west side and admire the view up Ludgate Hill to St Paul's to get an impression of what the cathedral must have looked like when it was first built, rising above the huddle of rooftops and the spires of the lesser Wren churches; the black spire situated to the left of the dome belongs to one of these churches, **St Martin Ludgate**.

Hidden behind you off Fleet Street is **St Bride's** (p152). Its steeple is the tallest of any Wren church and was supposedly the model for the tiered wedding cake. Take the first left off Fleet Street for a closer look. The church was burnt out during the Blitz, so the interior is a reconstruction, albeit a lovely one. Visit the crypt museum to find out about the construction of the church (several generations of wall are exposed, along with various artefacts) and the life and death of Fleet Street – a facsimile of the 30 December 1940 *Evening News* gives a graphic description of the devastation wreaked by one particular wartime raid.

Retrace your steps to Ludgate Circus and climb Ludgate Hill, braving the crowds on the cathedral steps to enter **St Paul's** (p162). You can easily spend a couple of hours here, enough for a climb up to the famous Whispering Gallery to look down within the cathedral, then on up and outside for the giddying views of the City from the Gold Gallery (more than 500 steps from the ground), and finally back down into the crypt beneath. Check out the skull and crossbones on the lintel. In the crypt, Nelson's grand monument is right beneath the central dome, while Wren's tomb is tucked modestly away at the east end in the south aisle.

Leaving the cathedral, turn right and pass through **Temple Bar**, another Wren creation. This gateway once stood at the western end of Fleet Street to mark the boundary between the City of London and Westminster, but it impeded the traffic and was removed by the Victorians. It returned in 2004 to become the entrance to the new Paternoster Square, home to the London Stock Exchange.

Grab a coffee and cross the square to emerge on Newgate Street. Opposite is **Christ Church**, which was almost destroyed during World War II. The ruined nave is now a rose garden; take a seat and sip your coffee. The surviving tower is a spectacular private home, its ten storeys linked by a lift.

Head east along Angel Street, across Aldersgate Street, to Gresham Street. First you'll see **St Anne & St Agnes**, with a leafy churchyard and regular classical recitals. Further along Gresham Street, catch a glimpse

of the tower of **St Alban Wood Street**, like Christ Church now a private house. Continue past **St Lawrence Jewry** – the church of the Corporation of London – to Moorgate, crossing into Lothbury to enter **St Margaret Lothbury** (7606 8330, www.stml.org.uk). This has one of the loveliest interiors of any Wren church, with an impressive wood screen by the great man himself.

Retrace your steps to Moorgate and turn left down Prince's Street to enter Bank tube. Take the Mansion House exit, following the path around to **St Stephen Walbrook** (39 Walbrook, 7606 3998, www.ststephenwalbrook.net), the most grandiose Wren church, a mass of creamy stone with a soaring dome, fabulously bulbous pulpit and incongruous modern altar by Henry Moore.

Turn left out of the church and left again into Cannon Street. Just past Cannon Street station, take another left on to St Swithin's Lane and head downstairs into the brick-vaulted cellar bistro of the Don (the Courtyard, 20 St Swithin's Lane, 7626 2606,

St Mary-le-Bow p56

www.thedonrestaurant.com),
where serious lunches are served
to bibulous bankers until 3pm on
weekdays. Turn left back on to
Cannon Street, then duck left
into Abchurch Lane. **St Mary
Abchurch** (7626 0306) is a real
gem, with a shallow, painted dome
and a beautiful reredos by Grinling
Gibbons. It was shattered into 2,000
pieces by a wartime bomb and
painstakingly pieced back together.

Back on Cannon Street, head
east to reach the top end of London
Bridge. Cross the street using the
underpass, turning left off King
William Street into Monument
Street. The **Monument** (p161)
is the world's tallest isolated stone
column, built to commemorate the
Great Fire. It was designed by
Wren and his associate Robert
Hooke. Brave the 311 steps up to
be rewarded with spectacular views
over the City and the Thames.

Get back on to Cannon Street and
head west to Bow Lane, topped and
tailed by churches from Wren's
office: at the southern end, **St
Mary Aldermary** (7248 4906,
www.stmaryaldermary.co.uk) has
flamboyant Gothic vaulting; at the
northern end, **St Mary-le-Bow** is
famous for its bells, but it's a post-
war reconstruction inside.

Retrace your steps down Bow
Lane, this time turning right into
Queen Victoria Street to reach
Peter's Hill and the Millennium
Bridge. Cross the river, turning east
off the bridge for Shakespeare's
Globe (p65). Overshadowed by the
theatre, **49 Bankside** is identified
by a plaque to be the house from
which Wren watched St Paul's
rise across the river. This seems
unlikely, given the house and
cathedral were completed in the
same year, but the views are
superb. Buy an ice-cream to munch
from one of the vans while waiting
for the riverbus at Bankside Pier.

Take the Thames Clipper (p214)
east to Masthouse Pier, from which
it's a ten-minute walk along the
river path to Island Gardens. Stock
up on fluids from the kiosk, soak
up the views of the **Old Royal
Naval College** (p185), then
cross under the river using the
Greenwich Foot Tunnel. Emerging
from the tunnel, pass the *Cutty
Sark* (still under refurbishment)
and turn left into College
Approach. The College is one of the
most extensive groups of baroque
public buildings in England and
survives much as Wren planned
it. The first building on your left
is the wonderful new **Discover
Greenwich** (see box p187), which
has superb displays, some giving
engaging explanations of Wren's
work on the hospital. Don't miss
the Painted Hall (most of the rich
decoration inside is trompe l'oeil),
which was built to Wren's designs
between 1696 and 1704, and you
won't be able to miss the stunning
colonnades leading south.

Continue through the college
to the eastern gate, turn right into
Park Row and enter Greenwich
Park. Crowning the hilltop is the
Royal Observatory (National
Maritime Museum, p186), where
crowds wait to stand astride the
Prime Meridian Line. Carry on to
enter **Flamsteed's House**, the
only bit of the complex by Wren.
Built for the first Astronomer
Royal, it's a dainty contrast to
the Royal Naval College, the
living quarters cosily domestic.
Only the Octagon room hints at
Wren's flair.

It's been a long day, so treat
yourself to a drink and some food.
As you head back to the Cutty
Sark, it might be time to explore
the other appealing aspect of
Discover Greenwich: an attached
café, restaurant and bar called the
Old Brewery (p186).

London by Area

Tate Modern p67

The South Bank

Tourists have been coming to the South Bank for centuries, but the entertainments have changed a little. **Shakespeare's Globe** has risen again, but for the associated prostitutes, gamblers and bear-baiting you'd need a time machine. Instead, enjoy a revitalised cultural hub – the **Southbank Centre**, **BFI Southbank** cinema complex and **Hayward** gallery – or join the multitude strolling the broad riverside walkway between Tower Bridge (p162) and Westminster Bridge. This strings together fine views and must-see attractions such as **Tate Modern**, and the **London Eye**.

Sights & museums

City Hall
Queen's Walk, SE1 2AA (www.london. gov.uk). London Bridge tube/rail. **Open** 8.30am-6pm Mon-Thur; 8.30am-5.30pm Fri. **Admission** free. **Map** p61 F2 ❶

Designed by Foster & Partners, this 45m-tall, eco-friendly rotund glass structure leans 31° away from the river. Home to London's metropolitan government, it has a huge aerial photo of the city you can walk on in the lower ground floor Visitor Centre and a café. Next door, Potters Fields Park and outdoor amphitheatre the Scoop host events through the summer.

Design Museum
Shad Thames, SE1 2YD (7403 6933, www.designmuseum.org). Tower Hill tube or London Bridge tube/rail. **Open** 10am-5.45pm daily. **Admission** £11; free-£10 reductions. **Map** p61 F2 ❷

The temporary exhibitions in this white 1930s building (previously a banana warehouse) focus on modern and contemporary industrial and fashion design, architecture, graphics and multimedia developments. The smart Blueprint Café has a fine balcony overlooking the river, and you can buy design books and items relating to current shows in the museum shop. In 2011, Terence Conran made a major donation that will enable the museum to move to new premises in the former Commonwealth Institute by 2014. **Event highlights** 'Designers in Residence' (until 27 Jan 2013).

Fashion & Textile Museum

83 Bermondsey Street, SE1 3XF (7407 8664, www.ftmlondon.org). London Bridge tube/rail. **Open** 11am-6pm Tue-Sat. **Admission** £7; free-£4 reductions. **Map** p61 F4 ③

As flamboyant as its founder, fashion designer Zandra Rhodes, this pink and orange museum holds 3,000 of Rhodes's garments, some on permanent display, and her archive of paper designs, sketchbooks, silk screens and show videos. There is also a shop, a little café and changing exhibitions exploring the work of particular trend-setters or themes such as the development of underwear.

Florence Nightingale Museum

St Thomas's Hospital, 2 Lambeth Palace Road, SE1 7EW (7620 0374, www.florence-nightingale.co.uk). Westminster tube or Waterloo tube/rail. **Open** 10am-5pm daily. **Admission** £5.80; free-£4.80 reductions; £16 family. **Map** p60 A3 ④

The nursing skill and zeal that made Nightingale a Victorian legend are honoured here. Reopened for the centenary of her death in 1910, the museum is now a chronological tour through her family life, the Crimean War and health reforms. Among the period mementoes are her slate and her pet owl, Athena.

Garden Museum

Lambeth Palace Road, SE1 7LB (7401 8865, www.gardenmuseum.org.uk). Lambeth North tube or Waterloo tube/rail. **Open** 10.30am-5pm Mon-Fri; 10.30am-4pm Sat; closed 1st Mon of mth. **Admission** £6; free-£5 reductions. **Map** p60 A4 ⑤

The world's first horticulture museum fits neatly into the old church of St Mary's. A 'belvedere' gallery, built out of eco-friendly wood sheeting, contains the permanent collection of art, antique tools and horticultural memorabilia, while the ground floor hosts temporary exhibitions. In the small back garden, a replica 17th-century knot garden was created in honour of John Tradescant, intrepid plant-hunter and gardener to Charles I. Tradescant is buried here. A stone sarcophagus contains the remains of William Bligh, captain of the mutinous HMS *Bounty*.

Golden Hinde

St Mary Overie Dock, Cathedral Street, SE1 9DE (7403 0123, www.golden hinde.com). London Bridge tube/rail. **Open** 10am-5.30pm daily. **Admission** £6; free-£4.50 reductions; £18 family. **Map** p61 E2 ⑥

This replica of Drake's 16th-century flagship is so meticulous it was able to reprise the privateer's circumnavigatory voyage. At weekends, the ship swarms with junior pirates. **Event highlights** 'Living History Experiences'; book well in advance.

Hayward

Southbank Centre, Belvedere Road, SE1 8XX (0844 875 0073, www.south bankcentre.co.uk). Waterloo tube/rail or Embankment tube. **Open** 10am-6pm Mon-Thur, Sat, Sun; 10am-10pm Fri. **Admission** varies. **Map** p60 A2 ⑦

This versatile art gallery continues its excellent programme of contemporary exhibitions, often with a strong interactive element. Casual visitors can hang out in the industrial-look café-bar downstairs, or visit free contemporary exhibitions in the inspired Project Space – take the stairs up from the glass foyer extension.

HMS Belfast

Morgan's Lane, Tooley Street, SE1 2JH (7940 6300, www.iwm.org.uk). London Bridge tube/rail. **Open** Mar-Oct

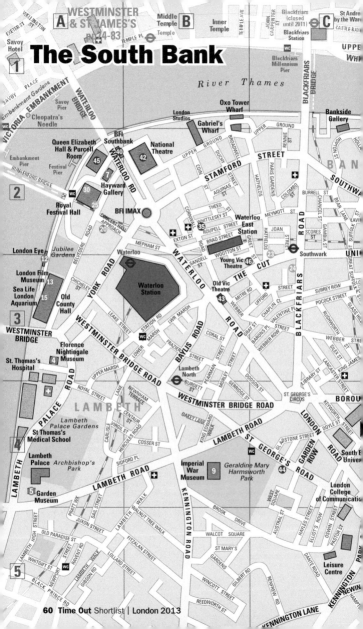

The South Bank

River Thames

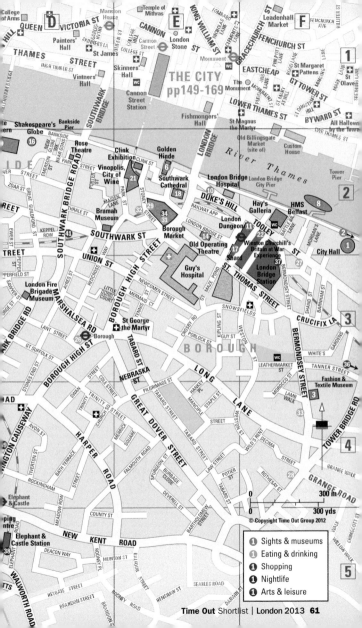

10am-6pm daily. *Nov-Feb* 10am-5pm daily. **Admission** £13.50; free-£10.80 reductions. **Map** p61 F2 ❽

This 11,000-ton light cruiser is the last surviving big gun World War II warship in Europe. Built in 1938, the *Belfast* escorted Artic convoys to Russia, and supported the Normandy landings. It now makes an unlikely playground for kids, who tear round its guns, bridge and engine room. An interactive display in the Operations Room has a radar simulation and you can play at controlling the Fleet.

Imperial War Museum

Lambeth Road, SE1 6HZ (7416 5320, www.iwm.org.uk). Lambeth North tube or Elephant & Castle tube/rail. **Open** 10am-6pm daily. Closed Jan-July 2013. **Admission** free. *Special exhibitions* prices vary. **Map** p60 B4 ❾

Antique guns, tanks, aircraft and artillery are parked up in the main hall of this imposing edifice, which illustrates the history of armed conflict from World War I to the present day. The tone of the museum darkens as you ascend: the third-floor Holocaust Exhibition is not recommended for under-14s; Crimes against Humanity – a minimalist space in which a film exploring contemporary genocide and ethnic violence rolls relentlessly – is unsuitable for under-16s. The museum is closing its doors for the first half of 2013 for a major refurbishment, reopening in July. After the £35-million redesign, the entire lower ground floor will be devoted to the Great War, in time for the centenary of its outbreak.

London Bridge Experience

2-4 Tooley Street, SE1 2SY (0844 847 2287, www.thelondonbridgeexperience. com). London Bridge tube/rail. **Open** 10am-5pm Mon-Fri; 10am-6pm Sat, Sun. **Admission** £23; free-£21 reductions; £74 family. **Map** p61 E2 ❿

Old London Bridge, finished in 1209, was the first Thames crossing made of stone – and London's only Thames bridge until Westminster Bridge was finished in 1750. This kitsch, family-focused exhibition is a costumed tour of the crossing's past, as well as a scary adventure into the haunted foundations: dank, pestilential catacombs peopled by animatronic torture victims (suitable for over-11s only). There's also a museum section, with bridge-related artefacts.

London Dungeon

28-34 Tooley Street, SE1 2SZ (0871 423 2240, www.thedungeons.com). London Bridge tube/rail. **Open** times vary, check website for details. **Admission** £23.52; £17.52-£21 reductions. **Map** p61 F2 ⓫

These railway arches contain a jokey celebration of torture, death and disease. Visitors are led through dry-ice past graves and corpses to experience nasty symptoms in the Great Plague exhibition: an actor-led medley of boils, projectile vomiting and worm-filled skulls. The Great Fire gets the treatment too, and Bloody Mary has joined the Ripper and Sweeney Todd in the rogues' gallery of infamy.

London Eye

Jubilee Gardens, SE1 7PB (0870 500 0600, www.londoneye.com). Waterloo tube/rail or Westminster tube. **Open** *Sept-Mar* 10am-8.30pm daily. *Apr-June* 10am-9pm daily. *July, Aug* 10am-9.30pm daily. **Admission** £18.60; free-£15 reductions. **Map** p60 A3 ⓬

It's hard to believe this giant wheel was only meant to turn for five years: it has proved so popular that no one wants it to come down, and refurbishment to fit it for another two decades was completed in 2012. A 'flight' takes half an hour, allowing plenty of time to get your snaps of the landmarks – if you pick a clear day, a circuit affords predictably great views of the city. Some people book in advance (taking a gamble with the weather), but you can turn up and queue for a ticket on the day – there can be long waits in summer.

London Eye

EXPLORE FROM THE INSIDE OUT

Time Out Guides written by local experts

Our city guides are written from a unique insider's perspective by teams of local writers.

Covering 50 destinations, the range includes the official London 2012 guide.

visit timeout.com/shop

London Film Museum

County Hall, Riverside Building, SE1 7PB (7202 7040, www.londonfilm museum.com). Westminster tube or Waterloo tube/rail. **Open** 10am-5pm Mon-Fri; 10am-6pm Sat, Sun. **Admission** £13.50; free-£11.50 reductions. **Map** p60 A3 ⓭

The London Film Museum celebrates the silver screen with props from *Star Wars*, *Superman* and *The Italian Job*, as well as the Rank gong. There's a gallery dedicated to animation, and you can watch interviews with the stars and clips from TV series that made it into film. A permanent exhibition, 'Charles Chaplin: The Great Londoner', focuses on the silent film star, who was born nearby.

Old Operating Theatre, Museum & Herb Garret

9A St Thomas's Street, SE1 9RY (7188 2679, www.thegarret.org.uk). London Bridge tube/rail. **Open** 10.30am-5pm daily. **Admission** £5.90; free-£4.90 reductions; £13.80 family. No credit cards. **Map** p61 E2 ⓮

The atmospheric tower that houses this salutary reminder of antique surgical practice used to be part of the chapel of St Thomas's Hospital. Visitors enter by a vertiginous wooden spiral staircase to view an operating theatre dating from 1822 (before the advent of anaesthetics), with tiered viewing seats for students. As fascinatingly gruesome are the operating tools, which look like torture implements.

Sea Life London Aquarium

County Hall, Riverside Building, Westminster Bridge Road, SE1 7PB (0871 663 1678, www.sealife.co.uk). Westminster tube or Waterloo tube/rail. **Open** *July, Aug* 10am-8pm daily. *Sept-June* 10am-6pm Mon-Thur, Sun; 10am-7pm Fri, Sat. **Admission** £19.80; free-£14.40 reductions; £68.40 family. Cheaper tickets available online, see website. **Map** p60 A3 ⓯

This is one of Europe's largest aquariums and a hit with kids. Inhabitants are grouped by geographical origin, beginning with the Atlantic, where blacktail bream swim alongside the Thames Embankment. There are poison arrow frogs, crocodiles and piranha in the 'Rainforests of the World' exhibit. The Ray Lagoon is still popular, though touching the friendly flatfish is no longer allowed (it's bad for their health). Starfish, crabs and anenomes can be handled in special open rock pools instead, and the clown fish still draw crowds. There's a mesmerising Seahorse Temple, a tank full of turtles and enchanting Gentoo penguins. The centrepieces, though, are the two massive Pacific and Indian Ocean tanks, with menacing sharks quietly circling fallen Easter Island statues and dinosaur bones.

Shakespeare's Globe

21 New Globe Walk, SE1 9DT (7401 9919, www.shakespearesglobe.com). Southwark tube or London Bridge tube/rail. **Open** *Exhibition* 10am-5pm daily. *Globe tours* Oct-Apr 10am-5pm daily. May-Sept 9.30am-12.30pm Mon-Sat; 9.30-11.30am Sun. *Rose Theatre tours* May-Sept 1-5pm Mon-Sat; noon-5pm Sun. **Admission** £12.50; free-£11 reductions; £28 family. **Map** p61 D2 ⓰

The original Globe Theatre, co-owned by Shakespeare and where many of his plays were first staged, burned down in 1613. Nearly 400 years later (it celebrated its 15th birthday in 2012), the Globe was rebuilt not far from its original site, using construction methods and materials as close to the originals as possible. It's a fully operational theatre, with historically authentic performances mixed with brand-new plays in a season running from June through to autumn. There's an exhibition on the reconstruction and Renaissance London in the UnderGlobe, and guided tours (lasting an hour and a half) run all year, visiting the nearby site of the Rose Theatre during Globe matinées.

The Rise & Rise of the Shard

A new landmark for London.

You can't miss the Shard (listings right), which is, after all, the point of the structure. It shoots to the sky 'like a shard of glass' – in the words of its architect, Renzo Piano, who envisaged his enigmatic, glass-covered, spire-like tower as 'a vertical city', combining private and public spaces.

Since 2009, Londoners have watched as first a concrete and steel skeleton grew skywards, and then its glass shell began to appear. In 2010, when it was still a concrete core, the Shard overtook One Canada Square (p182) as London's tallest building. In December 2011, it became the tallest building in the EU. The Shard reached its full height in March 2012, when its 217-foot, 500-tonne spire was winched into place. At 1,016 feet, It had been hoped that the Shard would be the tallest building in Europe, but Moscow's Mercury City Tower, scheduled for completion at the end of 2012, will be higher at 1,089 feet. The Shard may also be beaten by the the Hermitage Plaza in 2016; at a planned 1,050 feet, it will take the EU crown.

The Shard's slim, slightly irregular pyramid has 87 floors. Floors 75-87 accommodate the spire. Below, floors 68-72 are viewing galleries. From February 2013, high-speed lifts will whisk visitors up to see what are set to be the most stunning 360-degree, 40-mile views of London and its surrounds. Beneath them are flats and the the 200-room, five-star Shangri-La, set to become one of London's landmark hotels. There are more restaurants on floors 31-33, which features a spectacular glass atrium as a centrepiece. Offices occupy the lower floors.

The Shard opens in July 2012.

Shard

*32 London Bridge Street, SE1 9SS
(www.the-shard.com). London Bridge
tube/rail.* **Map** p61 E2 ⑰
See box left.

Southwark Cathedral

*London Bridge, SE1 9DA (7367
6700, www.southwark.anglican.org).
London Bridge tube/rail.* **Open** 9am-
5pm daily (closing times vary on
religious holidays). **Admission**
free; suggested donation £4.
Map p61 E2 ⑱
The oldest bits of this building date
back more than 800 years. The retro-
choir was the setting for several
Protestant martyr trials during the
reign of Mary Tudor. The courtyard is
one of the area's prettiest places for a
rest, especially during the summer.
Inside, there are memorials to
Shakespeare, John Harvard (benefactor
of the American university) and Sam
Wanamaker (the force behind the
reconstruction of the Globe); Chaucer
features in the stained glass. There are
displays throughout the cathedral
explaining its history.

Tate Modern

*Bankside, SE1 9TG (7887 8888,
www.tate.org.uk). Southwark tube or
London Bridge tube/rail.* **Open** 10am-
6pm Mon-Thur, Sun; 10am-10pm Fri,
Sat. *Tours* hourly, 11am-3pm daily.
Admission free. *Special exhibitions*
prices vary. **Map** p61 D2 ⑲
Thanks to its industrial architecture,
this powerhouse of modern art is awe-
inspiring even before you enter. It
ceased operating as Bankside Power
Station in 1981, then opened as a spec-
tacularly popular museum in 2000. The
huge turbine hall houses the Unilever
Series of temporary, large-scale installations (Tino Sehgal has the space until
28 October 2012), while the permanent
collection draws from the Tate's magnificent collection of international modern art to display the likes of Matisse,
Rothko, Bacon, Twombly and Beuys.

Since spring 2011, you've also been
able to see Picasso's *Nude, Green
Leaves & Bust* in a room dedicated to
the artist. There are vertiginous views
down inside the building from outside
the galleries, which group artworks
according to movement (Surrealism,
Minimalism, Post-war Abstraction).
The tanks that once housed oil to
power the gnerators have been converted into performance and event-based
art spaces. The Tate-to-Tate boat service (£5 adult) – polka-dot decor by
Damien Hirst, bar on board – links
with the London Eye (p62) and Tate
Britain (left) every 20 minutes.
Event highlights 'William Klein/
Daido Moriyama' (10 Oct 2012-1
Apr 2013); 'A Bigger Splash: Painting
After Performance Art' (14 Nov 2012-
1 Apr 2013).

Topolski Century

*150-152 Hungerford Arches, SE1 8XU
(7620 1275, www.topolskicentury.org.
uk). Waterloo tube/rail.* **Open** 11am-
7pm Mon-Sat; noon-6pm Sun.
Admission free. **Map** p60 A2 ⑳
Just inland from the Royal Festival
Hall, this expansive mural depicts the
extraordinary jumble of 20th-century
events through the roughly painted
faces of Bob Dylan, Winston Churchill
and many, many others. It's the work
of Polish-born expressionist Feliks
Topolski, who made his name as a war
artist in World War II – he was an eye
witness to the horrors of Belsen.

Vinopolis

*1 Bank End, SE1 9BU (7940 8300,
www.vinopolis.co.uk). London Bridge
tube/rail.* **Open** 2-10pm Thur, Fri; noon-
10pm Sat; noon-6pm Sun. **Admission**
£22.50-£40. **Map** p61 E2 ㉑
Glossy Vinopolis is more of an introduction to wine-tasting than a resource for
cognoscenti, but you do need to have
some prior interest to get a kick out of
it. Participants are introduced to sys-
tematic wine tasting and then given a
wine glass. Exhibits are set out by coun-

try, with opportunities to taste wine or champagne from different regions. Gin crashes the party courtesy of a Bombay Sapphire cocktail, and you can also sample Caribbean rum, whisky and beer.

Winston Churchill's Britain at War Experience

64-66 Tooley Street, SE1 2TF (7403 3171, www.britainatwar.co.uk). London Bridge tube/rail. **Open** *Apr-Oct* 10am-5pm daily. *Nov-Mar* 10am-4.30pm daily. **Admission** £12.95; free-£6.50 reductions; £29 family. **Map** p61 F3 ㉒

This old-fashioned exhibition recalls the privations endured by the British during World War II. Visitors descend from street level in an ancient tube lift to a reconstructed tube station shelter. The experience continues with Blitz-time London: real bombs, rare documents, photos and reconstructed shopfronts. Displays on rationing and food production are fascinating, and the set-piece bombsite quite disturbing.

Eating & drinking

Borough Market (p70) is great for gourmet snackers, while the cluster of chain eateries beside and beneath the Royal Festival Hall, includes Wagamama, Strada and, our pick, **Canteen** (right).

Anchor & Hope

36 The Cut, SE1 8LP (7928 9898). Southwark or Waterloo tube/rail. **Open** 5-11pm Mon; 11am-11pm Tue-Sat; 12.30-5pm Sun. **££**. **Gastropub. Map** p60 C2 ㉓

This monument to all things meaty, seasonal and British put Waterloo on the gastronomic map a few years back, and it still offers a lively dining experience – serving large cuts of beef, lamb or game in a plain but relaxed setting. It's a very popular place, but doesn't take evening bookings – so you'll often have to wait an hour at the noisy bar; weekday lunches are quieter. Sundays have a single 2pm sitting.

Baltic

74 Blackfriars Road, SE1 8HA (7928 1111, www.balticrestaurant.co.uk). Southwark tube. **Open** noon-3pm, 5.30-11.15pm Mon-Sat; noon-10.30pm Sun. **£££. Eastern European**. **Map** p60 C3 ㉔

This stylish spot (in the high-ceiling restaurant, a stunning chandelier is made of hundreds of amber shards) remains London's brightest star for east European food. The menu gives the best of eastern Europe – from Georgian-style lamb with aubergines to Romanian sour cream *mamaliga* (polenta) – a light, modern twist. Great cocktails, many vodkas, eclectic wines and friendly service add to the appeal.

Canteen

Royal Festival Hall, Belvedere Road, SE1 8XX (0845 686 1122, www.canteen.co.uk). Waterloo tube/rail. **Open** 8am-11pm Mon-Fri; 9am-11pm Sat, Sun. **££. British. Map** p60 A2 ㉕

Busy Canteen is furnished with utilitarian oak tables and benches. Dishes range from a bacon sandwich and afternoon jam scones to full roasts. Classic breakfasts (eggs benedict, welsh rarebit) are served all day, joined by the likes of macaroni cheese or sausage and mash from lunchtime.

Gladstone Arms

64 Lant Street, SE1 1QN (7407 3962). Borough tube. **Open** noon-11pm Mon-Fri; noon-midnight Sat; noon-10.30pm Sun. *Food served* noon-10pm daily. **Map** p61 D3 ㉖

While the Victorian prime minister still glares from the massive mural on the outer wall, inside is funky, freaky and candlelit. Gigs (blues, folk, acoustic) take place at one end of a tiny space; opposite, a bar dispenses ales and lagers. Retro touches include an old 'On Air' studio sign and pies as bar snacks.

Magdalen

152 Tooley Street, SE1 2TU (7403 1342, www.magdalenrestaurant.co.uk).

London Bridge tube/rail. **Open** noon-2.30pm, 6.30-10pm Mon-Fri; 6.30-10pm Sat. **£££**. **British**. Map p61 F3 ㉗
The atmosphere at Magdalen is low key and quite romantic, with tea lights flickering on white-clothed tables and classical music playing quietly. The menu may be short, but it is creative. Ingredients are chosen with evident care and treated with respect, neither too fussily nor too plainly. Service is friendly and suitably straightforward. The set lunch is a bargain.

M Manze

87 Tower Bridge Road, SE1 4TW (7407 2985, www.manze.co.uk). Bus 1, 42, 188. **Open** 11am-2pm Mon; 10.30am-2pm Tue-Thur; 10am-2.15pm Fri; 10am-2.45pm Sat. **£**. No credit cards. **Pie & mash**. Map p61 F4 ㉘
The finest remaining purveyor of the dirt-cheap traditional food of London's working classes. This Manze is not only the city's oldest pie shop, established back in 1902, but also in its own functional way the most beautiful, with marble-top tables and spick-and-span tiles. Expect scoops of mash, beef pies and liquor (a thin parsley sauce); for the brave, the stewed eels are a must.

Roast

Floral Hall, Borough Market, Stoney Street, SE1 1TL (7940 1300, www. roast-restaurant.com). London Bridge tube/rail. **Open** 7-11am, noon-2.45pm, 5.30-11pm Mon, Tue; 7-11am, noon-3.45pm, 5.30-11pm Sat; 11.30am-3pm, 4-9.45pm Sun. **£££**. **British**. Map p61 E2 ㉙
A big airy restaurant by Borough Market, Roast gets crammed on market days, but the staff cope admirably. The same pricey but extensive carte is served at lunch and dinner; set-price menus aren't much of a bargain either. Portions, though, are hearty. Cold poached Devon sea trout is typical, with Neal's Yard cheeses and fruit desserts for pudding. Add to this an impressive drinks list, including a

fine roster of teas, and you have a great all-round British restaurant.

Skylon

Royal Festival Hall, Belvedere Road, SE1 8XX (7654 7800, www.dand dlondon.com). Waterloo tube/rail. **Open** 11am-midnight daily. *Food served* noon-11pm daily. **£££**. **Brasserie/bar**. Map p60 A2 ㉚
For connoisseurs of London, there aren't many better views from than from the huge riverside windows. Sit near the bar counter (between two restaurant areas) to watch buses, bridges and boats while supping finely crafted cocktails. Despite the room's aircraft-hangar proportions, screens and bronze accents keep the feel intimate. Prices are high, and the food not always impressive.

Tapas Brindisa

18-20 Southwark Street, SE1 1TJ (7357 8880, www.brindisa.com). London Bridge tube/rail. **Open** 11am-11pm Mon-Sat. **£££**. **Tapas**. Map p61 E2 ㉛
Top-quality ingredients have always been the key at Brindisa, but its genius lies in the ability to assemble them into delicious and deceptively simple tapas. The set-up here is as basic as the food: there's a bar area dotted with high tables, and a close-packed, concrete-floored dining room at the other end. Both are generally thronged.

Wine Wharf

Stoney Street, Borough Market, SE1 9AD (7940 8335, www.winewharf. com). London Bridge tube/rail. **Open** 4-11.30pm Mon, Tue; noon-11.30pm Wed-Sat. **Wine bar**. Map p61 E2 ㉜
An extension of the wine-tasting attraction Vinopolis (p67), Wine Wharf inhabits two industrial-chic storeys of a reclaimed Victorian warehouse. The 250-bin list stretches to 1953 d'Yquem and serious champagne but, with nearly half the wines by the glass, you can probably afford to experiment a little.

LONDON BY AREA

For a similar take on beer, try neighbouring Brew Wharf (7378 6601, www.brewwharf.com).

Zucca

184 Bermondsey Street, SE1 3TQ (7378 6809, www.zuccalondon.com). London Bridge tube/rail or Bermondsey tube. **Open** 12.30-3pm, 6.30-10pm Tue-Sat; 12.30-3pm Sun. **££. Italian.** **Map** p61 F4 ③③

If only more restaurants had Zucca's approach: good food at great prices, served by interested staff with a genuine regard for diners. It sounds simple, yet it's pretty rare. The modern Italian menu is partnered by an all-Italian wine list, and the staff are happy to enlarge on both. The restaurant is open-plan, with the kitchen completely exposed to view, and the decor runs to shiny white surfaces with occasional splashes of intense orange.

Shopping

London's *bouquinistes* sell second-hand books and old prints from trestles by the **BFI** (p72), and the **Fashion & Textile Museum** (p59) presides over a few boutiques on Bermondsey Street.

Borough Market

Southwark Street, SE1 1TL (7407 1002, www.boroughmarket.org.uk). London Bridge tube/rail. **Open** 11am-5pm Thur; noon-6pm Fri; 8am-5pm Sat. **Map** p61 E2 ③④

Despite demolitions to make way for a rail viaduct overhead, London's busiest foodie market remains a major tourist attraction. Gourmet goodies – rare-breed meats, fruit and veg, cakes and preserves, oils and teas – run the gamut from Flour Power City Bakery's organic loaves to Neal's Yard Dairy's speciality British cheese; none of it comes cheap, but quality is high. The market opens on Thursday, which is quieter than the always-mobbed weekends – Saturday is monstrously busy.

Konditor & Cook

22 Cornwall Road, SE1 8TW (7261 0456, www.konditorandcook.com). Waterloo tube/rail. **Open** 7.30am-6.30pm Mon-Fri; 8.30am-2.30pm Sat. **Map** p60 B2 ③⑤

Gerhard Jenne caused a stir when he opened this bakery on a South Bank side street in 1993, selling gingerbread people for grown-ups and lavender-flavoured cakes. Success lay in lively ideas such as magic cakes that spell the recipient's name in a series of individually decorated squares. Quality pre-prepared salads and sandwiches are also sold.

Maltby Street

Maltby Street, Druid Street, Dockley Road & around (www.maltbystreet. com). London Bridge tube/rail. **Open** 9am-2pm Sat. **Map** p61 F3 ③⑥

Maltby Street is an unlikely place to find food retailers, but there's been a buzz about the Saturday openings since they began back in 2010. It's emphatically not a street market – merely a collection of rented railway arches where several Borough Market stalwarts had set up storage. When the traders – including well-known names like the Monmouth Coffee Company and Neal's Yard Dairy, along with smaller enterprises – decided to experiment with opening to the public, London's foodies had a new destination. The website has details of who is where.

Nightlife

As well as classical music and dance, the **Southbank Centre** (p73) programmes terrific rock, jazz and world music gigs.

Cable

33A Bermondsey Street, SE1 2EG (7403 7730, www.cable-london.com). London Bridge tube/rail. **Open** 10pm-6am Fri, Sat; 10pm-5am Sun. **Map** p61 F3 ③⑦

Zucca

All old-style brickwork and industrial air-con ducts, Cable has two dance arenas, a bar with a spot-and-be-spotted mezzanine, plenty of seats and a great covered smoking area. It has swiftly become a home for the capital's bass-hungry kids, as nights with names like Ergh, DNB Noize and Licked Beatz take over the weekends and shake the speaker stacks.

Corsica Studios

Units 4/5, Elephant Road, SE17 1LB (7703 4760, www.corsicastudios.com). Elephant & Castle tube/rail. No credit cards. **Map** p61 D5 ㊳

This flexible performance space is increasingly used as one of London's more adventurous live music venues and clubs, supplementing the bands and DJs with sundry poets, live painters and wigged-out projectionists. Its club nights are second to none: flagship night Trouble Vision boasts the best of bass.

Ministry of Sound

103 Gaunt Street, SE1 6DP (7740 8600, www.ministryofsound.com). Elephant & Castle tube/rail. **Map** p61 D4 ㊴

This refurbished clubbing powerhouse left the most important aspect of its success intact: the killer sound system. Playing on it across the Ministry's five rooms are guests that tend towards the stellar: Saturday nights boast big-name DJ takeovers from the likes of Afrojack, Laidback Luke, Roger Sanchez and Erick Morillo. Long-running trance night 'the Gallery' has made its home at Ministry of Sound on Fridays.

Arts & leisure

As well as the venues listed here, there are regular performances at **Shakespeare's Globe** (p65). Free-standing pit tickets are excellent value for money – it helps if it doesn't rain.

BFI Southbank

South Bank, SE1 8XT (7928 3535, 7928 3232 tickets, www.bfi.org.uk). Embankment tube or Waterloo tube/rail. **Map** p60 A2 ㊵

An esteemed London institution, with an unrivalled programme of retrospective seasons and previews, as well as regular director and actor Q&As. The riverside seating outside the under-powered main café is hugely popular, but the handsome cocktail bar/restaurant alongside the terrific Mediatheque (a free archive-viewing room) is better.

Made-for-IMAX kiddie pics and wow-factor documentaries are the usual fare at the nearby BFI IMAX (1 Charlie Chaplin Walk, 0870 787 2525), the biggest screen in the country, but there's a robust programme of monster-sized mainstream films too, including ace all-night screenings of film trilogies and tetralogies.

Event highlights London Film Festival (10-25 Oct 2012; Oct 2013).

Menier Chocolate Factory

51-53 Southwark Street, SE1 1RU (7907 7060, www.menierchocolate factory.com). Southwark tube or London Bridge tube/rail. **Map** p61 D2 ㊶

This fringe theatre, which has a fine bar-restaurant on the premises, has had a bit of a golden touch for West End musical transfers.

National Theatre

South Bank, SE1 9PX (7452 3400, 7452 3000 tickets, www.national theatre.org.uk). Embankment or Southwark tube, or Waterloo tube/rail. **Map** p60 B2 ㊷

This concrete monster is the flagship venue of British theatre. Three auditoriums allow for different kinds of performance: in-the-round, promenade, even classic proscenium arch. Nicholas Hytner's artistic directorship, with landmark successes such as Alan Bennett's *The History Boys*, has shown that the state-subsidised home of

British theatre can turn out quality drama at a profit. The Travelex season ensures a widening audience by offering seats for £12 (they get snapped up fast), £20 and £30, and there's free outdoor performances on the Watch This Space stage all summer.

Event highlights *People*, by Alan Bennett, directed by Nicholas Hytner (Nov 2012-Jan 2013); *The Captain of Kopenick* by Carl Zuckmayer, with Antony Sher (Jan-Apr 2013); *Children of the Sun* Howard Davies directs Maxim Gorky's play (Jan-Apr 2013); *Othello*, with Adrian Lester as Othello and Rory Kinnear as Iago (Apr-June 2013).

Old Vic

The Cut, SE1 8NB (0844 871 7628, www.oldvictheatre.com). Southwark tube or Waterloo tube/rail. **Map** p60 B3 ④③

The combination of Oscar-winner Kevin Spacey as artistic director and top producer David Liddiment at this grand, boxy 200-year-old theatre continues to be a commercial success, if not always a critical one. Programming runs from grown-up Christmas pantomimes to the Bridge Project, transatlantic collaborations on serious plays (Chekhov, Shakespeare) directed by Sam Mendes.

Event highlights The Old Vic Tunnels – under Waterloo station – host superb immersive/experimental theatre, music and other performance.

Siobhan Davies Dance Studios

85 St George's Road, SE1 6ER (7091 9650, www.siobhandavies. com). Elephant & Castle tube/rail. **Map** p60 C4 ②④

This award-winning venue, designed in consultation with dancers, not only meets their needs but looks amazing. Davies, who founded the company in 1988, often explores spaces outside her theatre, so check with the venue for performance details before setting out.

Southbank Centre

Belvedere Road, SE1 8XX (7960 4200 information, 0844 875 0073 tickets, www.southbankcentre.co.uk). Embankment tube or Waterloo tube/rail. **Map** p60 A2 ④⑤

In addition to the Hayward (p59), there are three main venues here: the Royal Festival Hall, a major venue with nearly 3,000 seats and the Philharmonia and the Orchestra of the Age of Enlightenment as residents; the Queen Elizabeth Hall, which can seat around 900; and the 365-capacity Purcell Room, for recitals. A £90m renovation a few years back improved the RFH, externally and acoustically, and since Jude Kelly took over as artistic director the programming has been rich in variety, with music and performance of all types, often appealingly themed into festivals. The RFH foyer stage hosts hundreds of free concerts each year, and the river terrace is thronged in good weather.

Event highlights Architectural installation *A Room for London* (until Dec 2012); FUNharmonics Family Concerts (13 May 2012-11 May 2013); Women of the World festival (29 Feb-10 Mar 2013).

Young Vic

66 The Cut, SE1 8LZ (7922 2922, www.youngvic.org). Southwark tube or Waterloo tube/rail. **Map** p60 B3 ④⑥

This Vic (which is actually well into middle age – it opened in 1970) has more youthful bravura than its sister up the road, packing out the open-air balcony at its popular bar-restaurant with a young crowd at weekends. They come to see European classics with a distinctly modern edge, new writing with an international flavour and the usually superb annual collaboration with the English National Opera (148).

Event highlights *Three Sisters* (8 Sept-31 Oct 2012); *Blackta* (1-17 Nov 2012); *The Changeling* (20 Nov-15 Dec 2012); *Going Dark* (10-22 Dec).

Trafalgar Square p79

Westminster & St James's

Westminster

For many the heart of London – if not Britain – Westminster is more formal than inviting. It is home to the **Houses of Parliament**, the seat of government power for 1,000 years; its **Big Ben** clocktower has starred in many holiday snaps. Britain's very first Parliament met in nearby **Westminster Abbey**, site of almost every British coronation. Here too are more photo opportunities in the shape of **Nelson's Column** and **Trafalgar Square**.

Sights & museums

Banqueting House

Whitehall, SW1A 2ER (0844 482 7777, www.hrp.org.uk). Westminster tube or Charing Cross tube/rail. **Open** 10am-5pm Mon-Sat. **Admission** £5; free-£4 reductions. **Map** p75 C2 ❶

This Italianate mansion was built in 1620 and is the sole surviving part of the Tudor and Stuart kings' Whitehall Palace. It features a lavish ceiling by Rubens that glorifies James I, 'the wisest fool in Christendom'. The hall is sometimes closed to host corporate dos. **Event highlights** Lunchtime concerts are held on the first Mon of every month, except Aug. Phone to check.

Churchill War Rooms

Clive Steps, King Charles Street, SW1A 2AQ (7930 6961, www.iwm.org.uk). St James's Park or Westminster tube. **Open** 9.30am-6pm daily. **Admission** £15.95; free-£12.80 reductions. **Map** p75 C2 ❷

Beneath Whitehall, the cramped and spartan bunker where Sir Winston Churchill planned the Allied victory in World War II remains exactly as he left it on 16 August 1945. The sense of wartime hardship is reinforced by wailing sirens and the great man's wartime speeches on the free audio guide.

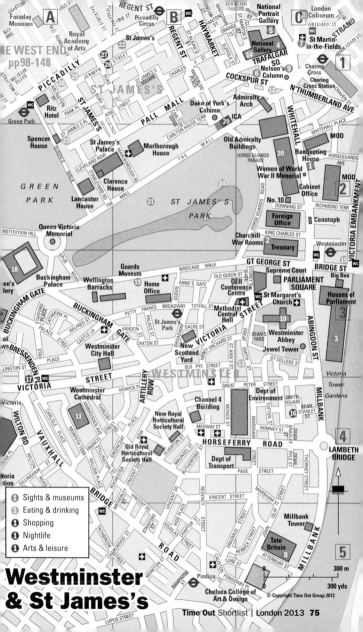

Westminster & St James's

Houses of Parliament

Parliament Square, SW1A 0AA (0844 847 1672 tours, www.parliament.uk). Westminster tube. **Open** (when in session) *House of Commons Visitors' Gallery* 2.30-10.30pm Mon, Tue; 11.30am-7.30pm Wed; 10.30am-6.30pm Thur; 9.30am-3pm Fri. *House of Lords Visitors' Gallery* 2.30-10.30pm Mon, Tue; 3-10pm Wed; 11am-7.30pm Thur; from 10am Fri. *Tours* 9.15am-4.30pm Sat & summer recess; check website for details. **Admission** *Visitors' Gallery* free. **Tours** £15; free-£10 reductions; £37 family. **Map** p75 C3 ❸

Visitors are welcome to observe the debates at the House of Lords and House of Commons – at noon on Wednesday Prime Minister's Question Time is reliably peppery – but tickets must be arranged in advance through your MP or embassy. The best times to visit are Saturdays or in summer recess, when tours – taking in ancient Westminster Hall – are organised (book ahead). The original Parliament buildings burnt down in 1834; the current neo-Gothic extravaganza was completed in 1860.

National Gallery

Trafalgar Square, WC2N 5DN (7747 2885, www.nationalgallery.org.uk). Leicester Square tube or Charing Cross tube/rail. **Open** 10am-6pm Mon-Thur, Sat, Sun; 10am-9pm Fri. *Tours* 11.30am, 2.30pm daily. **Admission** free. *Special exhibitions* prices vary. **Map** p75 C1 ❹

The National Gallery is one of the world's great repositories for art, with masterpieces from virtually every European school.

The modern Sainsbury Wing extension contains the gallery's earliest works: Italian paintings by the likes of Giotto and Piero della Francesca, as well as the Wilton Diptych, the finest medieval English picture in the collection.

In the West Wing are Italian Renaissance masterpieces by Correggio, Titian and Raphael, while the North Wing is home to 17th-century Dutch, Flemish, Italian and Spanish Old Masters, including works such as Rembrandt's *A Woman Bathing in a Stream*, as well as works by Turner and landscape artists Claude and Poussin.

In the East Wing are some of the gallery's most popular paintings: works by the French Impressionists and Post-Impressionists, including Monet's *Water-Lilies*, one of Van Gogh's *Sunflowers* and Renoir's *Les Parapluies*. You can't see everything in one visit, but free guided tours, audio guides and the superb Art Start computer help you make the best of your time.

Event highlights 'Seduced by Art: Photography Past and Present' (31 Oct 2012-20 Jan 2013).

National Portrait Gallery

St Martin's Place, WC2H 0HE (7306 0055, www.npg.org.uk). Leicester Square tube or Charing Cross tube/rail. **Open** 10am-6pm Mon-Wed, Sat, Sun; 10am-9pm Thur, Fri. **Admission** free. *Special exhibitions* prices vary. **Map** p75 C1 ❺

Portraits don't have to be stuffy. The NPG has everything from oil paintings of stiff-backed royals to photos of soccer stars and gloriously unflattering political caricatures. The portraits of musicians, scientists, artists, philanthropists and celebrities are arranged in chronological order from the top to the bottom of the building.

Event highlights 'The Queen: Art & Image' (until 21 Oct 2012); BP Portrait Award (mid June 2012-mid June 2013).

Routemaster buses (heritage)

Cockspur Street, Stops B & (opposite) S. **Map** p75 C1 ❻

See also box p78.

St Martin-in-the-Fields

Trafalgar Square, WC2N 4JJ (7766 1122, www.smitf.org). Leicester Square tube or Charing Cross tube/rail. **Open** 8am-6pm daily. *Brass Rubbing Centre* 10am-6pm Mon-Wed; 10am-8pm Thur-Sat; 11am-5pm Sun. **Admission** free. *Brass rubbing* £4.50. **Map** p75 C1 ❼

Houses of Parliament

The Routemaster Evolved

A contemporary update for a design classic.

The Routemaster, London's original hop-on, hop-off bus, was finally sent to the great garage in the sky in 2005 by the then mayor, Ken Livingstone. Noting the buses' perennial popularity, his successor, Boris Johnson, promised to bring a new generation of Routemasters to London's streets. The rounded, contemporary design, by Thomas Heatherwick, was unveiled in spring 2010 – not looking an awful lot like the traditional Routemaster, it has to be said, but at least passengers can still hop on and off at the back, which has a platform and pole like its predecessor.

According to Transport for London, the new Routemasters are 15 per cent more fuel efficient than other hybrid buses (of which London has many), 40 per cent more efficient than traditional double deckers and are much quieter on the streets.

Prototypes began plying route 38, from Victoria Station to Hackney, in February 2012. If you're determined to catch a new-style 38, you may have a long wait, though, as only eight buses were in operation at the time of writing.

Meanwhile, you can continue to experience the joy of the traditional Routemaster on two 'heritage routes'. Refurbished buses from the 1960-64 Routemaster fleet run on routes 9 (Aldwych via the Strand, Trafalgar Square and Piccadilly Circus to the Albert Hall) and 15 (from Trafalgar Square to Tower Hill, with glimpses of the Strand, Fleet Street and St Paul's Cathedral); head to stops B or S in the south-west corner of Trafalgar Square. Buses run every 15 minutes from 9.30am; fares match ordinary buses, but you must buy a ticket before boarding (see p214).

Built in 1726, St Martin's bright interior was recently restored, with Victorian furbelows removed and the addition of a strikingly plain altar window of the Cross, stylised as if rippling on water. In the crypt are a decent café and the London Brass Rubbing Centre.

Event highlights Candlelit evening concerts many Thur and Sat evenings throughout the year; see website for details.

Tate Britain

Millbank, SW1P 4RG (7887 8888, www.tate.org.uk). Pimlico tube. **Open** 10am-6pm daily; 10am-10pm 1st Fri of mth. *Tours* 11am, noon, 2pm, 3pm Mon-Fri; noon, 3pm Sat, Sun. **Admission** free. *Special exhibitions* prices vary. **Map** p75 C5 ❽

Tate Modern (p67) gets all the attention, but the original Tate Gallery has a broader and more inclusive brief. Housed in a stately Portland stone building on the riverside, it's second only to the National Gallery (p76) for British art in London. A £45m interior revamp began in February 2011 (it should be finished in 2013), but the superb collection of historic British art remains accessible – Hogarth, Gainsborough, Reynolds, Constable, and Turner (in the Clore Gallery), modern Brits Stanley Spencer, Lucian Freud and Francis Bacon, and Art Now installations that showcase up-and-comers. The handy Tate-to-Tate boat service (p214) zips east along the river to Tate Modern every 40mins.

Event highlights 'Pre-Raphaelites: Victorian Avant-Garde' (12 Sept 2012-13 Jan 2013).

Trafalgar Square

Leicester Square tube or Charing Cross tube/rail. **Map** p75 C1 ❾

Trafalgar Square was conceived in the 1820s as a homage to Britain's naval power. Always a natural gathering point – semi-pedestrianisation in 2003 made it more so – the square now regularly hosts celebrations, festivals and protests. The focus is Nelson's Column, a Corinthian pillar topped by a statue of naval hero Horatio Nelson, but the contemporary sculpture on the Fourth Plinth brings fresh colour.

Westminster Abbey

20 Dean's Yard, SW1P 3PA (7222 5152 information, 7654 4900 tours, www.westminster-abbey.org). St James's Park or Westminster tube. **Open** 9.30am-4.30pm Mon, Tue, Thur, Fri; 9.30am-7pm Wed; 9.30am-4.30pm Sat. *Abbey Museum, Chapter House & College Gardens* 10am-4pm daily. **Admission** £16; free-£13 reductions; £32 family. *Abbey Museum* free. *Tours* £3. **Map** p75 C3 ❿

The cultural significance of the Abbey is hard to overstate. Edward the Confessor commissioned it, but it was only consecrated on 28 December 1065, eight days before he died. William the Conqueror had himself crowned here on Christmas Day 1066, followed by every British king and queen since – bar two. This is also where, in spring 2011, HRH Prince William married Kate Middleton. In addition, many notables are interred in the abbey – Poets' Corner is always a draw. The Abbey Museum occupies one of the oldest parts of the Abbey: you'll find effigies of British monarchs, among them Edward II and Henry VII, wearing the actual robes they wore in life.

Westminster Cathedral

42 Francis Street, SW1P 1QW (7798 9055, www.westminstercathedral.org. uk). Victoria tube/rail. **Open** 7am-6pm Mon-Fri; 8am-6.30pm Sat; 8am-7pm Sun. *Exhibition* 10am-5pm Mon-Fri; 10am-6p m Sat, Sun. *Bell tower* 9.30am-4.30pm daily. **Admission** free; donations appreciated. *Exhibition* £5; free-£2.50 reductions. *Bell tower & exhibition* £8; free-£4 reductions. **Map** p75 A4 ⓫

With domes, arches and a soaring tower, the architecture of England's most important Catholic church (built

1895-1903) has a Byzantine look heavily influenced by Hagia Sophia. A brooding, dark ceiling sets off mosaics and marble columns with Eric Gill's savage *Stations of the Cross* at their head. A lift runs up the 273ft bell tower, for great views, and an exhibition shows off holy relics, a Tudor chalice and the architect's original model.

Eating & drinking

Albannach

66 Trafalgar Square, WC2N 5DS (7930 0066, www.albannach.co.uk). Charing Cross tube/rail. **Open** noon-1am Mon-Wed; 11am-3am Thur, Fri; 3pm-3am Sat; 11am-10.30pm Sun. **Cocktail bar. Map** p75 C1 ⑫
Albannach specialises in Scotch whiskies and cocktails based on Scotch, and the impressive location – facing right on to Trafalgar Square – will help you overlook the loud office groups and the kitsch of kilted staff and an illuminated reindeer.

Cinnamon Club

Old Westminster Library, 30-32 Great Smith Street, SW1P 3BU (7222 2555, www.cinnamonclub.com). St James's Park or Westminster tube. **Open** 7.30-9.30am, noon-2.45pm, 6-10.45pm Mon-Fri; noon-2.45pm, 6-10.45pm Sat. **££££. Indian. Map** p75 C3 ⑬
Aiming to create a complete Indian fine-dining experience, Cinnamon Club provides cocktails, fine wines, tasting menus, breakfasts (Indian, Anglo-Indian, British), private dining-rooms and all attendant flummery in an impressive, wood-lined space. Executive chef Vivek Singh devises innovative dishes, including a well-priced set meal.

National Dining Rooms

Sainsbury Wing, National Gallery, Trafalgar Square, WC2N 5DN (7747 2525, www.thenationaldiningrooms. co.uk). Charing Cross tube/rail. **Open** Bakery 10am-5.30pm Mon-Thur, Sat, Sun; 10am-8.30pm Fri; 10am-7.30pm Sat. *Restaurant* noon-3.15pm Mon-Thur, Sat, Sun; noon-3.30pm, 5-7pm Fri. Bakery **£**. Restaurant **£££**. **British**. **Map** p75 C1 ⑭
Oliver Peyton's restaurant in the National Gallery offers far better food than the usual museum fare, albeit at a price: oak-smoked Cornish duck, pea shoots with quince jelly and aval fries, perhaps, followed by wild wood pigeon with currant and beetroot glaze. The few window seats have prized views over Trafalgar Square and the bakery ably fulfils the cakes-and-cuppa role of the traditional museum café.

St Stephen's Tavern

10 Bridge Street, SW1A 2JR (7925 2286). Westminster tube. **Open** 10am-11.30pm Mon-Thur, Sat; 10.30am-12.15am Fri; 10.30am-11pm Sun. **Pub. Map** p75 C3 ⑮
Done out with dark woods, etched mirrors and lovely Arts and Crafts-style wallpaper, this is a handsome pub. The food is reasonably priced and the ales are excellent, but expensive. Brilliantly located by Big Ben, it's neither too touristy nor as busy as you might fear.

Arts & leisure

St John's, Smith Square

Smith Square, SW1P 3HA (7222 1061, www.sjss.org.uk). Westminster tube. **Map** p75 C4 ⑯
With four distinctive towers, this elegant church was finished in 1728. It now hosts classical concerts more or less every night, including occasional recitals on its magnificent Klais organ. In the crypt is the Footstool restaurant.

Victoria Palace Theatre

Victoria Street, SW1E 5EA (0844 248 5000, www.victoriapalacetheatre.co.uk). Victoria tube/rail. **Map** p75 A4 ⑰
Billy Elliot, scored by Elton John, is set during the 1984 coal miners' strike. A working-class lad loves ballet – to the consternation of his salt-of-the-earth dad. Production subject to change.

St James's

Traditional, quiet and exclusive, St James's is where **Buckingham Palace** presides over lovely **St James's Park**. Everything is dignified and unhurried, whether you're shopping at **Fortnum's** and on **Jermyn Street**, or entertaining in **Dukes** or the **Wolseley**.

Sights & museums

Buckingham Palace & Royal Mews

The Mall, SW1A 1AA (7766 7300 Palace, 7766 7301 Queen's Gallery, 7766 7302 Royal Mews, www.royal collection.org.uk). Green Park tube or Victoria tube/rail. **Open** Times vary; check website for details. **Admission** Prices vary; check website for details. **Map** p75 A3 ⑱

The London home of the Queen is open to the public each year while the family are away on their summer holidays; you'll be able to see the State Apartments, which are still used to entertain dignitaries and guests of state. At other times of year, visit the Queen's Gallery to see the Queen's personal collection of treasures, including paintings by Rembrandt, Sèvres porcelain and the Diamond Diadem crown. Further along Buckingham Palace Road, the Royal Mews is the home of the royal Rolls-Royces, the splendid royal carriages and the horses that pull them.

Event highlights The Changing of the Guard (except in rain: 11.30am alternate days, daily Apr-July).

Guards Museum

Wellington Barracks, Birdcage Walk, SW1E 6HQ (7414 3428, www.the guardsmuseum.com). St James's Park tube. **Open** 10am-4pm daily. **Admission** £4; free-£2 reductions. **Map** p75 B3 ⑲

This small museum tells the 350-year story of the Foot Guards, using flamboyant uniforms, medals, period paintings and intriguing memorabilia, such as the stuffed body of Jacob the Goose, the Guards' Victorian mascot.

Household Cavalry Museum

Horse Guards, Whitehall, SW1A 2AX (7930 3070, www.householdcavalry. co.uk). Westminster tube or Charing Cross tube/rail. **Open** Apr-Oct 10am-6pm daily. Nov-Mar 10am-5pm daily. **Admission** £6; free-£4 reductions; £15 family. **Map** p75 C2 ⑳

The Household Cavalry, the Queen's official guard, tell their stories through video diaries at this small but entertaining museum. Separated from the stables by a mere pane of glass, you'll also get a peek – and sniff – of the huge horses that parade outside daily.

Event highlights Changing of the Guard (except in rain: 11am Mon-Fri; 10am Sat).

St James's Park

St James's Park or Westminster tube. **Map** p75 B2 ㉑

The central lake of lovely St James's Park is home to numerous species of wildfowl, including pelicans that are fed at 3pm daily, and the bridge across gives glimpses west of Buckingham Palace. Just across the Mall, Green Park is featureless by comparison, but has gained a new memorial – to World War II Bomber Command, set to be unveiled on 28 June 2012.

St James's Piccadilly

197 Piccadilly, W1J 9LL (7734 4511, www.st-james-piccadilly.org). Piccadilly Circus tube. **Open** 8am-6.30pm daily. **Admission** free. **Map** p75 B1 ㉒

Consecrated in 1684, St James's is the only church Sir Christopher Wren built on a new site. A calming place with few frills, it is home to the William Blake Society (he was baptised here) and hosts a churchyard market (antiques, Tue; arts and crafts, Wed-Sat).

Event highlights Free classical recitals (1.10pm Mon, Wed, Fri).

Inn the Park

Eating & drinking

Dukes Bar

35 St James's Place, SW1A 1NY
(7491 4840, www.dukeshotel.co.uk).
Green Park tube. **Open** 2pm-midnight
Mon-Thur, Sun; noon-midnight Fri, Sat.
Cocktail bar. Map p75 A2 ㉓
This titchy bar looks like an upper-class
Georgian sitting room. Dukes' dry mar-
tinis are flamboyantly made at your
table – you pay for the privilege, but this
is one of London's most soothing and
elegant drinking experiences.

Inn the Park

St James's Park, SW1A 2BJ (7451
9999, www.innthepark.com). St James's
Park tube. **Open** 8-11am, noon-3pm,
6-8.30pm Mon-Fri; 9-11am, noon-4pm,
6-8.30pm Sat, Sun. **££-£££**. **British**
café-restaurant. Map p75 B2 ㉔
Self-service customers fight over tables
at the back, while the front terrace by
the lake is reserved for the fatter of wal-
let. The restaurant is open from (build
your own) breakfast to dinner, with the
accent on in-season, British ingredients. While the food quality sometimes
disappoints, the location never does.

Wiltons

55 Jermyn Street, SW1Y 6LX (7629
9955, www.wiltons.co.uk). Green Park
or Piccadilly Circus tube. **Open** noon-
2.30pm, 6-10.30pm Mon-Fri. **££££**.
British. Map p75 A1 ㉕
If you want to glimpse a vanishing way
of life, head for Wiltons: 'noted since
1742 for the finest oysters, fish and
game'. The cossetting service and the
muted decor are perfect for anyone
who finds the 21st century a bit much.

Wolseley

160 Piccadilly, W1J 9EB (7499 6996,
www.thewolseley.com). Green Park tube.
Open 7am-midnight Mon-Fri; 8am-
midnight Sat, Sun. **££££**. **Brasserie**.
Map p75 A1 ㉖
In a gorgeous room, the Wolseley shim-
mers with 1920s glamour, its dining

room filled with lively social energy
and battalions of waiters. It's a sought-
after venue at all times of day: breakfast, brunch, lunch, tea or dinner.

Shopping

Fortnum & Mason

181 Piccadilly, W1A 1ER (7734 8040,
www.fortnumandmason.co.uk). Green
Park or Piccadilly Circus tube. **Open**
10am-8pm Mon-Sat; noon-6pm Sun.
Map p75 A1 ㉗
In business for over 300 years, F&M is
a stunning department store: a spiral
staircase sweeps through the four-
storey building, light flooding down
from a central glass dome. The classic
eau de nil blue and gold colour scheme
with flashes of rose pink is everywhere,
both as decor and on the packaging
of the fabulous ground-floor treats –
chocolates, preserves and, of course, tea.

Jermyn Street

Green Park or Piccadilly Circus tube.
Map p75 A1 ㉓
Hilditch & Key (nos.37 & 73), Emma
Willis (no.66) and Turnbull & Asser
(nos.71-72) continue the bespoke tradi-
tion the street is known for. Bates the
Hatter has moved its topper-shaped
sign to join H&K at no.73. Charles
Tyrwhitt has a store at nos.98-100.

Arts & leisure

ICA

The Mall, SW1Y 5AH (7930 0493,
7930 3647 box office, www.ica.org.uk).
Piccadilly Circus tube or Charing Cross
tube/rail. **Open** *Galleries* (during
exhibitions) noon-7pm Wed, Fri-Sun;
noon-9pm Sun. **Admission** exhibitions
vary. Map p75 B1 ㉙
Founded in 1947 by an arts collective,
the Institute for Contemporary Arts
hosts arthouse cinema, performance
art, exhibitions and edgy club nights.
After management changes, the programme is shaping up – but public
funding was cut by 37% for 2012/13.

LONDON BY AREA

Wellington Arch p91

South Kensington & Chelsea

LONDON BY AREA

South Kensington

This area is home to the **Natural History Museum**, **Science Museum** and **V&A**; such is the wealth of exhibits in each you'd be foolish to try to 'do' more than one in any single day. The grandiose **Royal Albert Hall** and overblown, splendidly restored **Albert Memorial** also pay homage to the man behind it all, with **Kensington Gardens** a refreshing green backdrop. The Gardens are also the location of a newly refurbished **Kensington Palace**.

Sights & museums

Albert Memorial

Kensington Gardens, SW7 (7495 0916). South Kensington tube. **Map** p86 B1 ❶
An extraordinary memorial, with 180ft spire, unveiled 15 years after Prince Albert's death. Created by Sir George Gilbert Scott, it centres on a gilded, seated Albert holding a catalogue of the 1851 Great Exhibition, guarded on four corners by the continents of Africa, America, Asia and Europe. A tour guide points out the highlights (2pm, 3pm 1st Sun of mth; £6, £5 reductions).

Brompton Oratory

Thurloe Place, SW7 2RP (7808 0900, www.bromptonoratory.com). South Kensington tube. **Open** 6.30am-8pm daily. **Admission** free; donations appreciated. **Map** p86 C3 ❷
The second largest Catholic church in the country (after Westminster Cathedral, p79) was completed in 1884, but it feels older – partly because of its baroque Italianate style, partly because much of the decoration pre-dates the structure: such as Mazzuoli's late 17th-century apostle statues are from Siena cathedral. The Cardinal Newman Chapel opened in 2010.

Kensington Palace & Gardens

Kensington Gardens, W8 4PX (0844 482 7777, 0844 482 7799 reservations, www.hrp.org.uk). High Street Kensington or Queensway tube. **Open** *Mar-Oct* 10am-6pm daily. *Nov-Feb* 10am-5pm daily. **Admission** £12.50; free-£11 reductions; £34 family. **Map** p86 A1 ❸
See box p93.

Natural History Museum

Cromwell Road, SW7 5BD (7942 5000, www.nhm.ac.uk). South Kensington tube. **Open** 10am-5.50pm daily. **Admission** free. *Special exhibitions* prices vary. **Map** p86 B3 ❹
The NHM opened in a magnificent, purpose-built, Romanesque palazzo in 1881. Now, the vast entrance hall is taken up by a cast of a diplodocus skeleton, and to the left the Blue Zone has a 90ft model of a blue whale and often queues as long to see the animatronic *T Rex*. The Green Zone displays a cross-section through a giant sequoia tree – as well as an amazing array of stuffed birds, among which you can compare the fingernail-sized egg of a hummingbird with an elephant bird egg as big as a football – and another 22 million insect and plant specimens are housed (with the research scientists working on them) in the eight-storey, white Cocoon of the Darwin Centre. A new permanent gallery, Treasures, opening in November 2012, will group together prime objects from the collections, from the worlds of botany, entomology, mineralogy, zoology and palaeontology. Centre-stage will be Archaeopteryx lithographica, the fossil of the world's oldest bird, which lived 147 million years ago.
Event highlights 'Wild Planet' (23 Mar-30 Sept 2012); 'Cocoon' (until 15 Sept 2020); Treasure Gallery opens in Nov 2012.

Science Museum

Exhibition Road, SW7 2DD (7942 4000, 0870 870 4868 information, www.sciencemuseum.org.uk). South Kensington tube. **Open** 10am-6pm daily. **Admission** free. *Special exhibitions* prices vary. **Map** p86 B3 ❺
Only marginally less popular with the kids than its natural historical neighbour, the Science Museum celebrates technology in the service of daily life: from Puffing Billy, the world's oldest steam locomotive (built in 1815), via classic cars, to the Apollo 10 command module and a reconstruction of pioneering engineer James Watts' attic workshop. In the Wellcome Wing, the revamped Who Am I? gallery explores genetics, brain science and psychology, and the new, highly interactive Atmosphere, looks at the history of the science of climate change. Back in the main body of the museum, the third floor is dedicated to flight (with stunning new simulators) and the Launchpad gallery features levers, pulleys, explosions and all manner of experiments for kids.

Serpentine Gallery

Kensington Gardens, nr Albert Memorial, W2 3XA (7402 6075, www.serpentinegallery.org). Lancaster Gate or South Kensington tube. **Open** 10am-6pm daily. **Admission** free; donations appreciated. **Map** p86 B1 ❻
This secluded, small and airy gallery mounts rolling, two-monthly exhibitions by up-to-the-minute artists, along with the annual Serpentine Pavilion project (June-Sept), a temporary structure specially commissioned from an internationally renowned architect. The 2012 Pavilion was designed by Swiss architects Herzog & de Meuron and Chinese artist Ai Weiwei.
Event highlights The Serpentine Sackler Gallery opens in late 2012 in the nearby Grade II-listed Magazine – redesigned by starchitect Zaha Hadid.

Victoria & Albert Museum

Cromwell Road, SW7 2RL (7942 2000, www.vam.ac.uk). South Kensington tube. **Open** 10am-5.45pm Mon-Thur,

LONDON BY AREA

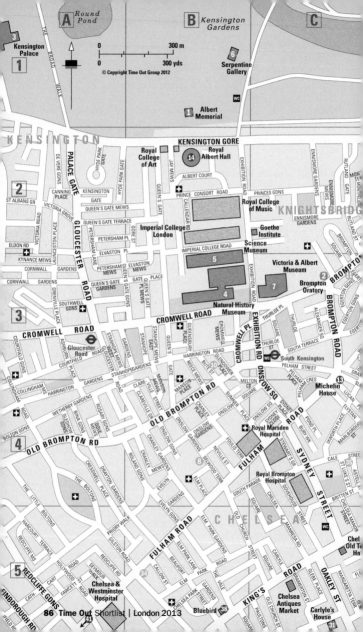

South Kensington & Chelsea

HYDE PARK

Serpentine

KNIGHTSBRIDGE

Harrods

BELGRAVIA

BELGRAVE SQUARE

Buckingham Palace Gardens

Royal Mews

GREEN PARK

Apsley House

Wellington Arch

Hyde Park Corner

Victoria Station

Victoria Coach Station

KING'S ROAD

Saatchi Gallery

PIMLICO ROAD

Royal Hospital Chelsea

National Army Museum

WESTMINSTER & ST JAMES'S pp74-83

①	Sights & museums
①	Eating & drinking
①	Shopping
①	Nightlife
①	Arts & leisure

Sat, Sun; 10am-10pm Fri. *Tours* hourly, 10.30am-3.30pm daily. **Admission** free. *Special exhibitions* prices vary.
Map p86 C3 **7**

The V&A is a superb showcase for applied arts from around the world, and its brilliant FuturePlan programme has revealed some stunning new galleries – not least the wonderfully visual Medieval & Renaissance Galleries. Among the unmissable highlights of the collection are the seven Raphael Cartoons (painted in 1515 as Sistine Chapel tapestry designs), the Great Bed of Ware and the splendid Ardabil carpet, the world's oldest floor covering. On the first floor are the Theatre and Performance Galleries, the William & Judith Bollinger Gallery of European jewellery (including diamonds that belonged to Catherine the Great) and the Gilbert Collection of gold snuffboxes and urns. There are also some superb architecture models.
Event highlights 'The Silent Traveller: Chiang Lee in Britain' 1933-1955 (23 Apr-9 Nov 2012); 'So peculiarly English: topographical watercolours' (7 June 2012-March 2013); V&A Illustration Awards (11 June-Dec 2012).

Eating & drinking

The fabled trio of tea rooms at the V&A (p85) are just a chandelier or two different from how they were in the 19th century. They're self-service. Expect to queue.

Anglesea Arms

15 Selwood Terrace, SW7 3QG (7373 7960, www.capitalpubcompany.com). South Kensington tube. **Open** 11am-11pm Mon-Sat; noon-10.30pm Sun.
Pub. Map p86 B4 **8**
Nearly 200 years old, the Anglesea was a local for Dickens and DH Lawrence. Aristocratic etchings and 19th-century London photographs adorn the dark, panelled wood walls, adding to the feel of a place lost in time. Real ales are the speciality: Brakspear Oxford Gold,

Hogs Back and Adnams among them. Food, served in a dining area with hearth fire, is traditional English; there's an outdoor terrace for summer.

Madsen

NEW *20 Old Brompton Road, SW7 3DL (7225 2772, www.madsen restaurant.com). South Kensington tube.* **Open** noon-11pm Mon-Thur; noon-midnight Fri, Sat; noon-5pm Sun.
£££. Scandinavian. Map p86 C3 **9**
Danes might feel frustrated that this chic, serene and very friendly café-cum-restaurant doesn't reflect the excitement surrounding Copenhagen's food scene, but the straightforward home cooking on offer – chicken breast fillet with horseradish cream sauce and roast root vegetables, pan-fried plaice with melted butter and carrots – is pleasing.

Oddono's

14 Bute Street, SW7 3EX (7052 0732, www.oddonos.co.uk). South Kensington tube. **Open** 10am-11pm Mon-Thur, Sun; 10am-midnight Fri, Sat. **£. Ice-cream. Map** p86 B3 **10**
Oddono's ice-cream wins awards for a reason. With a plain interior, this place is all about premium ingredients and classic flavours. Even on a grey day, regulars troop in for a fix of vaniglia made from Madagascan vanilla pods. The pistachio is some of the best anywhere, with generous sprinkles of the rich green nut.

Racine

239 Brompton Road, SW3 2EP (7584 4477). Knightsbridge or South Kensington tube, or bus 14, 74. **Open** noon-3pm, 6-10.30pm Mon-Fri; noon-3.30pm, 6-10.30pm Sat; noon-3.30pm, 6-10pm Sun. **£££. French. Map** p86 C3 **11**
Heavy curtains inside the door allow diners to make a grand entrance into Racine's warm 1930s retro atmosphere. The clientele is a mix of well-heeled locals and expats of all ages,

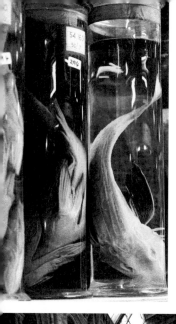

Natural History Museum p85

MONDEO

Science Museum p85

but there's plenty to enjoy from the menu: try a starter such as garlic and saffron mousse with mussels, or, for dessert, a clafoutis with morello cherries in kirsch.

Shopping

Conran Shop

Michelin House, 81 Fulham Road, SW3 6RD (7589 7401, www.conran.co.uk). South Kensington tube. **Open** 10am-6pm Mon, Tue, Fri; 10am-7pm Wed, Thur; 10am-6.30pm Sat; noon-6pm Sun. **Map** p86 C4 ⑬

Sir Terence Conran's flagship store in this lovely 1909 building showcases furniture and design for every room in the house, and the garden. Portable accessories, gadgets, books, stationery and toiletries make great gifts.

Arts & leisure

Royal Albert Hall

Kensington Gore, SW7 2AP (7589 3203 information, 7589 8212 box office, www.royalalberthall.com). South Kensington tube or bus 9, 10, 52, 452. **Map** p86 B2 ⑭

Another memorial to Queen Victoria's husband, this vast rotunda is best approached for the annual BBC Proms, despite acoustics that do orchestras few favours. Look out for recitals on the great Willis pipe organ and grand ballet extravaganzas at Christmas. **Event highlights** The Proms (mid July-mid Sept 2013).

Knightsbridge

Knightsbridge is about designer shops, many of them along **Sloane Street**, which leads down to Sloane Square (see p95), as well as two landmark department stores, **Harvey Nichols** and **Harrods**. Despite this, the area isn't particularly stylish. There are terrific people-watching opportunities, though.

Sights & museums

Apsley House

149 Piccadilly, W1J 7NT (7499 5676, www.english-heritage.org.uk). Hyde Park Corner tube. **Open** Nov-Mar 11am-4pm Sat, Sun. Apr-Oct 11am-5pm Wed-Sun. **Admission** £6.30; free-£5.80 reductions. **Map** p87 E1 ⑮

Called No.1 London because it was the first London building encountered on the road to the City from Kensington village, Apsley House was the Duke of Wellington's residence for 35 years. His descendants still live here, but several rooms are open to the public and give a superb feel for the man and his era.

Hyde Park

7298 2000, www.royalparks.gov.uk. Hyde Park Corner, Lancaster Gate or Marble Arch tube. **Map** p87 E1 ⑯

At 1.5 miles long and a mile wide, Hyde Park is one of the largest Royal Parks. It was a hotspot for demonstrations in the 19th century and remains so today – a march against war in Iraq in 2003 that finished here was the largest in British history. The legalisation of public assembly in the park led to the creation of Speakers' Corner in 1872 (close to Marble Arch tube), where political and religious ranters still have the floor, and Marx, Lenin, Orwell and the Pankhursts also spoke. Rowing boats and pedalos can be hired to venture among the ducks, swans and grebes on the Serpentine.

Wellington Arch

Hyde Park Corner, W1J 7JZ (7930 2726, www.english-heritage.org.uk). Hyde Park Corner tube. **Open** Apr-Oct 10am-5pm Wed-Sun. Nov-Mar 10am-4pm Sat, Sun. **Admission** £3.90; free-£3.50 reductions. **Map** p87 F1 ⑰

Built in the 1820s to mark Britain's triumph over Napoleonic France and initially topped by a vast statue of Wellington, since 1912 the bronze *Peace Descending on the Quadriga of War* has finished the Arch with a flourish. Three floors of displays cover its history and that of the Blue Plaques scheme (which puts their biographical details on the houses where famous people lived); the third floor has great views from its balcony.

Eating & drinking

Amaya

Halkin Arcade, Motcomb Street, SW1X 8JT (7823 1166, www. amaya.biz). Knightsbridge tube. **Open** 12.30-2.15pm, 6.30-11.30pm Mon-Sat; 12.45-2.45pm, 6.30-10.30pm Sun. **£££**. **Indian**. Map p87 E2 ⑲
Slinky by night, when its black leather seating, modish chandeliers and soundtrack of cool beats attract smooching couples, Amaya is light and breezy by day. From the open kitchen, black-aproned chefs display consummate skill at the tawa griddle, the tandoor oven and at the house-speciality charcoal grill.

Bar Boulud

Mandarin Oriental Hyde Park, 66 Knightsbridge, SW1X 7LA (7201 3899, http://danielnyc.com/barbouludhub.html). Knightsbridge tube. **Open** noon-2.30pm, 3.30-5pm, 5.30-10.30pm daily. **£££**.
French bistro. Map p87 D1 ⑲
Daniel Boulud, a French chef rated one of the rest restaurateurs in New York, has brought over some Big Apple style and French polish. The menu points to Lyon, the heart of French gastronomy, with amazing charcuterie and refined country classics, and to New York, with three types of burger. The service is well informed, well mannered and utterly professional, and the atmosphere refreshingly informal, with children genuinely welcomed.

Blue Bar

The Berkeley, Wilton Place, SW1X 7RL (7235 6000, www.the-berkeley.co.uk). Hyde Park Corner tube. **Open** 4pm-1am Mon-Sat; 4-11pm Sun. **Cocktail bar**. Map p87 E2 ⑳

It isn't just a caprice: this David Collins-designed bar lives up to its name. The sky-blue bespoke armchairs, the deep-blue ornate plasterwork and the navy-blue leather-bound menus combine with discreet lighting to striking effect. It's more a see and be seen place than somewhere to kick back, but don't let the celeb-heavy reputation put you off: the staff treat all customers like royalty and the cocktails they mix are a masterclass in sophistication.

Dinner by Heston Blumenthal

NEW *Mandarin Oriental Hyde Park, 66 Knightsbridge, SW1X 7LA (7201 3833, www.dinnerbyheston.com). Knightsbridge tube.* **Open** noon-2.30pm, 6.30-10.30pm daily. **££££**.
British. Map p87 D1 ㉑
With Heston Blumenthal now a fully-fledged celebrity, this warm, relaxing room is a hotspot attracting high-profile clientele. Dinner is not actually by Blumenthal, but under the command of Ashley Palmer-Watts, executive head chef of the Fat Duck group. The pair developed the menu together, taking inspiration from British culinary history, though the dishes are rendered in modern (rather than revolutionary) haute cuisine style.

Zuma

5 Raphael Street, SW7 1DL (7584 1010, www.zumarestaurant.com). Knightsbridge tube. **Open** *Restaurant* noon-2.45pm, 6-10.45pm Mon-Fri; 12.30-3.15pm, 6-45pm Sat; 12.30-3.15pm, 6-10.15pm Sun. *Bar* noon-11pm Mon-Fri; 12.30-11pm Sat; 12.30-10.30pm Sun. **££££**. **Japanese fusion/bar**. Map p87 D2 ㉒
One of London's smartest restaurants, there's more to this buzzy 'contemporary *izakaya*' (Japanese tapas bar, in effect) than its striking wood-and-stone interior. The surprise is that the mix of Japanese and fusion food on the long menu fully justifies high prices.

Palace Lives

Generations of royals called Kensington Palace home.

The newly restored Kensington Palace (p85) is now open to the public. This is not just another grand house with old furniture and paintings. Here, visitors follow a whimsical trail focused on four 'stories' of former residents. They unearth facts about them and their times through 'newspapers' – really handily placed crib sheets, relating the news of the day. There are whispering in the galleries and poignant reminiscences.

The first, and briefest, story is that of Princess Diana: stylised 'Diana' wallpaper lines a narrow corridor leading to a room containing some of her dresses.

The Queen's State Apartments are modest, liveable rooms. The lives featured here, we learn, are those of William and Mary, and Mary's sister, Queen Anne. Suitcases and sounds of the sea allude to William and Mary's arrival from the Netherlands to depose James II in the Glorious Revolution of 1688. William and Mary were childless and eventually succeeded by Anne. She had 17 pregnancies,

but only one child, the sickly Prince William, survived beyond infancy; doted on by his mother, he was the hope for the continuation of the Stuart line. But he took ill at his tenth birthday party, where it is said he overheated while dancing, leading to a fever and his death. The place settings for that doomed party are re-created here, along with dreamlike installations reflecting a childhood curtailed.

The King's State Apartments were created for George I and George II. George arrived from Hanover to take the throne following the death of Queen Anne without an heir. In contrast with the homely Queen's rooms, the grandeur of these semi-public spaces is palpable: the Presence Chamber, with its throne; the Privy Chamber for more intimate meetings; and the Gallery, with paintings by the likes of Tintoretto, used for chats with confidantes (you can still hear them today if you stand by the windows).

The fourth 'story', Victoria Revealed, traces the life of Queen Victoria through objects and extracts from her writings. Among the artefacts is her (tiny) wedding dress, jewellery and other gifts from Prince Albert, photographs of her children and dolls.

Much of the exhibition covers her private life: her love for Albert, their cosy domesticity, her devastation at his death and prolonged mourning. But major events of the period feature too, with a section devoted to the Great Exhibition and another to the Diamond Jubilee.

LONDON BY AREA

Shopping

Harrods

*87-135 Brompton Road, SW1X
7XL (7730 1234, www.harrods.
com). Knightsbridge tube.* **Open**
10am-8pm Mon-Sat; noon-6pm Sun.
Map p87 D2 ㉓

All the glitz and marble can be a bit
much, but in the store that boasts of selling everything, it's hard not to leave
with at least one thing you like. The food
halls are legendary, but it's on the fashion floors that Harrods comes into its
own, with well-edited collections from
the heavyweights – and a rather impressive new shoe department.

Harvey Nichols

*109-125 Knightsbridge, SW1X 7RJ
(7235 5000, www.harveynichols.com),
Knightsbridge tube.* **Open** 10am-8pm
Mon-Sat; noon-6pm Sun. **Map** p87 D2 ㉔

A worthy clutch of unique brands are
found over eight floors of beauty, fashion, food and home. The fashion floors
showcase emerging British talent
(Peter Pilotto, Mary Katrantzou), new
designers (Meadham Kirchoff, Brian
Reyes) and established favourites
(Donna Karan, Marc Jacobs). The food
market on the fifth floor stocks over
600 products, as well as being home to
a stylish bar, branches of Wagamama
and Yo! Sushi and the excellent Fifth
Floor restaurant.

Belgravia & Pimlico

This area is characterised by a
host of embassies and the fact
that everyone living here is very
rich. Enjoy strolling through tiny
mews, then settle into some plush
dining, drinking or shopping.

Eating & drinking

Boisdale

*13-15 Eccleston Street, SW1W 9LX
(7730 6922, www.boisdale.co.uk).
Victoria tube/rail.* **Open** noon-1am
Mon-Fri; 6pm-1am Sat. **Admission**
£5 before 10pm, then £12. **Whisky
bar**. **Map** p87 F3 ㉕

From the labyrinthine bar and restaurant spaces and heated cigar terrace to
overstated tartan accents, there's something brilliantly preposterous about
Boisdale. It's hard not to love a posh,
Scottish-themed enterprise that specialises in superb single-malt whiskies.
Additional appeal comes from live jazz
(six nights a week).

Nahm

*Halkin, Halkin Street, SW1X 7DJ
(7333 1234, www.halkin.como.bz).
Hyde Park Corner tube.* **Open** noon-
2.30pm, 7-10.45pm Mon-Fri; 7-10.45pm
Sat; 7-9.45pm Sun. **££££**. **Thai**.
Map p87 F2 ㉖

Done out in gold and bronze tones,
this elegant hotel dining room feels
opulent yet unfussy. Tables for two
look out over a manicured garden, and
the chance to share rare dishes of star-
tling flavour combinations from
David Thompson's kitchen always
makes for a memorable meal.
Thompson seeks to interpret historic
Thai cooking, yet flashes of inspiration bring the dishes firmly into the
modern era: for example, a chicken
and banana flower salad unusually,
but successfully, includes samphire
and palourdes clams.

Shopping

Daylesford Organic

*44B Pimlico Road, SW1W 8LJ
(7881 8060, www.daylesford
organic.com). Sloane Square tube.*
Open 8am-8pm Mon-Sat; 10am-4pm
Sun. **Map** p87 E4 ㉗

Part of a new wave of chic purveyors
of health food, this impressive offshoot of Lady Carole Bamford's
Cotswold-based farm shop is set over
three floors, and includes a café.
Goods include ready-made dishes, and
such store-cupboard staples as pulses
and pasta.

Elizabeth Street

Sloane Square tube. **Map** p87 F4 **㉘**
The Victoria Coach Station location doesn't inspire confidence, but Elizabeth Street sells show-stopping jewellery (Erickson Beamon, no.38), gorgeous invitations and correspondence cards (Grosvenor Stationery Company, no.47), quality cigars (Tomtom, no.63) and fine perfumes (Les Senteurs, no.71). There's also the only British outpost of French bakery Poilâne (no.46).

Chelsea

It's been more than four decades since *Time* magazine declared that London – by which it meant the **King's Road** – was 'swinging'. These days you're more likely to find suburban swingers wondering where it went than the next Jean Shrimpton, but places like **Anthropologie** have improved the retail opportunities and the **Saatchi Gallery** has put it back on the tourist map. Chelsea proper starts at **Sloane Square**, spoiled by traffic but redeemed by the edgy **Royal Court Theatre**.

Sights & museums

Chelsea Physic Garden

66 Royal Hospital Road, SW3 4HS (7352 5646, www.chelseaphysicgarden. co.uk). Sloane Square tube or bus 11, 19, 239. **Open** *Apr-Oct* noon-5pm Wed-Fri; noon-6pm Sun. **Admission** £8; free-£5 reductions. **Map** p87 D5 **㉙**
The capacious grounds of this gorgeous botanic garden are filled with healing herbs and vegetables, rare trees and dye plants. The garden was founded in 1673 by Sir Hans Sloane with the purpose of cultivating and studying plants for medical purposes.

National Army Museum

Royal Hospital Road, SW3 4HT (7730 0717, www.national-army-museum. ac.uk). Sloane Square tube or bus 11,
137, 170. **Open** 10am-5.30pm daily. **Admission** free. **Map** p87 D5 **㉚**
More entertaining than its rather dull exterior suggests, this museum of the history of the British Army kicks off with 'Redcoats', a gallery that starts at Agincourt in 1415 and ends with the American War of Independence. You'll also find some fingertips, frostbitten on Everest, and men of a certain age will welcome the exhibition of art from *Commando* comics.

Saatchi Gallery

Duke of York's HQ, SW3 4SQ (7823 2363, www.saatchi-gallery.co.uk). Sloane Square tube. **Admission** free. **Map** p87 E4 **㉛**
Charles Saatchi's gallery has three floors, providing more than 50,000sq ft of space for temporary exhibitions that generally show Saatchi's taste is broader than his reputation as a champion of Brit Art suggests. Still, some of his famous British acquisitions – notably Richard Wilson's brilliant sump-oil installation *20:50* – remain.

Eating & drinking

The art deco former garage **Bluebird** (350 King's Road, 7559 1000, www.danddlondon.com) has a fine modern European restaurant.

Gallery Mess

Saatchi Gallery, Duke of York's HQ, King's Road, SW3 4LY (7730 8135, www.saatchigallery.com). Sloane Square tube. **Open** 10am-9.30pm Mon-Sat; 10am-6.30pm Sun. **££. Brasserie**. **Map** p87 E4 **㉜**
The Saatchi Gallery (above) is home to a fabulous brasserie. There's a simple breakfast menu (pastries, eggs and toast or fry-up) to 11.30am, then lunch and dinner take over, with salads, pastas and burgers joined by daily specials: perhaps steamed salmon served in a yellow 'curry' broth or saddle of lamb drizzled with yoghurt. You can sit inside surrounded by modern art,

Ice-Cream Dreams

Suddenly, London has the taste for ice-cream, or, to be more precise, Italian-style *gelato*. We're starting to lose count of the number of new parlours to open in the capital, not least because some of our favourite old-timers, such as **Scoop** (p144). **Oddono's** (see p88) and **Gelato Mio** (204 Haverstock Hill, NW3 2AG, 7998 9276, www.gelatomio.co.uk) are expanding, while the Patisserie Valerie chain now has its own dedicated *gelateria* in Chelsea's **Gelateria Valerie** (right).

Then there's the fabulous ice-cream being sold in other eateries and shops, among them **William Curley** in Pimlico (198 Ebury Street, SW1W 8UN, 7730 5522, www.williamcurley. co.uk) and, in season, the Islington branch of **Paul A Young Fine Chocolates** (p174). And, we shouldn't forget old-school purveyor of Italian ice-cream and eats, **Marine Ices** (8 Haverstock Hill, NW3 2BLm 7482 9003, www.marineices.co.uk).

Competition keeps standards high, but has also encouraged the rise of more theatrical and attention-grabbing establishments: you can have your ice-cream frozen in front of your eyes in the chemistry-lab setting of Camden's **Chin Chin Laboratorists** (49-50 Camden Lock Place, NW1 8AF, 07885 604284, www.chinchinlabs. com), or have a 'vice cream' cocktail blowtorched by the fetish cap-wearing **Icecreamists** (p143) in Covent Garden.

but the grounds outside – littered with portable tables until 6pm in fair weather – are an attractive option.

Gelateria Valerie

9 Duke of York Square, SW3 4LY (7730 7978, www.patisserie-valerie. co.uk). Sloane Square tube. **Open** 7.30am-7.30pm daily. **£**. **Ice-cream**. **Open** 7.30am-7.30pm daily. **Map** p87 E4 ㉝

Gelato here is good, but it's the location that really sells Pâtisserie Valerie's gelateria. The impressive glass building has a long glass counter with tall swivel stools running along one window. Customers tuck into bowls of gelato while looking out on to Duke of York Square, while shoppers look back enviously. The patio is a relaxing place to sip Italian coffee too, if the weather allows.

Haché

329-331 Fulham Road, SW10 9QL (7823 3515, www.hacheburgers.com). South Kensington tube. **Open** noon-10.30pm Mon-Thur, Sun; noon-11pm Fri, Sat. **£**. **Burgers**. **Map** p86 B5 ㉞

Haché is French for 'chopped', but the only Gallic twist on the great American burger here is attention to detail. Rather than underpinning them with skewers, Haché's toasted ciabattas are left ajar so that you can admire the ingredients – they're worth admiring.

Tom's Kitchen

27 Cale Street, SW3 3QP (7349 0202, www.tomskitchen.co.uk). Sloane Square or South Kensington tube. **Open** 8-11am, noon-3pm, 6-11pm Mon-Fri; 10am-4pm, 6-11pm Sat, Sun. **£££**. **Brasserie**. **Map** p86 C4 ㉟

White-tiled walls, vast expanses of marble and a busy open kitchen ensure Tom Aitkens' place sounds full even when it isn't – for weekend lunches it can often be packed. The big draw here is the pancake: well over an inch thick and almost as big as the serving plate, it's categorically London's best. Lunch and dinner menus make the most of the wood-smoked oven, spit-roast and grill. Expect big-tasting comfort food.

Shopping

Anthropologie Decor
131-141 King's Road, SW3 5PW (7349 3110, www.anthropologie.eu). Sloane Square tube then bus 11, 19, 22, 319, 211. **Open** 10am-7pm Mon-Sat; noon-6pm Sun. **Map** p87 D5 ❸❻

This American shop, vintage-inspired and stylishly bohemian, has refocused to concentrate on homeware, with a bumper stock of haberdashery, wallpapers and design books. Fashion is at the other branch on Regent Street.

John Sandoe
10 Blacklands Terrace, SW3 2SR (7589 9473, www.johnsandoe.com). Sloane Square tube. **Open** 9.30am-6.30pm Mon-Sat; 11am-5pm Sun. **Map** p87 D4 ❸❼

Tucked away on a Chelsea side street, this 50-year-old independent looks just as a bookshop should. The stock is literally packed to the rafters, and of the 25,000 books here, 24,000 are a single copy – so there's serious breadth.

Shop at Bluebird
350 King's Road, SW3 5UU (7351 3873, www.theshopatbluebird.com). Sloane Square tube. **Open** 10am-7pm Mon-Sat; noon-6pm Sun. **Map** p86 B5 ❸❽

Part lifestyle boutique and part design gallery, the Shop at Bluebird offers a shifting showcase of clothing for men, women and children (Emma Cook, Peter Jensen, Marc Jacobs), accessories, books, furniture and gadgets. The shop has a bit of a retro feel, all vintage furniture, reupholstered seats and hand-printed fabrics.

Sloane Square
Sloane Square tube. **Map** p87 E4 ❸❾

The shaded benches and fountain in the middle of the square provide a lovely counterpoint to the looming façades of Tiffany & Co and the enormous 1930s Peter Jones department store, as well as the grinding traffic. Come summer, the brasserie terraces teem with stereotypical blonde Sloane Rangers sipping rosé; an artier crop of whatever's stylishly edgy will have taken up residence outside the Royal Court Theatre.

Arts & leisure

Cadogan Hall
5 Sloane Terrace, SW1X 9DQ (7730 4500, www.cadoganhall.com). Sloane Square tube. **Map** p87 E3 ❹❶

Built a century ago as a Christian Science church, this austere building has been transformed into a light and airy auditorium. Programming at the 905-capacity venue is mainly classical; acoustics are excellent.

Chelsea Football Club
Stamford Bridge, Fulham Road, SW6 1HS (0871 984 1905, www.chelseafc.com). Fulham Broadway tube. **Map** p86 A5 ❹❶

They may have lost a little ground in the Premiership, but Chelsea made up for it by winning the 2011/12 Champions League Final. You're unlikely to get tickets to see any league action, but you can check out the museum or seek tickets for European matches or cup ties against lower league opposition.

Royal Court Theatre
Sloane Square, SW1W 8AS (7565 5000, www.royalcourttheatre.com). Sloane Square tube. **Map** p87 E4 ❹❷

A hard-hitting theatre in a well-heeled location, the emphasis here has always been on new voices in British theatre – since John Osborne's *Look Back in Anger* in the theatre's inaugural year, 1956, there have been innumerable discoveries made here. Artistic director Dominic Cooke has injected plenty of politics into the programme. Expect to find rude, lyrical new work by first-time playwrights, as well as better established writers with a message.

Novello Theatre p148

The West End

Marylebone

There is relentless trade on Oxford Street, home to hip **Selfridges**, doughty **John Lewis** and chain flagships for **Uniqlo** and **Topshop**, but few locals esteem the historic thoroughfare. Despite the new Shibuya-style diagonal crossing at Oxford Circus, perhaps an inkling of future improvements, clogged pavements make for unpleasant shopping. Escape the crowds among the pretty boutiques on **Marylebone High Street** to the north. Among the sights, the **Wallace** is too often overlooked, and **Regent's Park** is one of London's finest green spaces.

Sights & museums

Madame Tussauds

Marylebone Road, NW1 5LR (0870 400 3000, www.madametussauds.com). Baker Street tube. **Open** times vary; check website for details. **Admission** £28.80; free-£24.60 reductions; £99 family. **Map** p99 A1 ❶

Madame Tussaud brought her show to London in 1802, 32 years after it was founded in Paris, and it's been here since 1884. There are 300 figures in the collection now, under various themes: 'A-list Party' (Brad, Keira, Kate Moss), 'Première Night' (Monroe, Chaplin, Arnie), 'By Royal Appointment' and so on. In the Chamber of Horrors in 'Scream', only teens claim to enjoy the floor drops and scary special effects; they're similarly keen on the Iron Man, Spiderman and an 18ft Hulk in Marvel Super Heroes 4D. Get here before 10am to avoid huge queues, and book ahead online to make prices more palatable.

Regent's Park

Baker Street or Regent's Park tube. **Open** 7am-dusk daily. **Map** p99 B1 ❷

Regent's Park is one of London's most popular open spaces. Attractions run from the animal noises and odours of

Marylebone & Mayfair

REGENT'S PARK

A **B** **C**

1 Sights & museums

2 Eating & drinking

3 Shopping

4 Nightlife

5 Arts & leisure

Numbered locations refer to the Marylebone and Mayfair sections on pp98-112

© Copyright Time Out Group 2012

WESTMINSTER & ST JAMES'S pp74-83

GREEN PARK

300 m

300 yds

War was presented in a way the whole family could engage in we shall be back

London Zoo (p171) to enchanting Open Air Theatre versions of *A Midsummer Night's Dream* that are an integral part of a London summer. Hire a rowing boat on the lake or just walk among the roses.

Wallace Collection

Hertford House, Manchester Square, W1U 3BN (7935 0687, www.wallace collection.org). Bond Street tube. **Open** 10am-5pm daily. **Admission** free. **Map** p99 A2 ❸

This handsome house, built in 1776 and being steadily returned to its original state after 'improvements' in previous generations, has an exceptional collection of 18th-century French paintings and objets d'art, as well as armour and weapons. Rooms contain Louis XIV and XV furnishings and Sèvres porcelain, while the galleries are hung with work by Titian, Velázquez, Gainsborough and Fragonard. Franz Hals's *The Laughing Cavalier* is one of the best known. After an 18-month refurbishment, the stunning Dutch Galleries, home to one of Europe's best collection of Dutch art, has reopened.

Eating & drinking

Artesian

Langham Hotel, 1C Portland Place, W1B 1JA (7636 1000, www.artesian-bar.co.uk). Oxford Circus tube. **Open** noon-2am Mon-Sat; noon-midnight Sun. **££££. Bar. Map** p99 C2 ❹

Order any three of the extraordinary cocktails here, add service, and you won't get much change from a £50 note. But you'll be drinking them in style: David Collins has done a fine job on the decor, the back bar theatrically lit by huge hanging lamps.

L'Autre Pied

5-7 Blandford Street, W1U 3DB (7486 9696, www.lautrepied.co.uk). Baker Street tube. **Open** noon-2.30pm, 6-10.30pm Mon-Sat; noon-3pm, 6.30-9.30pm Sun. **£££. Modern European. Map** p99 A2 ❺

L'Autre Pied offers nuanced cooking in handsome rooms. Despite the trappings of somewhere that takes food very seriously, it's an accessible and relaxing place to eat, and the kitchen rarely puts a foot wrong, displaying a light touch and subtle use of herbs.

Busaba Eathai

8-13 Bird Street, W1U 3DB (7518 8080/http://busaba.com). Bond Street tube. **Open** noon-11pm Mon-Thur; noon-11.30pm Fri, Sat; noon-10pm Sun. **Thai. Map** p99 B3 ❻

All the branches of this handsome Thai canteen are excellent and busy, but this one is superbly located for Oxford Street shoppers. Interiors in all branches combine shared tables and bench seats with a touch of dark-toned oriental mystique, and the dishes are always intriguing and well executed. **Other locations** throughout the city.

Comptoir Libanais

65 Wigmore Street, W1U 1PZ (7935 1110, www.lecomptoir.co.uk). Bond Street tube. **Open** 8am-10pm Mon-Fri; 10am-10pm Sat, Sun. **£. Lebanese. Map** p99 B3 ❼

Part canteen, part deli, Libanais is original, chic and bright, with cutlery in harissa tins and colourful murals in typical Arab advert style adorning the walls. Pick up a wrap (falafel, say, or chicken kofta) for lunch, pop by for mint tea and a rosewater macaroon in the afternoon, or linger over an informal dinner of moussaka or tagine with organic couscous or rice. Breads (baked in-house) and sweets are a key draw.

Fairuz

3 Blandford Street, W1U 3DA (7486 8108, www.fairuz.uk.com). Baker Street or Bond Street tube. **Open** noon-11.30pm Mon-Sat; noon-11pm Sun. **££. Lebanese. Map** p99 B2 ❽

The combination of Lebanese food, neighbourhood-taverna surroundings and West End location has helped this long-standing Marylebone favourite

Comptoir Libanais p101

retain its popularity. Its collection of mezes and mains is brilliantly executed.

La Fromagerie

2-6 Moxon Street, W1U 4EW (7935 0341, www.lafromagerie.co.uk). Baker Street or Bond Street tube. **Open** 8am-7.30pm Mon-Fri; 9am-7pm Sat; 10am-6pm Sun. **££**. **Café**. **Map** p99 A2 ❾

Famed with foodies for its dedicated cheese room, Patricia Michelson's high-end deli also dishes out freshly cooked, stylish café food. Its communal tables are often packed with devotees.

Golden Hind

73 Marylebone Lane, W1U 2PN (7486 3644). Bond Street tube. **Open** noon-3pm, 6-10pm Mon-Fri; 6-10pm Sat. **£**. **Fish & chips.** **Map** p99 B2 ❿

The pastel-hued art deco fryer at this chip shop is only used to store menus these days (the cooking's done in a back kitchen), but the Golden Hind still oozes local character, entirely in keeping with its Marylebone Lane location. Big portions hit the spot, and the staff really make a fuss of customers.

Purl

50 Blandford Street, W1U 7HX (7935 0835, www.purl-london.com). Bond Street tube. **Open** 5-11.30pm Mon-Thur; 5pm-midnight Fri, Sat. **Bar** **Map** p99 A2 ⓫

The four young chaps behind this speakeasy-style cocktail bar claim inspiration from the golden age of bartendingf. Accordingly, a lot of effort goes into each drink: for Mr Hyde's Fixer Upper, a hand-held food smoker pipes applewood smoke into a flask of rum, cola reduction and orange bitters. The flask is then sealed with candle-wax before being served with a goblet.

Shopping

Held at St Marylebone Parish Church on Saturdays, **Cabbages & Frocks** market (7794 1636, www.cabbagesandfrocks.co.uk) sells vintage clothing and snacks. On Sunday morning, **Marylebone Farmers' Market** is in Cramer Street car park at Moxton Street.

Cadenhead's Whisky Shop & Tasting Room

26 Chiltern Street, W1U 7QF (7935 6999, www.whiskytastingroom.com). Baker Street tube. **Open** 10.30am-6.30pm Mon-Fri; 10.30am-6pm Sat. **Map** p99 A2 ⓬

Cadenhead's is a rarity: an independent whisky bottler. The firm selects barrels from distilleries all over Scotland and bottles them without filtration or any other intervention. One of a kind.

John Lewis

278-306 Oxford Street, W1A 1EX (7629 7711, www.johnlewis.co.uk). Bond Street or Oxford Circus tube. **Open** 9.30am-8pm Mon-Wed, Fri; 9.30am-9pm Thur; 9.30am-7pm Sat; noon-6pm Sun. **Map** p99 B3 ⓭

Renowned for solid reliability, the courtesy of its staff and its 'never knowingly undersold' policy, John Lewis also deserves a medal for breadth of stock. The revamped ground-floor cosmetics hall, for example, has glamorous Crème de la Mer and Eve Lom, but also natural brands like Neal's Yard and Burt's Bees. The store is also a destination for those in search of fabrics and habadashery.

Margaret Howell

34 Wigmore Street, W1U 2RS (7009 9009, www.margarethowell.co.uk). Bond Street tube. **Open** 10am-6pm Mon-Wed, Fri, Sat; 10am-7pm Thur; noon-5pm Sun. **Map** p99 B2 ⓮

Howell's wonderfully wearable outfits are made in Britain and with an old-fashioned attitude to quality. These principles combine to create the best 'simple' clothes in London. Her pared-down approach means prices seem steep, but these are clothes that will get better with time.

Marylebone High Street

Bond Street or Baker Street tube.
Map p99 B2 🅕

With tube stations at its top and bottom, this is one of the most accessible shopping streets in town. Browse the likes of elegant lifestyle store Brissi (no.22), inspirational Daunt Books (no.83), the Scandinavian design classics at Skandium (no.86) and Kabiri's avant-garde jewellery (no.37). Need a snack? Detour to Marylebone Lane for 1950s timewarp café Paul Rothe & Son (no.35), via high-fashion artisan shoes at Tracey Neuls (no.29).

Selfridges

400 Oxford Street, W1A 1AB (0800 123 400, www.selfridges.com). Bond Street or Marble Arch tube. **Open** 9.30am-8pm Mon-Wed, Fri, Sat; 9.30am-9pm Thur; noon-6pm Sun. **Map** p99 A3 🅖

With its plethora of concession boutiques and collections from the hottest brands, Selfridges is as dynamic as a department store could be. While the basement is chock full of hip home accessores and stylish kitchen equipment, it's the fashion floors that really get hearts racing, with a winning combination of new talent, hip and edgy labels, high-street brands and high-end designers. Highlights include the extensive Shoe Galleries, while the 3rd Central contemporary collection is where you'll find the hippest brands of the day. Level 4 hits the new Toy Shop. Regularly changing pop-ups and special events keep customers on their toes.

Topshop

214 Oxford Street, W1W 8LG (0844 848 7487, www.topshop.com). Oxford Circus tube. **Open** 9am-9pm Mon-Wed, Fri, Sat; 9am-10pm Thur; 11.30am-6pm Sun. **Map** p99 C3 🅗

Topshop's massive, throbbing flagship is a teenage Hades at weekends, but there is absolutely nowhere on the high street that's more on-trend. You'll find a boutique of high-fashion designer capsule ranges, vintage clothes, and even a Hersheson hairstylist and a Metalmorphosis tattoo parlour among cheap and well-cut jeans, and all manner of other temptations. Topman is catching up with its sister, stocking niche labels such as Garbstore, and housing a trainer boutique, a suit section and a new personal shopping suite. Both shops are even more of a hive of activity during fashion week, when events are held.

Arts & leisure

Wigmore Hall

36 Wigmore Street, W1U 2BP (7935 2141, www.wigmore-hall.org.uk). Bond Street tube. **Map** p99 B2 🅓

Built in 1901 as the display hall for Bechstein Pianos, but now boasting perfect acoustics, art nouveau decor and an excellent basement restaurant, the Wiggy is one of the world's top chamber-music venues.

Mayfair

Mayfair still means money, but these days not necessarily stuffy exclusivity, with even the tailors of **Savile Row** loosening their ties a little. Even so, there's enough old-world decorum to satisfy the most fastidious visitor, from elegant shopping arcades to five-star hotels.

   Piccadilly Circus has undergone a £14-million revamp, with ugly pedestrian-funnelling and cyclist-shredding railings ripped out. Albert Gilbert's memorial fountain in honour of child labour abolitionist Earl Shaftesbury was erected in 1893. The statue on top was intended to represent the Angel of Christian Charity, but critics and public alike recognised a likeness to **Eros**, and the name has stuck. The illuminated advertising panels around the intersection appeared in the late 19th century and have been here ever since.

Sights & museums

Handel House Museum

25 Brook Street (entrance Lancashire Court), W1K 4HB (7399 1953, www. handelhouse.org). Bond Street tube. **Open** 10am-6pm Tue, Wed, Fri, Sat; 10am-8pm Thur; noon-6pm Sun. **Admission** £6; free-£4.50 reductions. **Map** p99 B3 ⑲

George Frideric Handel settled in this Mayfair house aged 37, remaining here until his death in 1759. The house has been beautifully restored with original and re-created furnishings, paintings and a welter of the composer's scores (in the same room as photos of Jimi Hendrix, who lived next door). There are recitals every Thursday.

Royal Academy of Arts

Burlington House, Piccadilly, W1J 0BD (7300 8000, www.royalacademy.org. uk). Green Park or Piccadilly Circus tube. **Open** 10am-6pm Mon-Thur, Sat, Sun; 10am-10pm Fri. **Admission** free. *Special exhibitions* prices vary. **Map** p99 C4 ⑳

Britain's first art school, founded in 1768, moved to the extravagantly Palladian Burlington House a century later, but it's now best known not for education but for exhibitions. You'll have to pay for blockbuster exhibitions in the Sackler Wing or main galleries, but shows in the John Madejski Fine Rooms – drawn from the RA's holdings ,which range from Constable to Hockney – are free.

Event highlights Summer Exhibition (June-Aug 2013).

Royal Institution & Faraday Museum

21 Albemarle Street, W1S 4BS (7409 2992, www.rigb.org). Green Park tube. **Open** 9am-9pm Mon-Fri. **Admission** free. **Map** p99 C4 ㉑

The Royal Institution has been at the forefront of scientific achievements for more than 200 years. Following a complete rebuild, you can enjoy the Michael Faraday Laboratory (a replica of the electromagnetic pioneer's workspace) and a fun new events programme.

Eating & drinking

Wild Honey (12 St George Street, W1S 2FB, 7758 9160, www.wild honeyrestaurant.co.uk) is a similarly affordable sister restaurant to the excellent **Arbutus** (see p130).

Bentley's Oyster Bar & Grill

11-15 Swallow Street, W1B 4DG (7734 4756, www.bentleysoysterbarand grill.co.uk). Piccadilly Circus tube. **Open** *Oyster Bar* 7.30-10.30am, noon-11pm Mon-Fri; noon-11pm Sat; noon-9.30pm Sun. *Restaurant* noon-2.30pm, 5.30-10.30pm Mon-Fri; 5.30-10.30pm Sat. **££££. Fish & seafood. Map** p99 C4 ㉒

There's something timeless about Richard Corrigan's restoration of this classic oyster house, which first opened its doors in 1916. While the first-floor dining rooms are more sedate and well mannered, the downstairs oyster bar is where the action is.

Burger & Lobster

NEW *29 Clarges Street, W1J 7EF (7409 1699, www.burgerandlobster.com). Green Park tube.* **Open** noon-10.30pm Mon-Sat; 10am-6pm Sun. **££. North American. Map** p99 B4 ㉓

It isn't hard to decide what to eat at Burger & Lobster, as there are only three choices – burger, lobster or lobster roll. A pub-style chalkboard at the entrance explains the menu: 'Burger or lobster or lobster roll, all with chips & salad, £20.' Upbeat and enthusiastic service adds to the lively din, and there's a distinct lack of stuffiness – it's hard to be formal when most of your fellow diners are wearing plastic bibs.

London Remembers

Few Londoners will ever forget the terrorist attacks of 7 July 2005, when 52 people were killed by suicide bombers. The city has a memorial to the tube and bus passengers who died. In the south-east corner of Hyde Park between the Lovers' Walk and busy Park Lane, the £1m monument consists of 52 ten-foot-tall, square steel columns, one for each of the fatalities. Each is marked with the date, time and location of that person's death; they're arranged in four groups, according to which of the four explosions killed the person in question. Designed by architects Carmody Groarke in close consultation with the victims' families, with Antony Gormley as an independent adviser, the monument is an austerely beautiful, quietly modern and human-scale tribute.

Elsewhere, London has a memorial to the 202 victims of the 2002 Bali bombings (just by the Churchill War Rooms, see p74), as well as a memorial garden for the victims of 9/11 (Grosvenor Square, near the US Embassy).

Interestingly, and despite widespread commemoration events for the 70th anniversary of the beginning of the Blitz (the 57 consecutive nights of German bombing which began on 7 September 1940), there is still no unified memorial to the perhaps 20,000 London civilians killed across the capital during this period.

LONDON BY AREA

Chisou

4 Princes Street, W1B 2LE (7629 3931, www.chisou.co.uk). Oxford Circus tube. **Open** noon-2.30pm, 6-10.15pm Mon-Sat. **££. Japanese**. Map p99 C3 ㉔
Chisou looks quiet, but inside it hums with activity. Salted belly pork, and the pure *ume cha* (rice in a hot broth with pickled plum) are highlights, and there's a serious saké and shochu list. Pop next door for noodles and *donburi*.

Connaught Bar

Connaught, Carlos Place, W1K 2AL (7499 7070, www.theconnaught.com). Bond Street tube. **Open** 4pm-1am Mon-Sat. **££££. Cocktail bar**. Map p99 B4 ㉕
The Connaught is one of London's most properly old-fashioned luxury hotels (p201) – but this is one hell of a sexy bar, with a sleek, black-and-chrome, cruise-liner style interior, and well-crafted cocktails to match. Across the corridor, the equally impressive Coburg Bar specialises in more traditional mixed drinks.

Galvin at Windows

Hilton, 22 Park Lane, W1K 1BE (7208 4021, www.galvinatwindows.com). Green Park or Hyde Park Corner tube. **Open** 11am-1am Mon-Wed; 11am-3am Thur, Fri; 3pm-3am Sat; 11am-10.30pm Sun. **Bar**. Map p99 B5 ㉖
Despite London's several new options for sky-high sipping (see box p164), this remains a remarkable site for a bar: 28 floors up, with a panoramic view of the capital, and a sleek interior that mixes art deco glamour with a hint of 1970s petrodollar kitsch. Obviously the drinks don't come cheap.

Hibiscus

29 Maddox Street, W1S 2PA (7629 2999, www.hibiscusrestaurant.co.uk). Oxford Circus tube. **Open** noon-2.30pm, 6.30-10pm Mon-Thur; 6-10pm Fri, Sat. **£££. Haute cuisine**. Map p99 C3 ㉗
Small and intimate, Hibiscus is one of the capital's most exciting places to eat.

Chef-patron Claude Bosi is a kitchen magician, playing with texture and flavour in ways that challenge and excite, without making diners feel they're in some weird experiment.

Momo

25 Heddon Street, W1B 4BH (7434 4040, www.momoresto.com). Piccadilly Circus tube. **Open** noon-5.30pm, 6.30-11.30pm Mon-Sat; 6.30-midnight Sun. **£££. North African**. Map p99 C4 ㉘

A big reputation, cool Marrakech-style decor, great Maghrebi soundtrack and some of the best North African food in London keep punters pouring in to Momo for an experience to savour. The alfresco terrace offers shisha pipes; downstairs is Mô Café (mint tea, wraps and meze) and Bazaar (books, CDs, furniture), plus the luxurious Kemia bar.

Only Running Footman

5 Charles Street, W1J 5DF (7499 2988, www.therunningfootman.biz). Green Park tube. **Open** 7.30am-11.30pm daily. **Pub**. Map p99 B4 ㉙

Reopening a few years back after a huge refurb, this place looks as if it's been here forever. On the ground floor, jolly chaps prop up the mahogany bar, enjoying three decent ales on draught and an extensive menu: anything from a posh cheddar and pickle sandwich to linguine with lobster and clams. Upstairs is a more formal restaurant.

Pollen Street Social

8-10 Pollen Street, W1S 1NG (7290 7600, www.pollenstreetsocial.com). Oxford Circus tube. **Open** noon-midnight Mon-Sat. **££££. Modern European**. Map p99 C3 ㉚

Owner Jason Atherton earned plaudits for his innovative small dishes at Gordon Ramsay's Maze. Here dishes remain tiny, but they are also pretty, daring and always a delightful surprise. Choose a selection of savoury dishes (seafood is a strength) and then move to the dessert bar, where you can chat to the chefs as they prepare more-ish sweets such as 'PBJ' (peanut butter and jelly as a frozen dessert).

Scott's

20 Mount Street, W1K 2HE (7495 7309, www.scotts-restaurant.com). Bond Street or Green Park tube. **Open** noon-10.30pm Mon-Sat; noon-10pm Sun. **££££. Fish & seafood**. Map p99 B4 ㉛

Of the celebrity hangouts in the capital, Scott's is the one that most justifies the hype: from the greeting by the doorman to the look-at-me contemporary British art on the walls and the glossy Rich List crowd. The food – perhaps tiny boar sausages with chilled rock oysters – gets better and better.

Sketch: The Parlour

9 Conduit Street, W1S 2XJ (0870 777 4488, www.sketch.uk.com). Oxford Circus tube. **Open** 10am-9pm Mon-Sat. **£££. Café**. Map p99 C3 ㉜

Of the three parts of Pierre Gagnaire's legendarily expensive Sketch, which also include Gallery's destination dining and Lecture Room's haute-beyond-haute cuisine, Parlour appeals the most for its tongue-in-cheek sexiness. Saucy nudes illustrate the chairs, and the chandelier appears to be covered with red fishnet tights. The menu includes simple hearty dishes and quirky high-concept creations, such as the club sandwich with red-and-green bread and a layer of stencilled jelly on top.

Tibits

12-14 Heddon Street, W1B 4DA (7758 4110, www.tibits.ch). Oxford Circus tube. **Open** 9am-10.30pm Mon-Wed; 9am-midnight Thur-Sat; 10am-10.30pm Sun. **££. Vegetarian**. Map p99 C4 ㉝

It's all California-cool in this groovy vegetarian export from Switzerland. The buffet-cum-pay-per-100g concept left us sceptical at first, but the global offerings have proven to be notches above the usual all-you-can-eat gaff.

Dover Street Market

Shopping

b store

4A Savile Row, W1S 3PR (7734 6846, www.bstorelondon.com). Oxford Circus tube. **Open** 10.30am-6.30pm Mon-Fri; 10am-6pm Sat. **Map** p99 C4 ㉔

A platform for cutting-edge designers in the heartland of traditional tailoring, b store is the place to preview next big things, with pieces from recent fashion graduates sitting alongside established iconoclasts such as Peter Jensen and Opening Ceremony. The eponymous own label, offering stylish basics and shoes, is going from strength to strength.

Browns

23-27 South Molton Street, W1K 5RD (7514 0000, www.brownsfashion.com). Bond Street tube. **Open** 10am-6.30pm Mon-Wed, Fri, Sat; 10am-7pm Thur. **Map** p99 B3 ㉟

Among the 100-odd designers jostling for attention in Joan Burstein's five interconnecting shops (menswear is at no.23) are Chloé, Christopher Kane, Marc Jacobs, Balenciaga and Todd Lynn, with plenty of fashion exclusives. Browns Focus at no.38 sells last season's leftovers. Shop 24 (p112) is her latest initiative.

Burlington Arcade

Piccadilly, W1 (7630 1411, www. burlington-arcade.co.uk). Green Park tube. **Open** 8am-6.30pm Mon-Sat; 11am-5pm Sun. **Map** p99 C4 ㊱

The Royal Arcades are a throwback to shopping past: Burlington is the largest and, commissioned by Lord Cavendish in 1819, oldest of them. Highlights include collections of classic watches at David Duggans, fragrance house Penhaligon, iconic British luxury luggage brand Globe-Trotter and Sermoneta, selling Italian leather gloves in a range of bright colours… and the top-hatted beadles who keep order.

Dover Street Market

17-18 Dover Street, W1S 4LT (7518 0680, www.doverstreetmarket.com). Green Park tube. **Open** 11am-6pm Mon-Wed; 11am-7pm Thur-Sat. **Map** p99 C4 ㊲

Comme des Garçons designer Rei Kawakubo's six-storey space combines the edgy energy of London's indoor markets – concrete floors, Portaloo dressing-rooms – with rarefied labels. All 14 of the comme des garçons labels are here, alongside exlusive lines from designers such as Lanvin and Azzedine Alaïa.

Elemis Day Spa

2-3 Lancashire Court, W1S 1EX (7499 4995, www.elemis.com). Bond Street tube. **Open** 9am-9pm Mon-Sat; 10am-6pm Sun. **Map** p99 B3 ㊳

This leading British spa brand's exotic, unisex retreat is tucked away down a cobbled lane off Bond Street. The elegantly ethnic treatment rooms are a lovely setting in which to relax and enjoy a spot of pampering, from wraps to results-driven facials.

Grays Antique Market & Grays in the Mews

58 Davies Street, W1K 5LP; 1-7 Davies Mews, W1K 5AB (7629 7034, www. graysantiques.com). Bond Street tube. **Open** 10am-6pm Mon-Wed, Fri; 10.30am-7.30pm Thur; 11am-5pm Sat; No credit cards. **Map** p99 B3 ㊴

More than 200 dealers run stalls in this smart covered market – housed in a Victorian lavatory showroom – selling everything from antiques, fine art and jewellery to vintage fashion.

Miller Harris

21 Bruton Street, W1J 6QD (7629 7750, www.millerharris.com). Bond Street or Green Park tube. **Open** 10am-6pm Mon-Sat. **Map** p99 B4 ㊵

Grasse-trained British perfumer Lyn Harris's distinctive, long-lasting scents are made with quality natural extracts and oils, and delightfully packaged.

LONDON BY AREA

Mount Street

Bond Street or Green Park tube.
Map p99 B4 ④

Mount Street, with its dignified Victorian terracotta façades and by-appointment art galleries, master butcher Allens (no.117) and cigar shop Sautter (no.106), has taken on a new, cutting-edge persona. At no.12, near the Connaught's cool cocktail bars (p108), Balenciaga has set its super-chic clothes in a glowing sci-fi interior. Here too are Britain's first Marc by Marc Jacobs (nos.24-25), revered shoe-designer Christian Louboutin (no.17) and a five-floor Lanvin (no.128). Further delights (such as Rick Owens) are on South Audley Street.

Paul Smith Sale Shop

23 Avery Row, W1X 9HB (7493 1287, www.paulsmith.co.uk). Bond Street tube.
Open 10.30am-6.30pm Mon-Wed, Fri, Sat; 10.30am-7pm Thur; noon-6pm Sun.
Map p99 B3 ④

Samples and last season's stock can be found at a 30-50% discount. You'll find clothes for men, women and children, as well as a range of accessories.

Postcard Teas

9 Dering Street, W1S 1AG (7629 3654, www.postcardteas.com). Bond Street or Oxford Circus tube. **Open** 10.30am-6.30pm Mon-Sat. **Map** p99 B3 ④

The range in this exquisite little shop isn't huge, but it is selected with care – usually from single estates. There's a central table for those who want to try a pot. Tea-ware and accessories are also sold, and there are tastings on a Saturday morning (10-11am).

Savile Row

Oxford Circus or Piccadilly Circus tube.
Map p99 C4 ④

Even Savile Row is moving with the times. US import Abercrombie & Fitch has been ensconced here for a few years now, not far from the cutting-edge and iconoclastic designers (the likes of Ute Ploier, Opening Ceremony,

Peter Jensen) of b store at no.24A. Be reassured: expensive bespoke tailoring remains the principal activity, with the workaday task of shopping for a suit transformed into an almost other-worldly experience at such emporia as Gieves & Hawkes (no.1) or, erstwhile tailor to Sir Winston Churchill, Henry Poole (no.15).

Shop 24

24 South Molton Street, W1K 5RD (7514 0032, www.brownsfashion.com). Bond Street tube. **Open** 10am-6.30pm Mon-Wed, Fri, Sat; 10am-7pm Thur. **Map** p99 B3 ④

Proving that simple ideas are the best, Browns (p111) has opened a boutique selling 'the staple items you can't live without'. The idea is that you can come here for all your wardrobe essentials, albeit luxurious ones. Looking for the ultimate Breton top? How about the melt-in-the-hands cashmere version by Vince? Or the perfect cotton T-shirt? Try a James Pearse.

Uniqlo

311 Oxford Street, W1C 2HP (7290 7701, www.uniqlo.co.uk). Bond Street or Oxford Circus tube. **Open** 10am-9pm Mon-Sat; 11.30am-6pm Sun.
Map p99 B3 ④

There are three outposts of Uniqlo, Japan's biggest clothes retailer, on Oxford Street alone – but this one is 25,000sq ft and three storeys of flag-ship. Not as cheap as Primark and more stylish, Uniqlo sells simple, single-colour staples for men and women.

Fitzrovia

West of Tottenham Court Road and north of Oxford Street, Fitzrovia – once a gathering point for radicals, writers and boozers, mostly in reverse order – retains sufficient traces of bohemianism to appeal to the media types that now frequent it. Some of the capital's best hotels and restaurants cluster at Charlotte Street, but these days **Bradley's** or the **Long Bar** are more satisfying places to have a drink than the Fitzroy Tavern or Wheatsheaf.

Sights & museums

All Saints

7 Margaret Street, W1W 8JG (7636 1788, www.allsaintsmargaretstreet. org.uk). Oxford Circus tube. **Open** 7am-7pm daily. **Admission** free. **Map** p114 B4 ❶
This 1850s church was designed by William Butterfield, one of the great Gothic Revivalists. Behind the polychromatic brick façade, the shadowy, lavish interior is one of the capital's ecclesiastical triumphs, with luxurious marble, flamboyant tile work and glittering stones built into its pillars. A three-year restoration project was completed in late 2011.

BBC Broadcasting House

Portland Place, Upper Regent Street, W1A 1AA (0370 901 1227, www.bbc. co.uk/showsandtours/tours). Oxford Circus tube. **Open** *Tours only* Sun. **Admission** £11.75; £8.25-£10.75 reductions. **Map** p114 A4 ❷
Each Sunday there are tours of the various radio stations in the BBC's HQ. Completed in 1932, it was Britain's first purpose-built broadcast centre. Booking ahead, possible from the website, is essential. Tours are also available at west London's BBC Television Centre (Wood Lane, Shepherd's Bush, W12 7RJ, 0370 901 1227).

BT Tower

60 Cleveland Street, W1. Goode Street tube. **Map** p114 B3 ❸
The BT Tower (formerly the Post Office Tower) was designed to provide support for radio, TV and telephone aerials. It was opened in 1964 and its crowning glory was a revolving restaurant, closed to the public in 1971 after a bomb attack by the Angry Brigade.

The building was Grade II-listed in 2003, but remains accessible only for private functions.

Pollock's Toy Museum

1 Scala Street (entrance Whitfield Street), W1T 2HL (7636 3452, www.pollockstoymuseum.com). Goode Street tube. **Open** 10am-5pm Mon-Sat. **Admission** £5; free-£4 reductions. **Map** p114 C4 ❹
Housed in a creaky Georgian townhouse, Pollock's is named after one of the last Victorian toy theatre printers. By turns beguiling and creepy, the museum is a nostalgia-fest of old board games, tin trains, porcelain dolls and Robertson's gollies.

Royal Institute of British Architects

66 Portland Place, W1B 1AD (7580 5533, www.architecture.com). Great Portland Street tube. **Map** p114 A3 ❺
Temporary exhibitions are held in RIBA's Grade II-listed HQ, which houses a bookshop, café and library, and hosts an excellent lecture series.

Eating & drinking

Benito's Hat

56 Goode Street, W1T 4NB (7637 3732, www.benitos-hat.com). Goode Street tube. **Open** 11.30am-10pm Mon-Wed, Sun; 11.30am-11pm Thur-Sat. **£.** **Burritos**. **Map** p114 B4 ❻
London's TexMex eateries are ten a peso at the moment, but Benito's Hat is one of the best – no wonder that it has expanded into Covent Garden and on to Oxford Street, as well as maintaining this original branch. The production line compiles some of the best burritos in town, and a few cocktails, and Mexian beer are served if you choose to eat in.

Bradley's Spanish Bar

42-44 Hanway Street, W1T 1UT (7636 0359). Tottenham Court Road tube. **Open** noon-11pm Mon-Sat; noon-10pm Sun. **Pub**. **Map** p114 C5 ❼

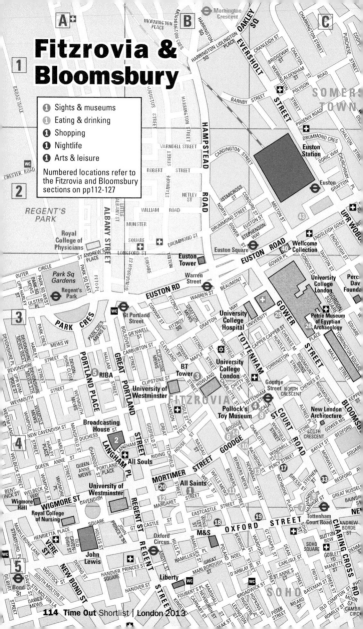

Fitzrovia & Bloomsbury

- **1** Sights & museums
- **1** Eating & drinking
- **1** Shopping
- **1** Nightlife
- **1** Arts & leisure

Numbered locations refer to the Fitzrovia and Bloomsbury sections on pp112-127

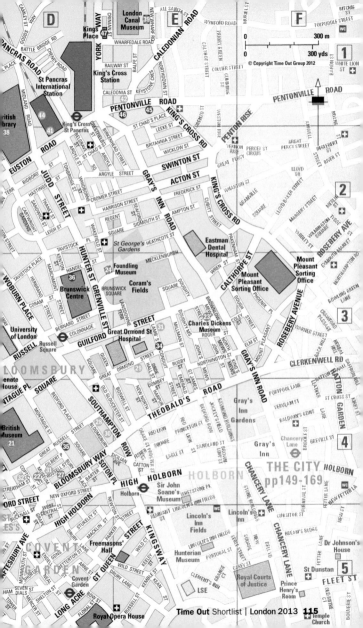

There's a touch of the Barcelona dive bar about this pub, and San Miguel on tap, but it ain't really Spanish. Not that the hotchpotch of local workers, shoppers and exchange students who fill the cramped two-floor space care.

Dabbous

NEW *39 Whitfield Street, W1T 2SF (7323 1544, www.dabbous.co.uk). Goodge Street tube.* **Open** noon-2.30pm, 5.30-10pm Tue-Sat. **££££. Modern European.** Map p114 C4 ⑧

Chef-proprietor Ollie Dabbous pairs a casual vibe – concrete floors, industrial ducting, bare lights, distressed metal screens – with an outstanding kitchen that can best be described as 'Modernist'. Dabbous has applied an almost Japanese appreciation of simplicity to small, artfully arranged dishes. Be warned that while the menu prices initially seem very reasonable, the tapas-sized portions mean that most diners will need to order four or five dishes each.

Hakkasan

8 Hanway Place, W1T 1HD (7927 7000). Tottenham Court Road tube. **Open** noon-3pm, 6-11pm Mon-Wed; noon-3pm, 6pm-midnight Thur, Fri; noon-4pm, 6pm-midnight Sat; noon-4pm, 6-11pm Sun. **££££. Chinese.** Map p114 C4 ⑨

The moody, nightclub feel of this glam take on the Shanghai teahouse still pulls a lively, monied crowd for high-ticket dining. Enjoy the experience for less by visiting for the lunchtime dim sum. The bar (which opens later than the restaurant) is also very chic.

Lantana

13 Charlotte Place, W1T 1SN (7637 3347, www.lantanacafe.co.uk). Goodge Street tube. **Open** 8am-6pm Mon, Tue; 8am-10.30pm Wed-Fri; 9am-5pm Sat, Sun. **£. Café.** Map p114 B4 ⑩

The super salads (smoky aubergine or a crunchy sugar snap and red cabbage combo, for example), cakes and sunny breakfasts have drawn throngs of regulars to this Antipodean-style eaterie ever since it opened. The espresso machine is the coffee connoisseur's choice – La Marzocco – and the beans come from the excellent Monmouth.

Long Bar

Sanderson, 50 Berners Street, W1 3NG (7300 1400, www.sanderson london.com). Oxford Circus or Goodge Street tube. **Open** 11am-midnight Mon-Wed; 11am-1am Thur-Sat; noon-10.30pm Sun. **Bar.** Map p114 B4 ⑪

The Long Bar's early noughties glory days may be a faded memory, but there's still easy glamour for the taking. The bar is indeed long – a thin onyx affair – but nabbing one of the eyeball-backed stools is unlikely. Try the lovely courtyard instead, where table service, candlelight and watery features make a much nicer setting.

Match Bar

37-38 Margaret Street, W1G 0JF (7629 7551, www.matchbar.com). Oxford Circus tube. **Open** 11am-midnight Mon-Sat; 4pm-midnight Sun. **Cocktail bar.** Map p114 B4 ⑫

London's Match cocktail bars celebrate the craft of the bartender with a selection of authentic concoctions, such as juleps and fizzes, made from high-end liquor. DJs spin from 7.30pm Thur-Sat.

Newman Arms

23 Rathbone Street, W1T 1NG (7636 1127, www.newmanarms.co.uk). Goodge Street or Tottenham Court Road tube. **Open** noon-12.30am Mon-Fri. **Pub.** Map p114 C4 ⑬

The cabin-like Newman Arms has had the decorators in, but is still in touch with its history: a poster for Michael Powell's *Peeping Tom*, filmed here in 1960, faces a black-and-white portrait of former regular George Orwell. In the Famous Pie Room upstairs (you may have to book), pies with a variety of fillings cost around a tenner, and there are good beers on tap downstairs.

Social p118

Salt Yard

54 Goodge Street, W1T 4NA (7637 0657, www.saltyard.co.uk). Goodge Street tube. **Open** noon-11pm Mon-Fri; 5-11pm Sat. **££. Spanish-Italian tapas.** **Map** p114 B4 ⑭

The artful menu of Iberian and Italian tapas standards served at this dark, calm and classy joint is aimed at diners in search of a slow lunch or lightish dinner. Fine selections of charcuterie and cheese front the frequently changing menu, which features the likes of tuna carpaccio with baby broad beans, and ham croquettes with manchego. A top choice for fuss-free tapas.

Sochu Lounge

Basement, Roka, 37 Charlotte Street, W1T 1RR (7580 9666, www.shochu lounge.com). Tottenham Court Road or Goodge Street tube. **Open** 5.30pm-midnight Mon-Sat; 5.30-11pm Sun. **Bar.** **Map** p114 C4 ⑮

Beneath landmark Japanese restaurant Roka, the chic Shochu Lounge offers drinks based on the vodka-like distilled spirit of the same name. Sochu is often overlooked for its better-known counterpart, saké, but it's here used in healthy tonics, in cocktails and sold by the 50ml measure. The full Roka menu is available.

Yalla Yalla

12 Winsley Street, W1W 8HQ (7637 4748, www.yalla-yalla.co.uk). Oxford Circus tube. **Open** 10am-midnight Mon-Sat; 10am-10pm Sun. **£. Lebanese.** **Map** p114 B5 ⑯

Yalla Yalla offers a delectable selection of meze (each wonderfully presented, with slick garnishes of olive oil, herbs and pomegranate seeds where appropriate) and heartier main courses based around the grill. The sticky chicken wings with pomegranate syrup are excellent, as is the grilled halloumi with olives and mint. For dessert, don't miss the honeyed vanilla ice-cream topped with caramelised nuts and dried fruit.

Shopping

Contemporary Applied Arts

2 Percy Street, W1T 1DD (7436 2344, www.caa.org.uk). Goodge Street or Tottenham Court Road tube. **Open** 10am-6pm Mon-Sat. **Map** p114 C4 ⑰

This airy gallery, run by the charitable arts organisation, represents more than 300 makers. Work embraces both the functional (jewellery, textiles, tableware) and unique decorative pieces.

HMV

150 Oxford Street, W1D 1DJ (0843 221 0289, www.hmv.com). Oxford Street or Tottenham Court Road tube. **Open** 9am-8.30pm Mon-Wed, Fri, Sat; 9am-9pm Thur; 11.30am-6pm Sun. **Map** p114 B5 ⑱

HMV is the last of the mammoth music stores on Oxford Street. Plenty of space is given over to DVDs and games upstairs, but world, jazz and classical have a whole floor in the basement – and the ground floor is packed with pop, rock and dance music, including vinyl.

Nightlife

100 Club

100 Oxford Street, W1D 1LL (7636 0933, www.the100club.co.uk). Oxford Circus or Tottenham Court Road tube. **Map** p114 C5 ⑲

Perhaps the most adaptable venue in London, this wide, 350-capacity basement room has provided a home for trad jazz, pub blues, northern soul and, famously, punk.

Social

5 Little Portland Street, W1W 7JD (7636 4992, www.thesocial.com). Oxford Circus tube. **Map** p114 B4 ⑳

A discreet, opaque front hides this daytime diner and DJ bar of supreme quality, a place that still feels, a decade after Heavenly Records opened it, more like a displaced bit of Soho than a resident of Fitzrovia.

Bloomsbury

In bookish circles, Bloomsbury is a name to conjure with: it is the HQ of London University and home to the superb **British Museum**. The name was famously attached to a group of early 20th-century artists and intellectuals (Virginia Woolf and John Maynard Keynes among them), and more recently to the (Soho-based) publishing company that gave us Harry Potter. It is an area that demands an idle browse: perhaps the bookshops of Great Russell Street, Marchmont Street or Woburn Walk, maybe along lovely Lamb's Conduit Street.

Sights & museums

British Museum

Great Russell Street, WC1B 3DG (7323 8299, www.britishmuseum.org). Russell Square or Tottenham Court Road tube. **Open** 10am-5.30pm Mon-Wed, Sat, Sun; 10am-8.30pm Thur, Fri. *Great Court* 9am-6pm Mon-Wed, Sun; 9am-11pm Thur-Sat. **Admission** free; donations appreciated. *Special exhibitions* prices vary. **Map** p115 D4 ㉑

The British Museum is a neoclassical marvel that was built in 1847, and topped off 153 years later with the magnificent glass-roofed Great Court. The £100m roof surrounds the domed Reading Room, where Marx, Lenin, Dickens, Darwin, Hardy and Yeats once worked. Star exhibits include ancient Egyptian artefacts – the Rosetta Stone on the ground floor, mummies upstairs – and Greek antiquities that include the stunning marble friezes from the Parthenon. The King's Library is a calm home to a 5,000-piece collection devoted to the formative period of the museum (a replica Rosetta Stone is here, if the real one's too crowded). You won't be able to see everything in one day, so buy a guide and pick some showstoppers, or plan several visits. Free eyeOpener

tours offer introductions to particular world cultures. The museum is undergoing extension work in its north-west corner, which should create new temporary galleries and education spaces for 2013.
Event highlights Shakespeare: Staging the World (19 July-25 Nov 2012).

Cartoon Museum

35 Little Russell Street, WC1A 2HH (7580 8155, www.cartoonmuseum.org). Tottenham Court Road tube. **Open** 10.30am-5.30pm Tue-Sat; noon-5.30pm Sun. **Admission** £5.50; free-£4 reductions. **Map** p115 D4 ㉒

On the ground floor of this former dairy, a brief chronology of British cartoon art is displayed, from Hogarth via Britain's cartooning 'golden age' (1770-1830) to examples of wartime cartoons, ending up with modern satirists such as Ralph Steadman and the *Guardian's* Steve Bell, alongside fine temporary exhibitions. Upstairs is a celebration of UK comics and graphic novels.

Charles Dickens Museum

48 Doughty Street, WC1N 2LX (7405 2127, www.dickensmuseum.com). Chancery Lane or Russell Square tube. **Open** 10am-5pm daily. **Admission** £6; free-£5 reductions; £15 family. **Map** p115 E3 ㉓

London is scattered with plaques marking addresses where the peripatetic Charles Dickens lived, but this is the only one of them still standing. He lived here from 1837 to 1840, during which time he wrote *Nicholas Nickleby* and *Oliver Twist*. Ring the doorbell to gain access to four floors of Dickensiana, collected over the years from various other of his residences.

Foundling Museum

40 Brunswick Square, WC1N 1AZ (7841 3600, www.foundlingmuseum. org.uk). Russell Square tube. **Open** 10am-5pm Tue-Sat; 11am-5pm Sun. **Admission** £7.50; free-£5 reductions. **Map** p115 D3 ㉔

The People's Supermarke

The People's Supermarket, Lamb's Conduit Street p122

Returning to England from America in 1720, Captain Thomas Coram was appalled by the number of abandoned children on the streets and persuaded artist William Hogarth and composer GF Handel to become governors of a new hospital for them. Hogarth decreed the hospital should also be Britain's first public art gallery, and work by Gainsborough and Reynolds is shown upstairs. The most heart-rending display is a tiny case of mementos that were all that mothers were allowed to leave the children they abandoned here. The café is charming.

Grant Museum of Zoology

Rockefeller Building, University College London, University Street, WC1E 6DE (3108 2052, www.ucl.ac.uk/museums/ zoology). Euston tube/rail or Goodge Street tube. **Open** 1-5pm Mon-Fri. **Admission** free. **Map** p115 C3 ㉕

Reopened in 2011 in an Edwardian former library, the much-loved Grant Museum of animal skeletons, taxidermy specimens and creatures preserved in fluid retains the air of the house of an avid Victorian collector. The collection includes remains of many rare and extinct animals, such as a dodo and a full skeleton of the zebra-like quagga, hunted out of existence in the 1880s, as well as bisected heads and a jar full of moles.

Petrie Museum of Egyptian Archaeology

University College London, Malet Place, WC1E 6BT (7679 2884, www.petrie.ucl.ac.uk). Goodge Street or Warren Street tube. **Open** 1-5pm Tue-Sat. **Admission** free; donations appreciated. **Map** p114 C3 ㉖

Where the Egyptology collection at the the British Museum (p119) is strong on the big stuff, this fabulous hidden museum is dim case after dim case of minutiae. Among the oddities are a 4,000-year-old skeleton of a man ritually buried in a pot. Wind-up torches help you peer into the gloomy corners.

St George's Bloomsbury

Bloomsbury Way, WC1A 2HR (7242 1979, www.stgeorgesbloomsbury.org.uk). Holborn or Tottenham Court Road tube. **Open** times vary; phone for details. **Admission** free. **Map** p115 D4 ㉗

Consecrated in 1730, St George's is a grand and typically disturbing work by Nicholas Hawksmoor, with an offset, stepped spire that was inspired by Pliny's account of the Mausoleum at Halicarnassus. Highlights include the mahogany reredos, and 10ft-high sculptures of lions and unicorns clawing at the base of the steeple. There are guided tours and regular concerts.

Eating & drinking

Right opposite the front gates of the British Museum (p119), the Grade II-listed **Museum Tavern** (49 Great Russell Street, WC1B 3BA, 7242 8987) has a good range of ales.

All Star Lanes

Victoria House, Bloomsbury Place, WC1B 4DA (7025 2676, www.allstar lanes.co.uk). Holborn tube. **Open** 5-11.30pm Mon-Wed; 5pm-midnight Thur; noon-2am Fri, Sat; noon-11pm Sun. **Bar & bowling**. **Map** p115 D4 ㉘

Walk past the lanes and smart, diner-style seating, and you'll find yourself in a comfortable, subdued side bar with chilled glasses, classy red furnishings, an unusual mix of bottled lagers and impressive cocktails. There's an American menu and, at weekends, DJs.

Espresso Room

31-35 Great Ormond Street, WC1N 3HZ (07760 714883 mobile, www.the espressoroom.com). Holborn tube or bus 19, 38. **Open** 7.30am-5pm Mon-Fri. **£**. **Coffee bar**. **Map** p115 E3 ㉙

We're big fans of this minuscule coffee bar, which serves excellent espressos, faultless flat whites and a few snacks. Carefully selected and roasted beans, top-notch execution – come here for one of London's finest brews.

Hummus Bros

*37-63 Southampton Row, WC1B 4DA
(7404 7079, www.hbros.co.uk). Holborn
tube.* **Open** 11am-9pm Mon-Fri. **£**.
Café. Map p115 D4 ㉚

The simple and successful formula at
this café/takeaway is to serve hou-
mous as a base for a selection of top-
pings, which you scoop up with
excellent pitta bread. The food is
nutritious and good value. There's a
second branch in Soho (88 Wardour
Street, 7734 1311) and a third in the
City (128 Cheapside, 7726 8011) –
handy for St Paul's (p162), but only
open weekday lunchtimes.

Lamb

*94 Lamb's Conduit Street, WC1N
3LZ (7405 0713, www.youngs.co.uk).
Holborn or Russell Square tube.* **Open**
noon-11.30pm Mon-Wed; noon-12.30am
Thur-Sat; noon-10.30pm Sun. **Pub**.
Map p115 E3 ㉛

Founded in 1729, this Young's pub is
the sort of place that makes you
misty-eyed for a vanishing era. The
Lamb found fame as a theatrical
haunt when the A-list included Sir
Henry Irving and sundry stars of
music hall; they're commemorated in
vintage photos, surrounded by well-
worn seats, polished wood and vintage knick-knacks.

Wagamama

*4 Streatham Street, WC1A 1JB
(7323 9223, www.wagamama.com).
Holborn or Tottenham Court Road
tube.* **Open** noon-11pm Mon-Sat;
noon-10pm Sun. **£. Noodle bar**.
Map p115 D4 ㉜

Since starting life in the basement
here in 1992, this chain of shared-table
restaurants has become a global phe-
nomenon, with branches as far as
Cyprus and Boston. The British
Wagamamas all serve the same menu:
rice plate meals and Japanese noodles,
cooked teppanyaki-style on a flat griddle or simmered in big bowls of spicy
soup, and served in double-quick time.

Shopping

Ask

*248 Tottenham Court Road, W1T
7QZ (7637 0353, www.askdirect.
co.uk). Tottenham Court Road tube.*
Open 10am-7pm Mon-Wed, Fri, Sat;
10am-8pm Thur; noon-6pm Sun.
Map p114 C4 ㉝

Some shops on Tottenham Court Road
– London's main street for consumer
electronics – feel gloomy and claustro-
phobic, and hit you with the hard sell.
Ask has four capacious, well-organised
floors that give you space to browse
stock that spans digital cameras, MP3
players, radios, laptops as well as hi-fis
and TVs with all the relevant accessories. Prices are competitive.

Lamb's Conduit Street

Holborn or Russell Square tube.
Map p115 E3 ㉞

Tucked away among residential back
streets, Lamb's Conduit Street is the
perfect size for a browse, whether you
fancy checking out quality tailoring at
Oliver Spencer (no.62), cult menswear
and cute women's knitwear from
Folk (no.49), cutting-edge design at
Darkroom (no.52) or even a recumbent
bicycle at Bikefix (no.48). Head off the
main drag to refuel at the Lamb (left)
or the Espresso Room (p121), pop into
the ethical new People's Supermarket
(nos.72-78), then go to Rugby Street for
homeware at Ben Pentreath (no.17) or
jewellery at Maggie Owen (no.13).

London Review Bookshop

*14 Bury Place, WC1A 2JL (7269 9030,
www.lrbshop.co.uk). Holborn tube.*
Open 10am-6.30pm Mon-Sat; noon-
6pm Sun. **Map** p115 D4 ㉟

An inspiring bookshop, from the stim-
ulating presentation to the quality of
the selection. Politics, current affairs
and history are well represented on
the ground floor, while downstairs,
audio books lead on to exciting poetry
and philosophy sections. There's a
lovely café too.

Skoob

Unit 66, Brunswick Centre, WC1N 1AE (7278 8760, www.skoob.com). Russell Square tube. **Open** 10.30am-8pm Mon-Sat; 10.30am-6pm Sun. **Map** p115 D3 ㊱

A back-to-basics concrete basement that showcases 50,000 titles covering virtually every subject, from philosophy and biography to politics and the occult. You probably won't find quite what you were looking for here – but you'll enjoy browsing, and you're almost certain to come away happily clutching something else.

Nightlife

Bloomsbury Bowling Lanes

Basement, Tavistock Hotel, Bedford Way, WC1H 9EU (7183 1979, www. bloomsburybowling.com). Russell Square tube. **Map** p115 D3 ㊲

A hip destination for local students and others wanting a late drink away from the buzz of Soho, the Lanes also puts on live bands and DJs on Monday, Friday and Saturday, sometimes with a 1950s theme. If you get bored of bands and bowling, hole up in a karaoke booth.

King's Cross

North-east of Bloomsbury, the once-insalubrious area of King's Cross is undergoing massive redevelopment around the grand **St Pancras International** station and well-established 'new' **British Library**. **King's Cross** station is also being refurbished, beginning with a stunning new concourse. The badlands to the north are being transformed (to the tune of £500m) into mixed-use nucleus King's Cross Central, including a new campus for the University of the Arts. **Kings Place** (see box p125) another sign of good things to come.

Sights & museums

St Pancras International

(Pancras Road, 7843 7688, www. stpancras.com; see also p212) welcomes the high-speed Eurostar train from Paris with William Barlow's gorgeous Victorian glass-and-iron train shed. For all the public art, high-end boutiques and eateries, the real attractions are the beautiful original trainshed roof and the recently reopened neo-Gothic **St Pancras Renaissance** hotel (see p204) that fronts the station. In early 2012, a stunning, honeycomb-like, curvaceous western concourse for **King's Cross** station, designed by John McAslan + Partners, opened.

British Library

96 Euston Road, NW1 2DB (7412 7332, www.bl.uk). Euston or King's Cross tube/rail. **Open** 9.30am-6pm Mon, Wed-Fri; 9.30am-8pm Tue; 9.30am-5pm Sat; 11am-5pm Sun. **Admission** free; donations appreciated. **Map** p115 D1 ㊳

'One of the ugliest buildings in the world,' opined a Parliamentary committee on the opening of the new British Library in 1997. Opinions have changed since then: the interior is a model of cool, spacious functionality, its focal point the King's Library, a six-storey glass-walled tower housing George III's collection in the central atrium. The BL holds more than 150 million items. In the John Ritblat Gallery, the library's main treasures are displayed: the Magna Carta, the Lindisfarne Gospels, original manuscripts from Chaucer and Beatles lyrics. Some great events too.

London Canal Museum

12-13 New Wharf Road, N1 9RT (7713 0836, www.canalmuseum.org.uk). King's Cross tube/rail. **Open** 10am-4.30pm Tue-Sun; 10am-7.30pm 1st Thur of the mth. **Admission** £4; free-£3 reductions. No credit cards. **Map** p115 E1 ㊴

The museum is housed in a former 19th-century ice warehouse, used by Carlo Gatti for his ice-cream, and includes an interesting exhibit on the history of the ice trade. The part of the collection looking at the history of the waterways and those who worked on them is rather sparse by comparison.

Wellcome Collection

183 Euston Road, NW1 2BE (7611 2222, www.wellcomecollection.org). Euston Square tube or Euston tube/rail. **Open** 10am-6pm Tue, Wed, Fri, Sat; 10am-10pm Thur; 11am-6pm Sun. **Admission** free. **Map** p114 C2 ⓴

Founder Sir Henry Wellcome, a pioneering 19th-century pharmacist and entrepreneur, amassed a vast, grisly and idiosyncratic collection of implements and curios – ivory carvings of pregnant women, used guillotine blades, Napoleon's toothbrush – mostly relating to the medical trade. It's now displayed in this swanky little museum, along with works of modern art. The temporary exhibitions are always wonderfully interesting, choosing subjects such skin, dirt or drugs.

Eating & drinking

The **Peyton & Byrne** café on the ground floor of the Wellcome Collection (above) is a handy stop. The new concourse at King's Cross has a good selection of places to eat, including a branch of **Benito's Hat** (see p113).

Booking Office

St Pancras Renaissance London, NW1 2AR (7841 3540, www.booking officerestaurant.com). King's Cross or St Pancras tube/rail. **Bar**. **Map** p115 D1 ㊶

Superlatives come easily when describing the Booking Office: epic, soaring, magnificent. As part of Sir Gilbert Scott's 1873 Midland Grand Hotel, it was designed to instill in passengers a sense of awe at the power of the railways. These days, it serves as an awe-inspiring bar, and the refit has made the most of the Victorians splendour.

Camino

3 Varnishers Yard, Regents Quarter, N1 9AF (7841 7331, www.camino.uk. com). King's Cross tube/rail. **Open** 8-11.30am, noon-3pm, 6.30-11pm Mon-Fri; 8-11.30am, noon-4pm, 6-11pm Sat; 8-11.30am, noon-4pm Sun. **£££**. **Spanish**. **Map** p115 E1 ㊷

A big, Spanish-themed bar-restaurant in the heart of the King's Cross construction zone, Camino is a shining example of the new King's Cross. In the bar you can order good tapas, but it's worth sitting down for a proper meal in the restaurant, where the cooking adheres to the central principle of traditional Spanish food: fine ingredients, simply cooked. Just opposite and run by the same people, the tiny Andalusian *bodega*-style Bar Pepito is dedicated to Spanish sherry (15 types are on offer).

Euston Tap

West Lodge, 190 Euston Rd, NW1 2EF (7387 2890, www.eustontap.com). Euston tube/rail. **Open** noon-11pm Mon-Fri; noon-midnight Sat; 2pm-midnight Sun. **Beer bar**. **Map** p115 C2 ㊸

A few yards from the station, this fantastic new beer bar occupies a small Grade II-listed Portland stone lodge – a relic from the original station built in the 1830s. The decor is a little worn, but there's an incredible selection of beers, with 19 rare craft beers on draught, guest beers from microbreweries and more than a hundred bottled varieties.

St Pancras Grand

Upper Concourse, St Pancras International, Euston Road, NW1 2QP (7870 9900, www.searcys.co.uk/ stpancrasgrand). King's Cross tube/rail. **Open** 7am-11pm Mon-Sat, 8am-11pm Sun. **£££**. **Brasserie**. **Map** p115 D1 ㊹

The St Pancras Grand evokes a grand European café, with a fabulous art

King's Place

A new space for the arts.

Scruffy and neglected, the streets around King's Cross Station have rarely had much to recommend them. However, the renovation of St Pancras Station has coincided with other new developments, of which the most impressive is tucked away up York Way.

Aware that office blocks are an 'unfriendly building type', property developer Peter Millican wanted Kings Place (p127) to be different from the norm. The building, designed by Dixon Jones, is tidily integrated with the adjacent canal basin. Above the airy lobby, the top seven floors of the building are given over to offices; the *Guardian* newspaper is the most high-profile resident. There's a gallery, a restaurant and a café on the ground floor. But the real appeal lies in the basement.

With just over 400 seats, the main hall is a subterranean beauty, dominated by wood carved from a single, 500-year-old oak tree and ringed by invisible rubber pads that kill unwanted noise that might interfere with the immaculate acoustics. There's also a versatile second hall and a number of smaller rooms, given over to workshops and lectures.

And the programming, overseen by Millican himself, is tremendous. It consists of long-weekend mini-series on diverse, classical-dominated themes. An innovation is the year-long sporadic concert series around a single composer (2012 saw Brahms Unwrapped). Other strands include chamber music on Sundays, and experimental music on Mondays, as well as the annual Kings Place Festival, held in September: 100 events in just four days. It's all part of an ethos that dares to be different.

Camino p124

deco-style interior and great views of the glass and steel roof of the train station. Sadly, the brasserie-style food has left something to be desired on recent visits.

Nightlife

Big Chill House
257-259 Pentonville Road, N1 9NL (7427 2540, www.bigchill.net). King's Cross tube/rail. **Open** 9am-midnight Mon-Wed; 9am-1am Thur; 9am-2am Fri; 11am-2am Sat; 11am-midnight Sun. **Map** p115 E1 ④⑤
A festival, record label, bar and club, the Big Chill empire rolls on. A good thing too, if it keeps offering such fine things as this three-floor space. There's a great terrace, but the real reasons to attend are the chill vibe and ace DJs. The programme is constantly being reworked and summer barbecue bashes from the Heatwave, Five Easy Pieces and Reggae Roast make the most of the terrace in summer.

Scala
275 Pentonville Road, N1 9NL (7833 2022, www.scala-london.co.uk). King's Cross tube/rail. **Map** p115 E1 ④⑥
One of London's best-loved gig venues, this multi-floored monolith is the frequent destination for one-off super-parties now that many of London's superclubs have bitten the dust. Built as a cinema shortly after World War I, it is surprisingly capacious and hosts a laudably broad range of indie, electronica, avant hip hop and folk. Its chilly air-conditioning is unrivalled anywhere else in the city – a definite boon should the summer get sultry.

Arts & leisure

Kings Place
90 York Way, N1 9AG (0844 264 0321, www.kingsplace.co.uk). King's Cross tube/rail. **Map** p115 D1 ④⑦
See box p125.

Place
17 Duke's Road, WC1H 9PY (7121 1000, www.theplace.org.uk). Euston tube/rail. **Map** p114 C2 ④⑧
For genuinely emerging dance, look to the Place. The theatre is behind the biennial Place Prize for choreography, which rewards the best in British contemporary dance as well as regular seasons of new work.

Soho

Forever unconventional, Soho remains London at its most game. Shoppers and visitors mingle with the musos, gays and boozers who have colonised the area since the late 1800s. If you want to drink or eat, you could hardly find a better part of London to do so. Have a wander among the skinny streets off **Old Compton Street**, Soho's main artery – and see if you can't still find yourself a bit of mischief.

Sights & museums

Leicester Square
Leicester Square tube. **Map** p128 C3 ①
See box p131.

Photographers' Gallery
NEW *16-18 Ramillies Street, W1A 1AU (0845 262 1618, www.photonet.org.uk). Oxford Circus tube.* **Open** 10am-6pm, Mon-Wed, Fri; 10am-8pm Thur; 11.30am-6pm Sun. **Map** p128 A1 ②
The new six-storey space for this excellent and long-established photographic gallery opened in early 2012. The UK's first public gallery to be dedicated to the medium, it hosts diverse exhibitions: in 2012, Edward Burtynsky's Oil portrayed the effect of oil on lives and landscapes, while the World in London project brought together specially commissioned portraits of 204 Londoners hailing from around the globe.

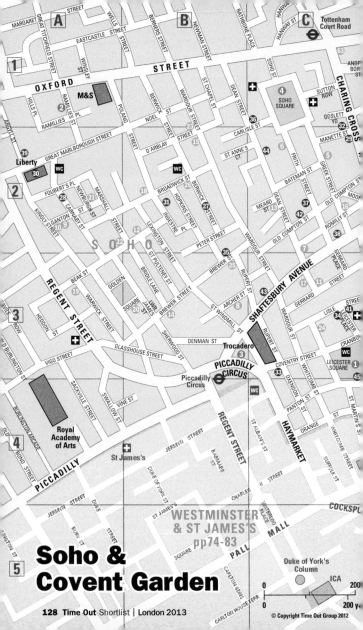

Soho & Covent Garden

© Copyright Time Out Group 2012

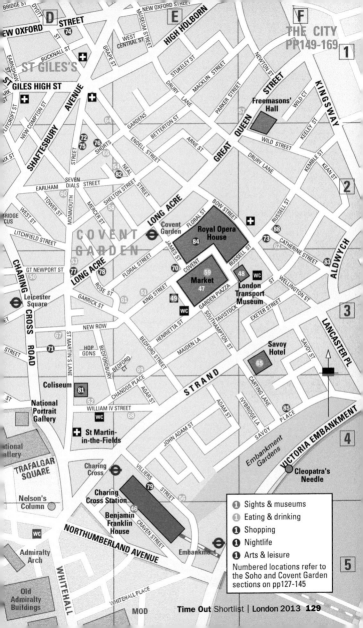

Sights & museums

Eating & drinking

Shopping

Nightlife

Arts & leisure

Numbered locations refer to the Soho and Covent Garden sections on pp127-145

Ripley's Believe It or Not!

*1 Piccadilly Circus, W1J 0DA
(3238 0022, www.ripleyslondon.com).
Piccadilly Circus tube.* **Open** 10am-
midnight daily (last entry 10.30pm).
Admission £25.95; free-£23.95
reductions; £81.95 family. **Map**
p128 B3 ❸

Over five floors of the Trocadero, this
'odditorium' follows a formula more or
less unchanged since Robert Ripley
opened his first display in 1933: an
assortment of 800 curiosities is displayed, ranging from a two-headed calf
to the world's smallest road-safe car.

Soho Square

Tottenham Court Road tube.
Map p128 C1 ❹

This tree-lined quadrangle was once
King's Square – a weather-beaten
Charles II stands at the centre, very at
home by the mock Tudor gardeners'
hut. On sunny days, the grass is covered with smoochy couples and the
benches fill up with snacking workers.

Eating & drinking

Since the 1950s, Gerrard and
Lisle Streets have been the centre
of **Chinatown**, marked by oriental
gates, stone lions and telephone
boxes topped with pagodas. Old-
style diners like Mr Kong (21 Lisle
Street, 7437 7341) and Wong Kei
(41-43 Wardour Street, 0871 332
8296) are still here, but we prefer
the likes of **Barshu** (right).

For quick, cheap eats, there's a
branch of **Hummus Bros** (p122)
on Wardour Street; for Thai food,
there's a branch of the excellent
Busaba Eathai (nos.106-110); for
late eats in the area, see box p140.

10 Greek Street

NEW *10 Greek Street W1D 4DH (020
7734 4677, www.10greekstreet.com).
Tottenham Court Road tube.* **Open**
noon-11.30pm Mon-Sat. **£££.**
Modern European. Map p128 C2 ❺

10 Greek Street at first appears to be yet
another trendy, no-bookings restaurant
in the same mould as, say, Spuntino
(p135) or Burger & Lobster (p106). You
can book for lunch, but not for dinner.
The look is a little spartan, with menus
on blackboards, though by night the
place takes on a certain low-lit ambi-
ence. Cooking can be excellent, too, with
the likes of smoked eel with horseradish
sauce and beetroot, followed by perfectly rendered duck breast.

Arbutus

*63-64 Frith Street, W1D 3JW (7734
4545, www.arbutusrestaurant.co.uk).
Tottenham Court Road tube.* **Open**
noon-2.30pm, 5-11pm Mon-Sat; noon-
3pm, 5.30-10.30pm Sun. **£££. Modern
European**. Map p128 C2 ❻

Providing very fine cooking at very fair
prices isn't an easy trick, but this place
makes it look easy. Although it's not
cheap to eat à la carte, the set lunch and
dinner are famously good value. It also
pioneered offering 250ml carafes for
sampling wine from the well-edited list.

Barshu

*28 Frith Street, W1D 5LF (7287 6688,
www.bar-shu.co.uk). Leicester Square
or Tottenham Court Road tube.* **Open**
noon-11pm Mon-Thur, Sun; noon-
11.30pm Fri, Sat. **££. Chinese**.
Map p128 C2 ❼

Since opening in 2006, Barshu has done
much to popularise Sichuan cuisine in
London. The cooking continues to thrill
and it is still an exceedingly charming
venue, its decor modelled on that of an
old Beijing teahouse. A dive into the
large menu reveals a number of 'blood
and guts' dishes: the likes of crunchy
ribbons of jellyfish with a dark vinegar
sauce and sesame oil.

Bocca di Lupo

*12 Archer Street, W1D 7BB (7734
2223, www.boccadilupo.com). Piccadilly
Circus tube.* **Open** 12.30-3pm, 5.30-
11pm Mon-Sat; noon-4pm Sun. **£££.**
Italian. Map p128 B3 ❽

A Better Leicester Square?

The square pulls its socks up.

Locals have for many years scorned the fast food, expensive cinemas and tacky pavement artists of Leicester Square. Apart from the tkts booth, selling cut-price, same-day theatre tickets, and Leicester Place's unlikely neighbours the Prince Charles cinema (see p139) and the French Catholic church of Notre Dame de France (no.5, 7437 9363, www.ndfchurch.org), with its Jean Cocteau murals, there was no reason to venture here. The green patch in the centre might be bearable on a sunny day, but woe betide anyone caught in the jostle of drunken suburban idiots and lost tourists at night.

When Westminster Council announced plans for an £18m redevelopment in 2008, there were serious doubts the fortunes of the square could be turned round. The idea of a new layout for the square's centre (improved lighting, modish 'ribbon' seating doubtless designed to prevent drunks and the homeless getting a good kip) conjured visions of another clean, characterless, commerce-friendly space. Certainly the pitch is high-end: the Grade II-listed, Frank Matcham-designed Hippodrome on the north-east corner is to reopen as a casino, and there are two new swish hotels: boutique **W Leicester Square** (see p206) from Starwood and the **St John Hotel** (see p204), an outpost of the nose-to-tail eating restaurant chain. But not all memories of the square's cheerfully tacky phase will be erased: the glockenspiel clock that used to command the attention of crowds outside the Swiss Centre every hour has returned, redesigned (27 bells, mechanical mountain farmers) but still chiming out the time on behalf of Switzerland Tourism.

LONDON BY AREA

Take an outstanding gastronomic tour of most of Italy's 20 regions with the starter-sized portions of Bocca di Lupo's 'degustation' menu – or larger portions for those who prefer a more traditional Italian meal – served up in an atmosphere of understated luxury at surprisingly reasonable prices.

Cha Cha Moon

15-21 Ganton Street, W1F 9BN (7297 9800). Oxford Circus tube. **Open** 11.30am-11pm Mon-Thur; 11.30am-11.30pm Fri, Sat; noon-10.30pm Sun. **£**. **Noodle bar**. **Map** p128 A2 ⑨

Like Wagamama (p122) before it, Alan Yau's Cha Cha Moon offers fast food of mixed Asian inspiration at low prices, served on long cafeteria-style tables. The main focus is excellent noodle dishes (around £5) from Hong Kong, Shanghai and elsewhere in China.

Dehesa

25 Ganton Street, W1F 9BP (7494 4170). Oxford Circus tube. **Open** noon-11pm Mon-Sat; noon-5pm Sun. **££**. **Spanish-Italian tapas**. **Map** p128 A2 ⑩

This informal yet sophisticated spot is a great place to relax with some non-run of the mill tapas dishes from Spain and Italy. The black-footed Ibérico pig (the place is named after its woodland home) appears in nutty-flavoured ham and other charcuterie, but local sourcing comes to the fore in tapas such as confit Old Spot pork belly with cannellini beans.

Experimental Cocktail Club

13A Gerrard Street, W1D 5PS (7434 3559, www.chinatownecc.com). Leicester Square tube. **Open** 6pm-3am Mon-Sat; 5-11pm Sun. **Cocktail bar**. **Map** p128 C3 ⑪

Quite fancy, a little French and fairly flipping phenomenal, the ECC is a stylish speakeasy spread over two floors of a townhouse. The main bar, occupying

the first floor, is classic, slightly colonial and cosy. Equally impressive is the intimate upstairs bar, complete with a small piano. The drinks, meanwhile, are extremely decent and the food is French and simple – boards of bread, cheese and charcuterie.

Fernandez & Wells

73 Beak Street, W1F 9SR (7287 8124, www.fernandezandwells.com). Oxford Circus or Piccadilly Circus tube. **Open** 7.30am-6pm Mon-Fri; 9am-6pm Sat; 9am-5pm Sun. **£**. **Café**. **Map** p128 B2 ⑫

If only there were more coffee bars like this in central London: one of its cheese toasties on sourdough bread or pastries make a fine breakfast. At lunch, seats are at a premium but worth the wait. The same people run a Spanish deli around the corner in Lexington Street; their St Anne's Court branch (no.16A) is nearby.

French House

49 Dean Street, W1D 5BG (7437 2799, www.frenchhousesoho.com). Leicester Square or Piccadilly Circus tube. **Open** noon-11pm Mon-Sat; noon-10.30pm Sun. **Pub**. **Map** p128 C2 ⑬

Titanic post-war drinkers, the Bacons and the Behans, frequented this small but significant boozer, while the venue's French heritage enticed De Gaulle to run his Resistance operation from the upstairs (the tiny but hip restaurant Polpetto, from the people behind Polpo, p135, was set to move out at the time of writing). Little has changed: beer is served in half pints and bottles of Breton cider are plonked on the famed back alcove table.

Hix/Mark's Bar

66-70 Brewer Street, W1F 9UP (7292 3518, www.marksbar.co.uk). Piccadilly Circus tube. **Open/food served** noon-1am Mon-Sat; 11am-11pm Sun. **£££**. **British/cocktail bar**. **Map** p128 B3 ⑭

In the dimly lit basement under Mark Hix's fine Soho restaurant, the superb Mark's Bar is a homage to New York –

albeit with a bar billiards table – from the tin ceiling tiles to the cocktails (try a lip-pursing Forbidden Sour). The ground-floor dining room is more modern and pared down, apart from crazy mobiles by Damien Hirst and Sarah Lucas. Prices are centre-of-town high, but the food is delightful: perhaps hanger steak with watercress, horseradish and beets, fish fingers with chips and mushy peas, or Blythburgh pork chop with wild fennel and Mendip snails. The top-notch puddings range from traditional to decidedly unusual (sea buckthorn berry posset).

Imli

167-169 Wardour Street, W1F 8WR (7287 4243, www.imli.co.uk). Tottenham Court Road tube. **Open** noon-11pm Mon-Sat; noon-10pm Sun. **£.** **Indian tapas. Map** p128 B2 ⑮
Indian tapas is the hook here, but Imli is no passing fad. Cut-price relative of Mayfair's classy Tamarind (20 Queen Street, 7629 3561), this restaurant has plenty of culinary zip. Three dishes amount to a filling two-course meal.

Maison Bertaux

28 Greek St, W1D 5DQ (7437 6007). Leicester Square tube. **Open** 9am-10pm Mon-Sat; 9am-8pm Sun. **£.** No credit cards. **Café. Map** p128 C2 ⑯
Oozing arty, bohemian charm, this café dates back to 1871 when Soho was London's little piece of the Continent. Battered bentwood tables and chairs add to the feeling of being in a pâtisserie in rural France. The provisions (cream cakes, greasy pastries, pots of tea) really aren't the point.

Manchurian Legends

12 Macclesfield Street, W1D 5BP (7437 8785). Leicester Square or Piccadilly Circus tube. **Open** noon-11pm daily. **££. Chinese. Map** p128 C3 ⑰
Manchurian Legends specialises in food from, er, Manchuria. Expect rich, warming, slow-cooked dishes, and plenty of pork belly. Some dishes are a major

departure from standard Chinatown fare, such as the sweet, sticky sauce covering a crispy, fatty lamb skewer sprinkled with cumin seeds and dried chilli. The service is friendly and geared to those unfamiliar with the cuisine.

Milk & Honey

61 Poland Street, W1F 7NU (7065 6840, www.mlkhny.com). Oxford Circus tube. **Open** (for non-members, 2hrs max, last admission 9pm) 6-11pm Mon-Sat. **Cocktail bar. Map** p128 B2 ⑱
You could walk past the inconspicuous door of this semi-mythical, dimly lit speakeasy every day and never know it was here. It's members-only most of the time, but mere mortals can pre-book a table until 11pm. What the place lacks in atmosphere in the early evening, it more than makes up for with outstanding cocktails.

NOPI

NEW *21 Warwick Street, W1B5NE (7494 9584, www.nopi-restaurant.com). Piccadilly Circus tube.* **Open** 8am-2.45pm, 5.30-11.30pm Mon-Fri; 9am-11.30pm Sat; 10am-4pm Sun. **££.** **Pan-Asian. Map** p128 A3 ⑲
NOPI is a fresh-faced addition to Soho's dining scene. Interior designer Alex Meitlis has taken elements of a traditional brasserie aesthetic into a light white space on the ground floor, while downstairs in the basement, communal tables sit next to the open kitchen, and the space doubles as a supplies store. Food is from diverse corners: you'll find the likes of Thai sticky rice porridge, cured halibut with lemony oil, shiso and samphire and rich burrata accoanied by toasted coriander and blood orange on the menu.

Nordic Bakery

14A Golden Square, W1F 9JG (3230 1077, www.nordicbakery.com). Oxford Circus or Piccadilly Circus tube. **Open** 8am-8pm Mon-Fri; 9am-7pm Sat; 10am-7pm Sun. **£. Café. Map** p128 B3 ⑳

Who Needs a Cinema?

Screening locations are getting creative.

Summer Screen at Somerset House

At unusual locations
Free Film Festivals
www.freefilmfestivals.org.
This enterprising community project puts on free outdoor screenings in interesting public spaces in south-east London: *Battleship Potemkin* on the roof of a Peckham multistorey car park, say.

On a rooftop
Rooftop Film Club
Queen of Hoxton, 1-5 Curtain Road, EC2A 3JX (7422 0958, www.rooftopfilmclub.com).
In summer, the rooftop garden at this bar/club/arts collective screens around five films a week. Everyone is issued with wireless headphones, and you can sip a beer or order some food while you watch.

In architectural splendour
Summer Screen at Somerset House
The Strand, WC2R 1LA, 7845 4600, www.somersethouse. org.uk/film

This summer season takes place in the lovely neoclassical courtyard of Somerset House; tickets sell out way in advance. Bring along a picnic and plenty of cushions.

Thames-side
More London Free Festival
www.morelondon.com.
A sunken outdoor amphitheatre beside City Hall, the Scoop hosts a series of free film events in summer.

On a barge
http://floatingcinema.info.
In summer the Floating Cinema plies London's waterways with screenings and events. In May 2012 an open architecture competition for a new permanent floating cinema was launched.

On the QT
Secret Cinema
www.secretcinema.org.
Venue and film are announced just 24 hours before curtain-up at these immersive club-like experiences, with dress code.

A haven of über-stylish Scandinavian cool warmed up with baskets, tea towels, denim aprons and a nature-inspired wall rug. Open sandwiches come on rye bread, and the fresh-out-of-the-oven cinnamon buns – thick, fluffy and oozing spicy sweetness – are the real deal.

Pitt Cue Co

NEW *1 Newburgh Street, W1F 7RB. Oxford Circus tube (no phone, www. pittcue.co.uk).* **Open** noon-3pm, 6-10pm Mon-Sat. **££**. **North American**. Map p128 A2 ㉑

This tiny place has a ground-floor takeaway and standing-room-only bar, with a dining room in the basement. No bookings are taken, but there's often a queue. So what's the attraction? Slow-cooked and grilled meat, often paired with tangy, sour slaws, pickles and a dash of heat. Pulled pork, beef brisket and beef ribs are dry-rubbed and smoked for hours, over charcoal or wood. St Louis ribs are slathered in sticky barbecue sauce. Eat-in meals are served in enamel dishes suggestive of prison plates, but prison food never tasted this good.

Polpo

41 Beak Street, W1F 9SB (7734 4479, http://polpo.co.uk). Piccadilly Circus tube. **Open** noon-11pm Mon-Sat; noon-4pm Sun. **££**. **Italian/wine bar**. Map p128 A2 ㉒

In an 18th-century townhouse that was once home to Canaletto, this is a charming *bacaro* (Venetian-style wine bar). The room has a fashionably distressed look, the wines (served in rustic jugs of 250ml or 500ml) are selected from four good importers, and the food is a procession of small dishes, all of them packed with flavour. Some choices are classic Venetian (such as the cicheti bar snack); others are more adventurous.

Princi

135 Wardour Street, W1F 0UF (7478 8888, www.princi.co.uk). Leicester Square or Tottenham Court Road

tube. **Open** 8am-midnight Mon-Sat; 8.30am-10pm Sun. **£**. **Bakery-café**. Map p128 B1 ㉓

Alan Yau teamed up with an Italian bakery for this busy venture. At the vast, L-shaped granite counter, choose from a broad range of savoury dishes, along with numerous cakes, tiramisu and pastries. The big slices of pizza have a springy base, the margherita pungent with fresh thyme; caprese salad comes with creamy balls of good buffalo mozzarella and big slices of beef tomato.

St John Hotel

1 Leicester Street, off Leicester Square, WC2H 7BL (7251 0848, www.stjohn hotellondon.com). Leicester Square or Piccadilly Circus tube. **Open** 8-10.30am, noon-3pm, 5.30pm-midnight daily. **£££**. **British**. Map p128 C3 ㉔

St John's menus – at the original in Clerkenwell (p157), at the Spitalfields branch and now here, in a spartan hotel (p204) – are masterpieces of brevity, with offal featuring heavily. A starter of 'pig's head, rabbit and radishes' might be followed by 'bacon and snails', both will be packed with earthy flavour. The resolutely British desserts are another St John strength.

Spuntino

61 Rupert Street, W1D 7PW (no phone, http://spuntino.co.uk). Piccadilly Circus tube. **Open** 11am-midnight Mon-Sat; noon-11pm Sun. **££**. **Italian**. Map p128 B3 ㉕

You can spot this speakeasy-style eaterie by the queue snaking out of the door – the signage certainly isn't clear. Inside, tattooed bar staff mix drinks and push bar snacks or bigger dishes across the steel-topped bar to customers. The narrow, dimly lit space is artfully contrived to look semi-derelict. Food is Italian with an American flavour and reasonably good value. Be prepared to arrive early (before 7pm) or you'll have to join the queue – reservations aren't accepted.

LONDON BY AREA

Yauatcha

*15-17 Broadwick Street, W1F 0DL
(7494 8888). Piccadilly Circus or
Tottenham Court Road tube.* **Open**
noon-11.45pm Mon-Sat; noon-10.30pm
Sun. **£££**. **Dim sum/tearoom**.
Map p128 B2 ㉖

This groundbreaking dim sum destination is a sultry lounge-like basement
den, with fish tanks and starry ceiling
lights, where young professionals, families of Chinese and suited business
people enjoy their succession of freshly
prepared – and highly impressive –
perennial favourites.

Shopping

There's a terrific West End branch
of **Anthropologie** (158 Regent
Street, W1B 5SW, 7529 9800,
www.anthropologie.co.uk; see
also p97).

Berwick Street

*Piccadilly Circus or Tottenham Court
Road tube.* **Map** p128 B2 ㉗

The buzzy street market (9am-6pm
Mon-Sat), in an area better known for
its lurid, neon-lit trades, is one of
London's oldest. Dating back to 1778,
it's still great for seasonal produce and
cheap fabric. The indie record shops
that used to be clustered here have
taken a pasting over the last few years,
but Revival Records (no.30) is full of
vinyl beans. Chris Kerr (no.52), son of
legendary 1960s tailor Eddie, is still
here, crafting brilliant bespoke suits.
There are lots of vintage shops too.

Carnaby Street

Oxford Street tube. **Map** p128 A2 ㉘

As famous as the King's Road back
when the Sixties Swung, Carnaby
Street was until a few years ago more
likely to sell you a postcard of the
Queen snogging a punk rocker than a
fishtail parka. But the noughties have
been kind and Carnaby is cool again.
Among classy chains (Lush, Muji),
Kingly Court (7333 8118, www.carna-
by.co.uk) is the real highlight, a three-
tiered complex containing a funky mix
of chains and independents.

Foyles

*113-119 Charing Cross Road, WC2H
0EB (7437 5660, www.foyles.co.uk).
Tottenham Court Road tube.* **Open**
9.30am-9pm Mon-Sat; noon-6pm Sun.
Map p128 C2 ㉙

Probably London's single most impressive independent bookshop, Foyles built
its reputation on the sheer volume and
breadth of its stock (there are 56 specialist subjects in this flagship store). Its five
storeys accommodate concessions too:
Ray's Jazz, London's least beardy jazz
shop, is on the third floor, there's
Unsworth's antiquarian booksellers and
the new Grant & Cutler foreign-lan-
guage bookstore. The first-floor café
hosts great low-key gigs and readings.

Liberty

*Regent Street, W1B 5AH (7734 1234,
www.liberty.co.uk). Oxford Circus tube.*
Open 10am-9pm Mon-Sat; noon-6pm
Sun. **Map** p128 A2 ㉚

A creaky, 1920s, mock Tudor department store masterpiece, Liberty has
upped its game over the last few
years – a store-wide 'renaissance' (in its
own words) that introduced a raft of
cool new contemporary labels and a
series of inspired events. Shopping
here is about more than just spending
money; artful window displays, exciting new collections and luxe labels
make it an experience to savour.
Despite being fashion-forward, Liberty
respects its dressmaking heritage with
a good haberdashery department.

Lucy in Disguise

*48 Lexington Street, W1F 0LR (7434
4086, www.lucyindisguiselondon.com).
Oxford Circus of Piccadilly Circus tube.*
Open 10am-7pm Mon-Wed, Fri, Sat;
10am-8pm Thur. **Map** p129 E5 ㉛

The vintage store owned by Lily Allen
and her half-sister Sarah Owen has come
into its own since moving to this

fabulous space. The shiny chequered floor and old chandeliers create a glamorous vibe in which to shop for good-quality vintage, from dresses by Pierre Cardin and Christian Dior to silk scarves and leather handbags. The Lucy In Disguise own label – new pieces inspired by vintage designs – is a real draw too

Nightlife

Borderline

Orange Yard, off Manette Street, W1D 4JB (0844 847 2465, www. meanfiddler.com). Tottenham Court Road tube. **Map** p128 C2 ③②

A cramped, sweaty dive bar-slash-juke joint, the Borderline has long been a favoured stop-off for touring American bands of the country and blues type, but you'll also find a variety of indie acts and singer-songwriters down here.

Comedy Store

1A Oxendon Street, SW1Y 4EE (0844 847 1728, www.thecomedystore.co.uk). Leicester Square or Piccadilly Circus tube. **Map** p128 C3 ③③

The Comedy Store made its name as the home of 'alternative comedy' in the 1980s. The venue has a gladiatorial semicircle of seats, and some of the circuit's best bills.

Leicester Square Theatre

6 Leicester Place, WC2H 7BX (0844 873 3433, www.leicestersquaretheatre. com). Leicester Square tube. **Map** p128 C3 ③④

The main auditorium programmes a good mix of big-name comedy (such as Michael McIntyre and Bill Bailey), cabaret (Miranda Sings, Impropera) and straight plays, but keep an eye on the goings-on in the little basement performance space, with its champagne bar.

Madame JoJo's

8-10 Brewer Street, W1F 0SE (7734 3040, www.madamejojos.com). Leicester Square or Piccadilly Circus tube. **Map** p128 B3 ③⑤

Famed nights at this red and shabby basement club include variety – Kitsch Cabaret is every Saturday night – but its long-running Tuesday nighter, White Heat, still books up-and- coming bands and DJs for a largely indie crowd.

Pizza Express Jazz Club

10 Dean Street, W1D 3RW (0845 602 7017, www.pizzaexpress.com). Tottenham Court Road tube. **Map** p128 C1 ③⑥

The upstairs restaurant (7437 9595) is a straightforward jazz-free pizza joint, but downstairs the 120-capacity basement venue is one of the best modern mainstream jazz venues in Europe.

Ronnie Scott's

47 Frith Street, W1D 4HT (7439 0747, www.ronniescotts.co.uk). Leicester Square or Tottenham Court Road tube. **Map** p128 C2 ③⑦

Opened (albeit on a different site) by the British saxophonist Ronnie Scott in 1959, this jazz institution was completely refurbished five years ago. The capacity was expanded to 250, the food got better and the bookings drearier. Happily, Ronnie's has got back on track, with jazz heavyweights once more dominating in place of the mainstream pop acts who held sway for a while.

Arts & leisure

Curzon Soho

99 Shaftesbury Avenue, W1D 5DY (0871 703 3988, www.curzoncinemas. com). Leicester Square tube. **Map** p128 C2 ③⑧

All the cinemas in the Curzon group programme a superb mix of shorts, rarities, double bills and mini-festivals, but the Curzon Soho is the best – not least because it has a good ground-floor café and decent basement bar.

London Palladium

Argyll Street, W1F 7TF (0844 412 2957, www.wizardofozthemusical.com). Oxford Circus tube. **Map** p128 A2 ③⑨

The home of Andrew Lloyd Webber's stage remake of MGM's 1939 blockbuster, *The Wizard of Oz*. The staging is pretty spectacular. Production is subject to change.

Odeon Leicester Square

Leicester Square, WC2H 7LQ (0871 224 4007, www.odeon.co.uk). Leicester Square tube. **Map** p128 C3 ⓴
This art deco masterpiece is London's archetypal red-carpet cinema for premieres. Catch one of the occasional silent movie screenings with live organ music if you can; otherwise, it will be a comfy viewing of a pricey current blockbuster.

Prince Charles Cinema

7 Leicester Place, Leicester Square, WC2H 7BY (7494 3654, www.princecharlescinema.com). Leicester Square tube. **Map** p128 C3 ⓵
The downstairs screen here offers the best value in town (£5.50-£10) for releases that have ended their first run elsewhere. The weekend singalong screenings are very popular – Singalong-a-*Grease* is the latest.

Prince Edward Theatre

28 Old Compton Street, W1D 4HS (0844 482 5151, www.jerseyboyslondon.com). Leicester Square or Piccadilly Circus tube. **Map** p128 C2 ⓶
The Prince Edward shows *Jersey Boys*, the story of Frankie Valli and the Four Seasons. The pace is lively, the sets gritty and the doo-wop standards ('Big Girls Don't Cry', 'Can't Take My Eyes Off You') superbly performed. Production subject to change.

Queen's Theatre

Shaftesbury Avenue, W1D 6BA (7907 7071, www.delfontmackintosh.co.uk). Leicester Square tube. **Map** p128 C3 ⓷
The capital's longest running musical, *Les Misérables*, offers quasi-operatic power ballads and some bona fide classics in a gritty tale of revolution and poverty. Production subject to change.

Soho Theatre

21 Dean Street, W1D 3NE (7478 0100, www.sohotheatre.com). Tottenham Court Road tube. **Map** p128 C2 ⓸
Its cool blue neon lights, front-of-house café and occasional late-night shows attract a younger, hipper crowd than most theatres. The Soho brings on aspiring writers through regular workshops, has regular solo comedy shows and has recently got really stuck in to cabaret.

tkts

Clocktower Building, Leicester Square, WC2H 7NA (www.officiallondontheatre.co.uk/tkts). Leicester Square tube. **Open** 10am-7pm Mon-Sat; 11am-4pm Sun. **Map** p128 C3 ⓹
Avoid getting ripped off by the touts and buy tickets here for West End blockbusters at much-reduced rates, either on the day or up to a week in advance. It's not uncommon to find the best seats sold at half price.

Covent Garden

Covent Garden is understandably popular with visitors. A traffic-free oasis in the heart of the city, replete with shops, cafés and bars – and the **London Transport Museum** – it centres on a restored 19th-century covered market, and has recently been the subject of a makeover (see box p145). On the west side, the portico of St Paul's **Covent Garden** hosts jugglers and escapologists. And if you're looking for great vocal performances rather than street performances, the **Royal Opera House** is here too.

Sights & museums

Presiding over the eastern end of Oxford Street, the landmark **Centre Point** tower now contains a public bar and restaurant (**Paramount**, p144).

West End Final

Where to eat, after hours.

For all London's excitement when it comes to cutting-edge nightlife, this really isn't a good city if you're looking to eat late. So when the **St John Hotel** restaurant (p135) opened in spring 2011, it felt rather as though it had invented quality late-night dining in the West End. Not only is the food very good, but it is served until 1.45am.

In fact, those with deep pockets already had a couple of excellent options. There are few better ways to impress a hungry weekend date than a late stop-off at **Hakkasan** (p116), the sleek and stylish basement cocktail bar and modern Chinese restaurant. Last orders are taken until 11.30pm from Sunday through to Wednesday, but as late as 12.30am on Thursday, Friday and Saturday. And for sheer sense of occasion, the lovely art deco interior of the **Wolseley** (p82) is perfect, with food orders taken until 11.45pm (10.45pm on Sunday).

Cheaper options can be found near Chinatown. The utilitarian **Café TPT** (21 Wardour Street, W1D 6PN, 7734 7980) takes orders for Chinese roast meats and seafood until 12.30am; but for exceedingly late closing times (3.30am daily), head to the **New Mayflower** (68-70 Shaftesbury Avenue, W1D 6LY, 7734 9207). Staff usually push set meals at tourists, but there are plenty of perfectly adequate Cantonese dishes on the menu.

Benjamin Franklin House

36 Craven Street, WC2N 5NF (7925 1405, www.benjaminfranklinhouse. org). Charing Cross tube/rail. **Open** pre-booked tours only, noon-5pm Wed-Sun. **Admission** £7; free-£5 reductions. **Map** p129 E5 ⑯

The house where Franklin lived from 1757 to 1775 can be explored on well-run, pre-booked multimedia 'experiences'. Lasting an intense 45 minutes, they are led by an actress in character as Franklin's landlady. Less elaborate 20-minute tours (£3.50) are given by house interns on Mondays.

Covent Garden Piazza

Covent Garden tube. **Map** p129 E3 ⑰ See box p145.

London Transport Museum

Covent Garden Piazza, WC2E 7BB (7379 6344, www.ltmuseum.co.uk). Covent Garden tube. **Open** 10am-6pm Mon-Thur, Sat, Sun; 11am-6pm Fri. **Admission** £13.50; free-£10 reductions. **Map** p129 F3 ⑱

Tracing the city's transport history from the horse age, this fine museum focuses on social history and design, illustrated by a superb array of buses, trams and trains. The collections are in broadly chronological order, beginning with the Victorian gallery and a replica of Shillibeer's first horse-drawn bus service from 1829.

Event highlights Depot guided tours (last Fri & Sat of the mth).

St Paul's Covent Garden

Bedford Street, WC2E 9ED (7836 5221, www.actorschurch.org). Covent Garden or Leicester Square tube. **Open** 8.30am-5pm Mon-Fri; 9am-1pm Sun. **Admission** free; donations appreciated. **Map** p129 E3 ⑲

Known as the Actors' Church, this magnificently spare building was designed by Inigo Jones for the Earl of Bedford in 1631. The thespians commemorated on its walls range from those lost in obscurity to those destined for immortality. Surely there's no more romantic tribute London than Vivien Leigh's plaque, simply inscribed with words from Shakespeare's *Antony & Cleopatra*: 'Now boast thee, death, in thy possession lies a lass unparallel'd.'

Eating & drinking

There's a busy **Masala Zone** (48 Floral Street, 7379 0101, www.masalazone.com; see also p171) near the Opera House and market.

Abeno Too

17-18 Great Newport Street, WC2H 7JE (7379 1160, www.abeno.co.uk). Leicester Square tube. **Open** noon-11pm Mon-Sat; noon-10.30pm Sun. **££**. **Japanese**. Map p129 D3 ⑤⓪
Okonomiyaki (hearty pancakes with nuggets of vegetables, seafood, pork and other titbits added to a disc of noodles) are cooked to order on hot-plates set into Abeno's tables and counter.

Clos Maggiore

33 King Street, WC2E 8JD (7379 9696, www.closmaggiore.com). Covent Garden or Leicester Square tube. **Open** noon-2.15pm, 5-11pm Mon-Sat; noon-2.30pm, 5-10pm Sun. **££**. **French**. Map p129 E3 ⑤①
Just off Covent Garden's bustling piazza, Clos Maggiore transports you to a picturesque corner of Provence. An elegant boxwood-lined dining room leads to an intimate indoor courtyard filled with fake blossoms and fairy lights. A Provençal-inspired menu highlights the provenance of produce, and those carefully sourced ingredients shine through in all of the dishes. Look out for the exceptionally good value set menu at lunchtime.

Les Deux Salons

42-44 William IV Street, WC2N 4DD (7420 2050, www.lesdeuxsalons.co.uk). Charing Cross tube/rail. **£££**. **French**. Map p129 D4 ⑤②

The decor is cliché on a grand scale – brass rails, tiled floor, red booths – but if you were expecting standard brasserie fare, think again. Patrick Demetre and Will Smith, the team behind Arbutus (p130) and Wild Honey (p106) aim higher, with the likes of ox cheek with watercress, bone marrow and a deceptively rich salsify salsa, followed, perhaps, by pale juicy pork belly pepped up with a slice of saucisson, crunchy spring greens, carrots and lentils. Carafes of 250ml make it easy to try a different wine with each course.

Dishoom

12 Upper St Martin's Lane, WC2H 9FB (7420 9320, www.dishoom.com). Covent Garden or Leicester Square tube. **Open** 8am-11pm Mon-Fri; 10am-11pm Sat; 10am-10pm Sun. **££**. **Pan-Indian**. Map p129 D3 ⑤③
Dishoom has got the look of a Mumbai 'Irani' café (the cheap, cosmopolitan eateries set up by Persian immigrants in the early 1900s) spot on. Solid oak panels, antique mirrors and ceiling fans say 'retro grandeur', and there's a fascinating display of old magazine covers, adverts and fading photos of Indian families. Parts of the menu are familiar street snacks (a terrific pau bhaji), but chocolate fondant, classy cocktails and intriguing lassi flavours move things upmarket.

Food for Thought

31 Neal Street, WC2H 9PR (7836 9072). Covent Garden tube. **Open** noon-8.30pm Mon-Sat; noon-5pm Sun. **£**. No credit cards. **Vegetarian café**. Map p129 E2 ⑤④
The menu of this much-loved and long-established veggie café changes daily, though you can expect three or four main courses, and a selection of salads and desserts. The laid-back premises are down a steep stairway that, during lunch, usually fills with a patient queue. The ground floor offers the same food to take away.

LONDON BY AREA

Giaconda Dining Room

9 Denmark Street, WC2H 8LS (7240 3334, www.giacondadining.com). Tottenham Court Road tube. **Open** noon-2.15pm, 6-9.15pm Tue-Fri; noon-2pm, 6-9.15pm Sat. **££. Modern European**. Map p129 D1 ⑤

A thoroughly likeable restaurant, despite being a little cramped. The food is what most people want to eat most of the time: the owners describe it as French-ish with a bit of Spain and Italy, meaning big-flavoured grills, fish and intriguing assemblages (chicken liver, chorizo, trotters and tripe, for instance).

Gordon's

47 Villiers Street, WC2N 6NE (7930 1408, www.gordonswinebar.com). Embankment tube or Charing Cross tube/rail. **Open** 11am-11pm Mon-Sat; noon-10pm Sun. **Wine bar**. Map p129 E4 ⑤

Gordon's has been serving drinks since 1890, and it looks like it – the place is a specialist in yellowing, candle-lit alcoves. The wine list doesn't bear expert scrutiny and the food is buffet-style, but atmosphere is everything, and this is a great, bustling place.

Great Queen Street

32 Great Queen Street, WC2B 5AA (7242 0622). Covent Garden or Holborn tube. **Open** noon-2.30pm, 6-10.30pm Mon-Sat; noon-3pm Sun. **££. British**. Map p129 F1 ⑤

The pub-style room here thrums with bonhomie. Ranging from snacks to shared mains, the menu is designed to tempt and satisfy rather than educate or impress. Booking is essential, and the robust food is worth it. At the Sunday lunch session, diners sit and are served together. The Dive bar downstairs serves snacks and drinks.

Hawksmoor Seven Dials

11 Langley Street, WC2H 9JJ (7856 2154, www.thehawksmoor.co.uk). Covent Garden tube. **Open** noon-3.30pm,

5.30-10.30pm Mon-Sat; noon-4.30pm Sun. **£££. Grill**. Map p129 E2 ⑤

Hawksmoor stands out as the benchmark to beat for best all-round bar and grill experience. The site's a real beauty, evocative of old New York with its speakeasy feel and old brickwork. The cocktails are masterfully concocted and the steaks are sublime, with clued-up staff keen to advise on the various cuts of meat and lengthy wine list.

Icecreamists

Market Building, Covent Garden Market, WC2E 8RF (8616 0721, www.theicecreamists.com). Covent Garden tube. **Open** noon-10.30pm daily. **£. Ice-cream**. Map p129 E3 ⑤

Although the black and electric-pink decor, thumping music and neon signage is more sex shop than ice-cream parlour, Icecreamists isn't all garish style over substance. The gimmick-laden *gelatos* are actually pretty good, with the sea salt lacing Sex, Drugs & Choc'n'Roll giving the creamy milk chocolate a superb lift.

Kopapa

32-34 Monmouth Street, WC2H 9HA (7240 6076, www.kopapa.co.uk). Leicester Square tube. **Open** 8.30am-11.30pm Mon-Fri; 10am-3pm, 3.30-10.45pm Sat; 10am-3pm, 3.30-9.45pm Sun. **££. Global**. Map p129 D2 ⑥

Kopapa serves breakfast, small dishes, great wines and great coffee, in a come-as-you-are café setting. Many of its bare tables are shared; around half are bookable, the rest are not. The lights are low, the seats close together. The coffees, smoothies and wines by the glass are all first rate, but it's fabulous tapas-style fusion food that really makes Kopapa stand out.

Lamb & Flag

33 Rose Street, WC2E 9EB (7497 9504). Covent Garden tube. **Open** 11am-11pm Mon-Thur; 11am-11.30pm Fri, Sat; noon-10.30pm Sun. **Pub**. Map p129 E3 ⑥

A pub for over 300 years and a fixture on Rose Street for longer, the unabashedly traditional Lamb & Flag is always a squeeze, but no one minds. The afternoon-only bar upstairs is 'ye olde' to a fault, and sweetly localised by pictures of passed-on regulars.

Opera Tavern

23 Catherine Street, WC2B 5JS (7836 3680, www.operatavern.co.uk). Covent Garden tube. **Open** noon-3pm, 5pm-12.30am Mon-Fri; noon-12.30am Sat; noon-5pm Sun. **££. Spanish-Italian tapas.** Map p129 F2 ⊕

Low-lit, bang on-trend and immediately appealing, this is a restaurant of real character. The grand old pub premises date from 1879, but received a major refit. It's equally accomplished as a bar and restaurant, with a menu that craftily meshes Italianate small plates and Spanish tapas.

Paramount

32nd floor, Centre Point, 101-103 New Oxford Street, WC1A 1DD (7420 2900, www.paramount.uk.net). Tottenham Court Road tube. **Open** 8am-1.30am Mon-Wed; 8am-2.30am Thur, Fri; 11.30am-2.30am Sat; noon-4pm Sun. **£££. Modern European.** Map p128 C1 ⊕

With its lofty location at the top of the landmark Centre Point building, it's not surprising that the handsome Tom Dixon-designed interior of this smart restaurant is upstaged by the superb view. Still, Colin Layfield's menu holds its own, with carefully constructed dishes that appeal to the eye and the tongue. The attached bar is open only to members or diners.

Rock & Sole Plaice

47 Endell Street, WC2H 9AJ (7836 3785, www.rockandsoleplaice.com). Covent Garden tube. **Open** 11.30am-10.30pm Mon-Sat; noon-9.30pm Sun. **££. Fish & chips.** Map p129 D1 ⊕

A chippie since 1874, this busy establishment has walls covered in theatre posters. The ground-floor tables are often all taken (check whether there's space in the basement), and the outside seats are never empty in summer.

Savoy Grill

100 Strand, WC2R 0EW (7592 1600, www.gordonramsay.com/thesavoygrill). Charing Cross tube/rail or Embankment tube. **Open** noon-3pm, 5.30-11pm Mon-Sat; noon-4pm, 6-10.30pm Sun. **£££. British.** Map p129 F3 ⊕

The glamour of the refurbished Savoy hotel (p206) demanded much of Gordon Ramsay's Savoy Grill, and he's largely delivered. The room is suitably low-lit, with the right balance of intimacy and openness. The menu is full of grills and seafood, but with more imaginative British dishes that show the kitchen's talent: a starter of potted salt beef was slow-cooked and tender, while mutton pie was a deliciously clever play on shepherd's pie. It's expensive but not overpriced. Book well ahead.

Scoop

40 Shorts Gardens, WC2H 9AB (7240 7086, www.scoopgelato.com). Covent Garden tube. **Open** noon-10.30pm daily. **£. Ice-cream.** Map p129 D2 ⊕

Frequent queues are a testament to the quality of the ice-cream, even dairy-free health versions, at this Italian artisan's shop. Flavours include a very superior Piedmont hazelnut type, which can be eaten in at a few tables or taken away.

J Sheekey

28-34 St Martin's Court, WC2N 4AL (7240 2565, www.j-sheekey.co.uk). Leicester Square tube. **Open** noon-3pm, 5.30pm-midnight Mon-Sat; noon-3.30pm, 6-11pm Sun. **£££. Fish & seafood.** Map p129 D3 ⊕

Sheekey's Oyster Bar opened in 2009, yet another enticement to visit this fine restaurant. Unlike many of London's period pieces (which this certainly is: it was chartered in the mid 19th century), Sheekey's buzzes with fashionable folk.

Market Makeover

Covent Garden has been transformed.

Icecreamists

Kurt Geiger

While all eyes have been focused on the new Westfield Stratford City, another shopping district has quietly been undergoing a nip and tuck. Covent Garden has been transformed from a slightly rough-edged cobbled square to a plumped-up, youthful shopping district.

Since 2006, property investor Capco has consumed great chunks of prime real estate in Covent Garden, scooping up property on the Piazza, King Street, James Street, Long Acre and beyond – £780 million of it, to be exact. And it's Capco's marketing and communications director, Bev Churchill, who is charged with re-editing the neighbourhood. One-time marketing director of Selfridges, she knows a thing or two about retail. And she certainly things big. A slew of shops have been replaced by high street heavyweights and luxury brands. Fred Perry, Whistles, L'Artisan Parfumier, Kurt Geiger, Rugby Ralph Lauren and Burberry Brit

have all appeared; last year, the world's largest **Apple Store** (see p146) set up shop and, perhaps most tellingly, the West Cornwall Pasty Co has become a Ladurée café, where waistcoat-wearing staff dispense dainty orange-blossom macaroons where steak and Stilton pastries were once shovelled out.

Russell Norman's **Da Polpo** (6 Maiden Lane, WC2E 7NA, 7836 8448), a sister restaurant of Polpo (see p135), opened in May 2011; and the **Icecreamists**' shock-concept ice-cream (see p143) sits in the Market Building.

But what of Covent Garden's bawdy personality? To Bev, it's all about plonking niche, indie shops, bars and restaurants up against luxury retailers and contemporary art, and also about uncovering what's already there. The Rugby store, a late-1600s townhouse with library-like rooms and grand façade, is a case in point. 'Covent Garden has great bone structure,' explains Bev. 'It just needed a little facelift.'

Even if you opt for the main restaurant, your party of four may be crammed on to a table for two, but the accomplished menu will take your mind off it, stretching from sparklingly simple seafood platters to dishes that are interesting without being elaborate.

Terroirs

5 William IV Street, WC2N 4DW (7036 0660, www.terroirswinebar. com). Charing Cross tube/rail. **Open** noon-11pm Mon-Fri; 11am-4pm Sat. **£££. Wine bar. Map** p129 E4 ㊿

Now extending over two floors, Terroirs is a superb and very popular wine bar that specialises in the new generation of organic and biodynamic, sulphur-, sugar- or acid-free wines. The list is only slightly shorter than the Bible and the food is terrific: a selection of French bar snacks, charcuterie and seafood. A new Columbia Road Market (p178) branch, Brawn, is as popular.

Wahaca

66 Chandos Place, WC2N 4HG (7240 1883, www.wahaca.co.uk). Covent Garden or Leicester Square tube. **Open** noon-11pm Mon-Sat; noon-10.30pm Sun. **£. Mexican. Map** p129 E3 ㊾

Wahaca has a look as cheery as its staff, created from lamps made out of tomatillo cans dotted with bottle tops, wooden crates packed with fruit, and tubs of chilli plants. The menu is really designed for sharing, tapas style, but you can choose one of the large plato fuertes (enchiladas, burritos or grilled dishes) if you want your own plate.

Shopping

Apple Store

1-7 The Piazza, WC2E 8HA (7447 1400, www.apple.com). Covent Garden tube. **Open** 9am-9pm Mon-Sat, noon-6pm Sun. **Map** p129 E3 ㊲

A temple to geekery, this is the world's biggest Apple Store, with separate rooms – set out over three storeys – devoted to each product line. The exposed brickwork, big old oak tables and stone floors make it an inviting place, and it's also the world's first Apple Store with a Start Up Room where staff will help set up your new iPad, iPhone, iPod or Mac, or transfer files from your old computer to your new one – all for free.

Cecil Court

www.cecilcourt.co.uk. Leicester Square tube. **Map** p129 D3 ㊶

Bookended by Charing Cross Road and St Martin's Lane, picturesque Cecil Court is known for its antiquarian book, map and print dealers. Notable residents include children's specialist Marchpane (no.16), the Italian Bookshop (no.5), Watkins (nos.19 & 21), for occult and New Age titles, and 40-year veteran David Drummond at Pleasures of Past Times (no.11), who specialises in theatre and magic.

Coco de Mer

23 Monmouth Street, WC2H 9DD (7836 8882, www.coco-de-mer.co.uk). Covent Garden tube. **Open** 11am-7pm Mon-Wed, Fri, Sat; 11am-8pm Thur; noon-6pm Sun. **Map** p129 D2 ㊲

London's most glamorous erotic emporium sells a variety of tasteful books, toys and lingerie, from glass dildos that double as objets d'art to crotchless culottes and corsets.

Hope & Greenwood

1 Russell Street, WC2B 5JD (7240 3314, www.hopeandgreenwood.co.uk). Covent Garden tube. **Open** 11am-7.30pm Mon-Fri; 10.30am-7.30pm Sat; noon-6pm Sun. **Map** p129 F2 ㊳

This adorable 1950s-style, letterbox-red cornershop is the perfect place to find the sherbets, chews and chocolates that were once the focus of a proper British childhood. Even the staff look the part: beautifully turned out in pinnies, ready to pop your sweets in a striped paper bag with a smile.

James Smith & Sons

*53 New Oxford Street, WC1A 1BL
(7836 4731, www.james-smith.co.uk).
Holborn or Tottenham Court Road
tube.* **Open** 9.30am-5.15pm Mon-Fri;
10am-5.15pm Sat. **Map** p129 D1 🔞

For more than 175 years, this charming shop, Victorian fittings still intact, has held its own in the niche market of umbrellas and walking sticks. Forget throwaway brollies that break at the first sign of bad weather and instead invest in a hickory-crooked City umbrella.

Monmouth Coffee House

*27 Monmouth Street, WC2H 9 EU
(7379 3516, www.monmouthcoffee.
co.uk). Covent Garden tube.* **Open** 8am-6.30pm Mon-Sat. **Map** p129 D2 🔞

Founded 30 years ago, Monmouth sets itself daunting standards for quality and ethical trading, and meets them consistently. This is pre-eminently a place for single-estate and co-operative coffees. You'll always find a good Kenyan coffee here, and Central and South America are represented by excellent ranges. Founder Anita Le Roy is an industry leader in the campaign to help growers improve quality and earn higher prices for their product. This branch, the original shop/café, is tiny and cosy.

Neal's Yard Dairy

*17 Shorts Gardens, WC2H 9UP
(7240 5700, www.nealsyarddairy.
co.uk). Covent Garden tube.* **Open** 11am-7pm Mon-Thur; 10am-7pm Fri, Sat. **Map** p129 D2 🔞

Neal's Yard buys from small farms and creameries and matures the cheeses in its own cellars until they're ready to sell. Names such as Stinking Bishop and Lincolnshire Poacher are as evocative as the aromas in the shop.

St Martin's Courtyard

*Between St Martin's Lane & Long Acre
(www.stmartinscourtyard.co.uk). Covent
Garden tube.* **Map** p129 D3 🔞

The two dozen shops in this courtyard development include Corgis, Banana Republic, and Twenty8Twelve. There are also good-quality Italian, British and Mexican restaurants.

Stanfords

*12-14 Long Acre, WC2E 9LP (7836
1321, www.stanfords.co.uk). Covent
Garden or Leicester Square tube.*
Open 9am-7.30pm Mon-Fri; 10am-8pm Sat; noon-6pm Sun. **Map** p129 D3 🔞

Three floors of travel guides, literature, maps, language guides, atlases and magazines. The basement houses the complete range of British Ordnance Survey maps, and you can plan your next move over Fairtrade coffee in the café.

Nightlife

Heaven

*Underneath the Arches, Villiers Street,
WC2N 6NG (7930 2020, www.heaven-
london.com). Embankment tube or
Charing Cross tube/rail.* **Map** p129
E4 🔞

London's most famous gay club is a bit like *Les Misérables* – it's camp, full of history and tourists love it. Popcorn on Mondays has long been a good bet, but it's really all about G-A-Y on Thursdays, Fridays and Saturdays. For as long as anyone can remember, divas with an album to flog (Madonna, Kylie, Girls Aloud) have turned up to play here at the weekend.

12 Bar Club

*Denmark Street, WC2H 8NL (7240
2622, www.12barclub.com). Tottenham
Court Road tube.* **Open** 7pm-3am Mon-Sat; 6pm-12.30am Sun. No credit cards.
Map p129 D1 🔞

This cherished hole-in-the-wall – if smoking were still allowed, this is the kind of place that would be full of it – books a grab-bag of stuff. The size (capacity 100, a stage that barely accommodates a trio) dictates a predominance of singer-songwriters.

Arts & leisure

Coliseum

St Martin's Lane, WC2N 4ES (0871 911 0200, www.eno.org). Leicester Square tube or Charing Cross tube/rail. **Map** p129 D4 **31**

Built as a music hall in 1904, the home of the English National Opera (ENO) is in sparkling condition following a renovation in 2004. The ENO itself is in solid shape under the youthful stewardship of music director Edward Gardner, with occasional duds offset by surprising sell-outs. All works are performed in English, and prices are generally cheaper than at the Royal Opera House.

Event highlights *Julius Caesar* (10 Oct-2 Nov 2012); *Medea* (15 Feb-16 Mar 2013).

Donmar Warehouse

41 Earlham Street, WC2H 9LX (0844 871 1624, www.donmarwarehouse. com). Covent Garden or Leicester Square tube. **Map** p129 E2 **32**

The Donmar is less a warehouse and more a boutique theatre. Artistic director Michael Grandage kept the venue on the fresh, intelligent path established by Sam Mendes, and his sucessor, Josie Rourke, promises to do the same. The Donmar's combination of artistic integrity and intimate size has proved hard to resist, with many high-profile film actors appearing, among them Nicole Kidman, Gwyneth Paltrow and Ewan McGregor.

Novello Theatre

Aldwych, WC2B 4LD (7907 7071, www.delfontmackintosh.co.uk). Covent Garden or Holborn tube. **Map** p129 F3 **33**

Michael Frayn's trouser-dropping sex farce, *Noises Off*, is about a hopeless bunch of actors on tour. Deliciously witty and painfully accurate, it is the ultimate West End comedy – a brilliantly structured three-act in-joke about luvvies backstage.

Royal Opera House

Bow Street, WC2E 9DD (7304 4000, www.roh.org). Covent Garden tube. **Map** p129 E2 **34**

The Royal Opera House was founded in 1732 on the profits of a production of John Gay's *Beggar's Opera*; the current building, built roughly 150 years ago but extensively remodelled, is the third on the site. Organised tours explore the massive eight-floor building, taking in the main auditorium, the costume workshops and sometimes a ballet rehearsal. The glass-roofed Floral Hall, the Crush Bar and the Amphitheatre Café Bar (with its terrace over the market) are open to the general public. Critics argue the programming can be a little spotty, especially given the famously elevated ticket prices at the top end. Never mind: there are still fine productions, many of them under the baton of Antonio Pappano. This is also home to the Royal Ballet.

Event highlights *The Nutcracker* (8 Dec-16 Jan 2013); Harrison Birtwistle's *The Minotaur* (17-28 Jan 2013).

Savoy Theatre

The Strand, WC2R 0ET (0844 847 2345, www.ambassadortickets.com). Charing Cross tube/rail. **Map** p129 F4 **35**

The Savoy is hosting a new production of Neil Simon's *The Sunshine Boys*, with Danny DeVito and Richard Griffiths. They play ageing vaudevillians Willie Clark and Al Lewis. The boys haven't spoken for years, but when CBS asks if they can reunite for a show on the history of comedy, they can't resist.

Theatre Royal Drury Lane

Catherine Street, WC2B 5JF (7907 7071, www.shrekthemusical.co.uk). Covent Garden tube. **Map** p129 F2 **36**

DreamWorks' *Shrek*, a scatologically jolly green giant of a stage show and Broadway hit, has taken off in the West End. *Shrek*'s farts-and-all humour and carnivalesque spirit have survived in David Lindsay-Abaire's book. Production subject to change.

Tower of London p162

The City

Holborn to Clerkenwell

The City of London collides with the West End in Holborn and Clerkenwell. Bewigged barristers inhabit the picturesque **Inns of Court**, while City boys head out from their loft apartments to the latest restaurant in one of London's foodiest areas – or to superclub **Fabric**.

Sights & museums

Courtauld Gallery

Strand, WC2R 1LA (7848 2526, www. courtauld.ac.uk/gallery). Temple tube. **Open** 10am-6pm daily. **Admission** £6; free-£4.50 reductions; free 10am-2pm Mon. **Map** p150 A4 **❶**

In the north wing of Somerset House (p154), the Courtauld's select collection of paintings has several works of world importance. There are outstanding works from earlier periods (don't miss Lucas Cranach's fine *Adam & Eve*), but the strongest suit is Impressionist and post-Impressionist paintings, such as Manet's astonishing *A Bar at the Folies-Bergère* and numerous works by Cézanne. Hidden downstairs, the sweet little gallery café is often overlooked.

Dr Johnson's House

17 Gough Square, EC4A 3DE (7353 3745, www.drjohnsonshouse.org). Chancery Lane tube or Blackfriars tube/rail. **Open** *May-Sept* 11am-5.30pm Mon-Sat. *Oct-Apr* 11am-5pm Mon-Sat. **Admission** £4.50; free-£3.50 reductions; £10 family. No credit cards. **Map** p150 B4 **❷**

The author of one of the first – surely the most significant and beyond doubt the wittiest – dictionary of the English language, Dr Samuel Johnson (1709-84) also wrote poems, a novel and one of the earliest travelogues. You can tour stately the Georgian townhouse where he came up with his inspired definitions

The City

1. Sights & museums
1. Eating & drinking
1. Shopping
1. Nightlife
1. Arts & leisure

THE WEST END pp98-148

THE SOUTH BANK pp58-73

River Thames

0   300 m
0   300 yds

© Copyright Time Out Group 2012

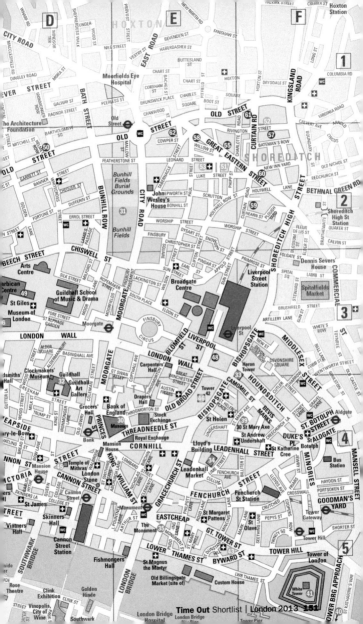

– 'to make dictionaries is dull work' was his definition of the word 'dull'.

Fleet Street

Chancery Lane or Temple tube.
Map p150 B4 ❸
The first printing press on this legendary street of newspapers was installed behind St Bride's Church (below) in 1500 by William Caxton's assistant, Wynkyn de Worde, but it wasn't until 1702 that London's first daily newspaper, the *Daily Courant*, rolled off the presses. By the end of World War II, half a dozen newspaper offices were churning out scoops between the Strand and Farringdon Road, but they gradually all moved away once Rupert Murdoch had won his bitter war with the print unions in the 1980s; the last of the news agencies, Reuters, followed in 2005. Fine buildings that remain from the roaring days of the industry include Reuters (no.85), the Daily Telegraph (no.135) and the jet-black Daily Express (nos.121-128).

Hunterian Museum

Royal College of Surgeons, 35-43 Lincoln's Inn Fields, WC2A 3PE (7869 6560, www.rcseng.ac.uk/museums). Holborn tube. **Open** 10am-5pm Tue-Sat. **Admission** free. No credit cards.
Map p150 A4 ❹
John Hunter (1728-93) was a pioneering surgeon and anatomist, and physician to King George III. His huge collection of medical specimens can be viewed in this two-floor museum. The grisly exhibits include various bodily mutations and the brain of 19th-century mathematician Charles Babbage.

Museum & Library of the Order of St John

St John's Gate, St John's Lane, EC1M 4DA (7324 4005, www.museumstjohn. org.uk). Farringdon tube/rail. **Open** 10am-5pm Mon-Sat. *Tours* 11am, 2.30pm Tue, Fri, Sat. **Admission** free; suggested donation £5, £4 reductions.
Map p150 C2 ❺

This museum celebrates the Order of St John. Now known for its ambulance service, the order's roots lie in the Christian medical practices developed during the Crusades of the 11th to 13th centuries. Artefacts related to the Order of Hospitaller Knights, from Jerusalem, Malta and the Ottoman Empire, are displayed: there's a separate collection relating to the evolution of the modern ambulance service. The museum reopened in 2010 after major refurbishment reorganised the galleries in the Tudor gatehouse and, across St John's Square, opened the Priory Church, its gorgeous garden and its 12th-century crypt to the public.

St Bartholomew-the-Great

West Smithfield, EC1A 9DS (7606 5171, www.greatstbarts.com). Barbican tube or Farringdon tube/ rail. **Open** 8.30am-5pm Mon-Fri (until 4pm Nov-Feb); 10.30am-4pm Sat; 8.30am-8pm Sun. **Admission** £4; free-£3 reductions; £10 family.
Map p150 C3 ❻
This atmospheric medieval church was chopped about during Henry VIII's reign: the interior is now firmly Elizabethan, although it also contains donated works of contemporary art and an ancient font. You may recognise the main hall from such movies as *Shakespeare in Love* and *Four Weddings & a Funeral*.

St Bride's Church

Fleet Street, EC4Y 8AU (7427 0133, www.stbrides.com). Temple tube or Blackfriars tube/rail. **Open** 8am-6pm Mon-Fri; 11am-3pm Sat; 10am-6.30pm Sun. Times vary Mon-Sat, so phone ahead. **Admission** free. No credit cards. Map p150 B4 ❼
St Bride's, 'the journalists' church', contains a shrine to hacks killed in action. The interior was rebuilt after Blitz bombing. Down in the crypt, a quietly excellent museum displays fragments of the churches that have existed on this site since the sixth century and

Here lieth the Body of
Mʳ ELY DYSON
late of this parish

St Bartholomew-the-Great

tells the story of the newspapers on Fleet Street. According to local legend, the spire was the inspiration for the classic tiered wedding cake.

Sir John Soane's Museum

13 Lincoln's Inn Fields, WC2A 3BP (7405 2107, www.soane.org). Holborn tube. **Open** 10am-5pm Tue-Sat; 10am-5pm, 6-9pm 1st Tue of mth. *Tours* 11am Sat. **Admission** free; donations appreciated. *Tours* free-£5. **Map** p150 A3 ❽

Architect Sir John Soane (1753-1837) was an obsessive collector of art, furniture and architectural ornamentation, partly for enjoyment and partly for research. He turned his house into an amazing museum to which 'amateurs and students' should have access. Much of the museum's appeal derives from the domestic setting, but the real wow is the Monument Court. At its lowest level is a 3,000-year-old sarcophagus of alabaster so fine that it's almost translucent, as well as the cell of Soane's fictional monk Don Giovanni. The first phase of a long-term programme of renovation and expansion will be completed in July 2012 (see box p160).

Event highlights Monthly candlelit tours – always book in advance.

Somerset House & the Embankment Galleries

Strand, WC2R 1LA (7845 4600, www.somersethouse.org.uk). Temple tube or Charing Cross tube/rail. **Open** 10am-6pm daily. **Admission** free. *Embankment Galleries* prices vary; see website for details. **Map** p150 A5 ❾

Architect Sir William Chambers spent the last 20 years of his life from 1775 working on this neo-classical edifice overlooking the Thames. Effectively the first purpose-built office block in the world, it was built to accommodate learned societies such as the Royal Academy, and also the Inland Revenue. The Inland Revenue is still here, but the rest of the building is open to the public. It houses the wonderful

Courtauld (p149) and has a beautiful courtyard with choreographed fountains, a terraced café and restaurant. It also hosts temporary exhibitions.

Temple Church & Inner Temple

Fleet Street, EC4Y 7BB (7353 8559, www.templechurch.com). Temple tube. **Open** 2-4pm Tue-Fri; phone or check website for details. **Admission** £4; free reductions. No credit cards. **Map** p150 B4 ❿

The quadrangles of Middle Temple (7427 4800, www.middletemple.org.uk) and Inner Temple (7797 8250, www.innertemple.org.uk) have been lodgings for training lawyers since medieval times, with Temple Church – the private chapel of the mystical Knights Templar, its structure inspired by Jerusalem's Church of the Holy Sepulchre – serving both. Its rounded apse contains the worn gravestones of several Crusader knights. Tours of Inner Temple can be arranged (minimum five people, £10 each; 7797 8241).

Event highlights Organ recitals in Temple Church (Wed lunchtimes).

Eating & drinking

Bistrot Bruno Loubet

Zetter, St John's Square, 86-88 Clerkenwell Road, EC1M 5RJ (7324 4455, www.thezetter.com). Farringdon tube/rail. **Open** 7-10.30am, noon-2.30pm, 6-10.30pm Mon-Fri, 7.30-11am, noon-3pm, 6-10.30pm Sat; 7.30am-11am, noon-3pm, 6-10pm Sun. **£££. Modern European**. **Map** p150 C2 ⓫

The menu at this bistro is thoughtfully constructed to satisfy novelty seekers, but won't scare off the conservative palate – you might find slow-cooked hare on the menu, but also the likes of confit lamb shoulder with white beans pepped up with North African preserved lemon and harissa. Playful French desserts are another strength. The staff are smiley and very efficient, and there's a buzz of happy diners.

Clerkenwell Kitchen

*27-31 Clerkenwell Close, EC1R 0AT
(7101 9959, www.theclerkenwellkitchen.
co.uk). Angel tube or Farringdon
tube/rail.* **Open** 8am-5pm Mon-Fri. **££.**
Eco-restaurant. Map p150 B2 ⑫
Tucked into an office development for
creatives, Clerkenwell Kitchen has a
ready supply of enthusiasts who pop
in for coffees, sandwiches, lunch meetings and quiet moments with the
Wi-Fi. High-quality, fair-priced meals
made with seasonal produce are served
from noon – restaurant-calibre food
served in a stylishly informal café setting, to be enjoyed with a glass of wine
or Meantime beer.

Le Comptoir Gascon

*61-63 Charterhouse Street, EC1M
6HJ (7608 0851, www.comptoir
gascon.com). Farringdon tube/rail.*
Open noon-2.15pm, 7-9.45pm Tue,
Wed; noon-2.15pm, 7-10.45pm Thur,
Fri; 9am-3pm, 7-10pm Sat. **££.**
French. Map p150 C3 ⑬
Comptoir is the modern rustic cousin
(dainty velour chairs, exposed pipes,
open brickwork, pottery dishes) of
the more serious-minded Club Gascon
(57 West Smithfield, 7796 0600, www.
clubgascon.com), but exudes as much
class and confidence as its forebear in
the presentation of delectable regional
specialities of Gascony. The posh café
vibe is enhanced by capable and amiable French staff.

Delaunay

NEW *55 Aldwych, WC2B 4BB (7499
8558, www.thedelaunay.com). Covent
Garden, Temple tube or Charing Cross
tube/rail.* **Open** 11.30am-midnight
Mon-Sat; 11.30am-11pm Sun. *Breakfast
served* 7-11.30am Mon-Fri; 8-11am Sat.
Brunch served 11am-5pm Sat, Sun.
Tea served 3-6.30pm daily. **£££.**
Brasserie. Map p150 A4 ⑭
Comparisons with the iconic Wolseley
(p83) are inevitable. The Delaunay is
also a 'grand café' in the Continental
mould, and the same owners created

and run both. The menu majors on
German classics, the likes of chou-
croute (warm sauerkraut with
sausages, salted meats and charcuterie) and a classic wiener schnitzel,
along with perfectly presented desserts
and cakes hailing from mittel-Europe.
Breakfast is a highlight: perfect
Viennoiserie, porridge, pancakes, eggs
every way, muesli, full English… and
of course, it also serves afternoon tea.

Eagle

*159 Farringdon Road, EC1R 3AL
(7837 1353). Farringdon tube/rail.*
Open noon-11pm Mon-Sat; noon-5pm
Sun. **££. Gastropub**. Map p150 B2 ⑮
Widely credited with being the first
gastropub (it opened in 1991), this is
still recognisably a pub that serves
quality food: noisy, often crowded,
with no-frills service and dominated by
an open range where T-shirted cooks
toss earthy grills in theatrical bursts of
flame. The Med-influenced menu stays
true to 'big flavours'.

Jerusalem Tavern

*55 Britton Street, EC1M 5UQ (7490
4281, www.stpetersbrewery.co.uk).
Farringdon tube/rail.* **Open** 11am-11pm
Mon-Fri. **Pub**. Map p150 C2 ⑯
Tilting, creaking and uneven, the tatty
Jerusalem serves sought-after ales
from Suffolk's St Peter's brewery. A
rag-tag and loyal crowd muses over the
Evening Standard crossword and, in
winter, a cosy fireplace encourages the
desire for warm sustenance. Haddock
and salmon fish cakes fit the bill nicely.

Look Mum No Hands

*49 Old Street, EC1V 9HX (7253 1025,
www.lookmumnohands.com). Barbican
tube or Old Street tube/rail.* **Open**
7.30am-10pm Mon-Fri; 9am-10pm
Sat; 10am-10pm Sun. **£. Café**.
Map p151 D2 ⑰
Look Mum is a cycle-friendly café-bar
with 'secure' cycle parking in a courtyard (bring your own lock anyway), a
one-person workshop and plenty of

LONDON BY AREA

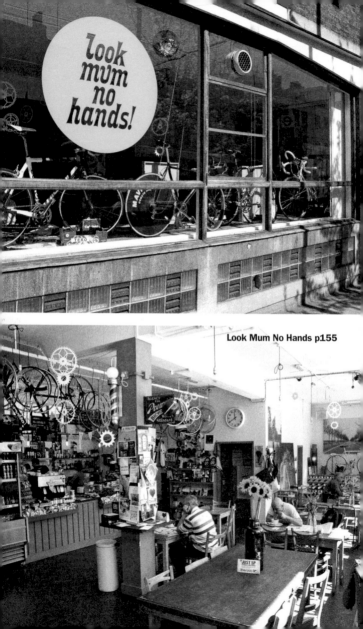

Look Mum No Hands p155

space to hang out, snack, use the Wi-Fi, and – in the evenings – drink bottled beer or well-priced wine. Live afternoon screenings of cycle races take place in the big main room. The food is simple – platters of cured meats or veggie platters, Greek salads, baked tarts, morning pastries and cakes.

Modern Pantry

47-48 St John's Square, EC1V 4JJ (7250 0833, www.themodernpantry. co.uk). Farringdon tube/rail. **Open** *Café* 8am-11pm Mon-Fri; 9am-11pm Sat; 10am-10pm Sun. *Restaurant* noon-3pm, 6-11pm Tue-Fri; 6-11pm Sat; 10am-4pm Sun.* **££. International**. **Map** p150 C2 ⓲

A culinary three-parter in a pair of Georgian townhouses that feels savvy and still of the moment a few years after opening. Both pantry (takeaway) and café are at street level; upstairs are adjoining, informal dining rooms. Service is spot on and the menu brilliantly fuses all kinds of ingredients. Weekend brunch is always special – but usually busy.

Morito

32 Exmouth Market EC1R 4QL (7278 7007). Farringdon tube/rail or bus 19, 38, 341. **Open** 5-11pm Mon; 12.30-3.30pm, 4.30-11pm Tue-Sat. **££.** **Tapas**. **Map** p150 B2 ⓳

While the busy, unassailably popular Moro (34-36 Exmouth Market, EC1R 4QE, 7833 8336, www.moro.co.uk) is all smart clothes and clattering expanse, Morito – Sam and Sam Clark's tapas venture next door – is tiny, pared-back and intimate. Wine is served by the tumbler, carafe or bottle, while draught beers come in third-of-a-pint '*chatos*'. From stools at the bright orange Formica bar, you can watch chefs cook at an open grill. As with Moro, the menu reaches far beyond Spain – the trademark cuisine is 'Moorish' (Spanish, but with heavy North African influences). It's all understated, but right on the money.

Prufrock Coffee

23-25 Leather Lane, EC1N 7TE (7242 0467, www.prufrockcoffee.com). Chancery Lane tube or Farringdon tube/rail. **Open** 8am-5pm Mon-Fri; 10am-4pm Sat. **£.** **Café**. **Map** p150 B3 ⓴

Even with London's recent growth of boutique coffee shops and professional baristas, Prufrock is a special place. It feels like an airy art gallery crossed with a laboratory: the high windows display an antique coffee machine, music is of the classical sort and the large counter in the middle holds an impressive array of hardware – an espresso machine, grinders, siphons with halogen beam heaters, Japanese pour-over filters, even a Trifecta. The man behind it, Gwilym Davies, was crowned World Barista Champion in 2009; his staff are every bit as good.

St John

26 St John Street, EC1M 4AY (7251 0848, www.stjohnrestaurant.com). Barbican tube or Farringdon tube/rail. **Open** noon-3pm, 6-11pm Mon-Fri; 6-11pm Sat; 1-3pm Sun. **£££.** **British**. **Map** p150 C2 ㉑

Leading light of the modern British cooking revival, St John is an austere-looking place, opened in 1995 in the shell of a smokehouse by chef-patron Fergus Henderson. Its spirit hasn't changed: the focus is on unusual seasonal British ingredients, simply cooked and presented. Less expensive is the short menu at the boisterous no-reservations bar. The new St John Hotel (p204) is in Soho.

Seven Stars

53 Carey Street, WC2A 2JB (7242 8521). Chancery Lane or Holborn tube. **Open** 11am-11pm Mon-Fri; noon-11pm Sat; noon-10.30pm Sun. **££.** **Gastropub**. **Map** p150 A4 ㉒

If you can squeeze into the small interior, you'll get a slice of low-rent, bohemian London: Roxy Beaujolais's pub is a fantastic social hub for local characters, from eccentric lawyers to burlesque babes. One of the few City pubs where your large burgundy will be well priced for top quality.

Three Kings of Clerkenwell

7 Clerkenwell Close, EC1R 0DY (7253 0483). Farringdon tube/rail. **Open** noon-11pm Mon-Fri; 7-11pm Sat. No credit cards. **Pub**. Map p150 B2 ㉓

Rhino heads, Egyptian felines and Dennis Bergkamp provide the decorative backdrop against which discerning boho regulars glug real ale, cider or lager, and tap the well-worn tables to gems from a superb jukebox.

Vinoteca

7 St John Street, EC1M 4AA (7253 8786, www.vinoteca.co.uk). Farringdon tube/rail. **Open** noon-11pm Mon-Sat; noon-5pm Sun. **Wine bar**. Map p150 C3 ㉔

Inspired by the Italian *enoteca* (a blend of off-licence and wine bar, with bar snacks), Vinoteca is in fact more of a gastropub in spirit. But even if you want no more to eat than bread and olive oil, come here for the impressive 200-bottle wine list, of which a range of 19 labels are available by the glass.

Ye Old Mitre

1 Ely Court, at the side of 8 Hatton Gardens, EC1N 6SJ (7405 4751). Chancery Lane tube or Farringdon tube/rail. **Open** 11am-11pm Mon-Fri. **Pub**. Map p150 B3 ㉕

The secluded location requires you to slink down an alleyway just off Hatton Garden, where you'll be transported to a parallel pub universe where the clientele are friendly and the staff (in pristine black and white uniforms) briskly efficient. Open only during the week, it's a pint-sized pub that's earned its top-notch reputation.

Zetter Townhouse

49-50 St John's Square, EC1V 4JJ (7324 4545, www.thezettertownhouse. com). Farringdon tube/rail. **Open** 10am-midnight Mon-Thur, Sun; 10am-1am Fri, Sat. **Bar**. Map p150 C2 ㉖

Spread across the ground floor of the Zetter hotel's new sister site (p209), this cosy cocktail lounge is a collaboration with the founders of 69 Colebrooke Row (p174). Colebrooke's head barman Tony Conigliaro is an expert alcohol alchemist renowned for creating left-field liquids and libations in his laboratory. Here the drinks list is unique, experimental yet refreshingly uncomplicated, with 13 house cocktails priced at £8.50. Switched-on staff are delighted to talk you through your tipple. You can turn up unannounced, but book ahead to be sure of a seat.

Shopping

A terrific collection of shops is scattered along **Exmouth Market**, the short pedestrianised street that's home to **Morito** (p157). They include little CD shop-cum-café **Brill** (no.27), jewellery at **ec one** (no.41) and terrific books at **Clerkenwell Tales** (no.30).

Kate Kanzier

67-69 Leather Lane, EC1N 7TJ (7242 7232, www.katekanzier.com). Chancery Lane tube or Farringdon tube/rail. **Open** 8.30am-6.30pm Mon-Fri; 11am-4pm Sat. Map p150 B2 ㉗

Adored for great-value directional footwear for women, Kate Kanzier is the place to visit for brogues, ballerinas, sandles and leather boots in a huge range of colours. Sexy high-heeled pumps in patent, suede, leather and animal prints are marked out by vintage designs. Handbags and clutches are also stocked.

Nightlife

Fabric

77A Charterhouse Street, EC1M 3HN (7336 8898, www.fabriclondon.com). Farringdon tube/rail. **Open** 10pm-6am Fri; 11pm-8am Sat; 11pm-6am Sun. Map p150 C3 ㉙

Fabric is the club most party people come to see in London: the main room has the stomach-wobbling Bodysonic dancefloor, the second is a rave-style warehouse, the third is where the cool stuff happens. Fridays belong to the bass: highlights include DJ Hype, who takes over all three rooms once a month for his drum 'n' bass and dubstep night Playaz. Saturdays rock to techy, minimal, deep house sounds. Recent years have also seen Fabric On + On dance marathons. Stellar DJs – and big queues – are a given.

Volupté

7-9 Norwich Street, EC4A 1EJ (7831 1622, www.volupte-lounge. com). Chancery Lane tube. **Open** 5pm-1am Tue-Thur; 5pm-3am Sat. **Map** p150 B3 ㉙

Expect to suffer extreme wallpaper envy as you enter the ground-floor bar, then descend to the club proper. Punters enjoy some of the best cabaret talent in town from tables set beneath absinthe-inspired vines. Nights include Harlem Swing Club.

The City

Fewer than 10,000 souls live within the Square Mile (1.21 square miles, in fact), but every working day the population increases tenfold, as bankers, brokers, lawyers and traders storm into their towering office blocks. The City still holds to boundaries set by the second-century walls of Roman Londinium (a few sections of which remain), although it then had six times more residents than now. The streets are full of historic gems, but the real crowd-pullers are **St Paul's** and the **Tower of London**.

Sights & museums

The art gallery at **Barbican** (£8-£10, free-£8 reductions; p167) has good exhibitions of art, design

and architecture, while the free Curve space shows excellent commissions. Of the three classic skyscrapers in the City – **Lloyd's** (p161), the **Gherkin** (real name **30 St Mary Axe**, p162) and **Tower 42** (the NatWest Tower) – only the latter is open to the public, with its bar, **Vertigo 42** (p165). However, the new **Heron Tower** (p161) is due to open a rooftop sushi restaurant and sky bar in summer 2012. See box p164.

Bank of England Museum

Entrance on Bartholomew Lane, EC2R 8AH (7601 5545, www.bankofengland. co.uk/museum). Bank tube/DLR. **Open** 10am-5pm Mon-Fri. **Admission** free. **Map** p151 E4 ㉚

Housed in the bank's former Stock Offices, this engaging museum explores the history of the national bank. As well as a rare opportunity to lift a 13kg gold bar (albeit one encased in a secure box you poke your hand into), you can learn about Kenneth Grahame: *The Wind in the Willows* author was a long-term employee here.

Bunhill Fields

Old Street tube/rail. **Admission** free. **Map** p151 E2 ㉛

The importance of this nonconformist burial ground was recognised in 2011, when it was protected from development by a Grade I listing. It's a moving little place, hemmed in by office walls and crammed with memorials to dead dissenters, such as John Bunyan, Daniel Defoe and William Blake. Opposite, the former home and chapel of John Wesley are now a museum of Methodism (49 City Road, 7253 2262, www.wesleyschapel.org.uk).

Guildhall Art Gallery & Clockmakers' Museum

Guildhall Yard, EC2P 2EJ (7332 3700, www.guildhall-art-gallery.org.uk). St Paul's tube or Bank tube/DLR. **Open** 10am-5pm Mon-Sat; noon-4pm Sun.

The Soane Next Door

A major expansion for the Soane's 200th anniversary.

A favourite of many locals, the little **Sir John Soane's Museum** (p154) has changed status over the years from a treasured secret to something approaching a must-visit. These days you can expect queues at the front door of this eccentric house of curiosities (more than 93,000 people visit each year).

In July 2012, the 200th anniversary of the building of the house will be marked by the completion of the first phase of an ambitious £7m restoration. A former staff lavatory will once again be the Tivoli Recess – the city's first gallery of contemporary sculpture, with a stained-glass window and skylights with plaster sunbursts. Further stained glass will illuminate the Shakespeare Recess, with William's likeness from his Stratford-upon-Avon tomb set there.

Less exciting, but arguably at least as important, is the use to which the next-door building (no.12) is going to be being put. The old entrance to the house – a narrow corridor where all those visitors had to sign in, buy their guides and postcards, and leave coats, bags and umbrellas with the volunteers – was far too cramped for the purpose. After the restoration is complete, you will leave your clutter at no.12, before strolling into the main house untrammelled and ready to be enthralled.

Once you've toured the house's treasures, seen the ingenious fold-out walls of paintings and admired the clever lighting effects and

archaeological oddments, you exit through no.12, past a new shop and an Exhibition Room that gives details on Soane and the objects you've just seen. (Soane wasn't much given to labelling, and the museum is obliged – by the 1833 Act of Parliament that set up the museum – to follow his lead.)

Over the years up to 2014, the entire second floor of Soane's house will open to the public – for the first time since his death in 1837. Working from watercolour paintings done in around 1825, the museum will recreate his bedroom, Model Room (containing 80 fine architectural models), the Oratory (a memorial to his dead wife, using what was already antiquarian stained glass) and the mirrored bookshelves of the Book Passage. Most typical of all will be one small feature of the the Ante Room: once restored, this space full of sculptures and plastercasts will also have a hole in the floor, through which Soane's modern-day guests will be able to peer into a Catacomb full of funerary urns from ancient Rome.

Admission free. *Temporary exhibitions* £5; free-£3 reductions. **Map** p151 D4 ③②

The City of London's gallery (free to enter since spring 2011) contains dull portraits of royalty and some former mayors, and plenty of wonderful surprises, including a brilliant Constable, high-camp Pre-Raphaelite works and various absorbing paintings of historic London. A sub-basement has the scant remains of a 6,000-seat Roman amphitheatre, built around AD 70. Across the big courtyard, the single-room Clockmakers' Museum (www.clockmakers.org, closed Sun, free admission) is a symphony of ticking, chiming clocks and watches.

Heron Tower

110 Bishopsgate, EC2M 4AY (www.herontower.com). Liverpool Street tube/rail. **Map** p151 E3 ③③

The 755ft-tall Heron Tower (radio mast included) opened in autumn 2011. On top of all the so-called office 'villages', a bit under 600ft up in the distinctive stepped roof, a Restaurant & Sky Bar will open to the public.

Lloyd's of London

1 Lime Street, EC3M 7HA (www.lloyds.com). Monument tube. **Map** p151 E4 ③④

Lord Rogers' high-tech building has all its mechanical services (ducts, stairwells, lift shafts) on the outside, a design that still looks modern after 25 years. The original Lloyd's Register, decorated with bas-reliefs of sea monsters and nautical scenes, is on nearby Fenchurch Street. No public access.

Monument

Monument Street, EC3R 8AH (7626 2717, www.themonument. info). Monument tube. **Open** 9.30am-5pm daily. **Admission** £3; free-£2 reductions. No credit cards. **Map** p151 E5 ③⑤

The Monument, the world's tallest freestanding stone column was designed by Sir Christopher Wren and his (often overlooked) associate Robert Hooke as a memorial to the Great Fire of London. It measures 202ft from the ground to the tip of the golden flame on the orb at its top, exactly the distance east to Farriner's bakery in Pudding Lane, where the fire is supposed to have begun on 2 September 1666. Reopened after a glorious £4.5m refurbishment, the Monument can now be climbed up a spiral interior staircase for fine views.

Museum of London

150 London Wall, EC2Y 5HN (7001 9844, www.museumoflondon. org.uk). Barbican or St Paul's tube. **Open** 10am-6pm daily. **Admission** free; suggested donation £3. **Map** p151 D3 ③⑥

This expansive museum (set in the middle of a roundabout) tells the whole history of London – with help from east London's Museum of London Docklands (182). Themes include 'London Before London' – flint axes, fossils, grave goods – and 'Roman London', which has a reconstructed dining room complete with mosaic floor. Also on the ground floor, sound effects and audio-visual displays illustrate the medieval city, along with cases of shoes and armour, and there's a moving exhibit on the Black Death, as well as a wonderful re-creation of the Vauxhall Pleasure Gardens. Rush downstairs for outstanding new galleries on modern London, opened in 2010. Among many fine exhibits are an unexploded Blitz bomb, an Alexander McQueen dress and a genuine 18th-century debtors' prison cell.

Postman's Park

St Paul's tube. **Map** p151 C3 ③⑦

This peaceful, fern-filled park near St Paul's contains the Watts Memorial to Heroic Sacrifice: a wall of Victorian ceramic plaques, each of which commemorates a fatal act of bravery by an ordinary person.

LONDON BY AREA

St Paul's Cathedral

Ludgate Hill, EC4M 8AD (7236 4128, www.stpauls.co.uk). St Paul's tube. **Open** 8.30am-4pm Mon-Sat. *Galleries, crypt & ambulatory* 9.30am-4.15pm Mon-Sat. **Admission** £12.50; free-£11.50 reductions; £29.50 family. *Tours* £3; £1-£2.50 reductions. **Map** p150 C4 **38**

A £40m restoration a few years ago left the main façade of St Paul's looking as brilliant as it must have when the first Mass was celebrated here in 1710. The vast open spaces of the interior contain memorials to national heroes such as Wellington and Lawrence of Arabia, as well as superb mosaics and gilt added by the Victorians. The Whispering Gallery, inside the dome, is reached by 259 steps from the main hall (the acoustics are so good a whisper can be clearly heard across the dome). Stairs continue up to first the Stone Gallery (119 steps), with its high external balustrades, then outside to the Golden Gallery (152 steps), with its giddying views. Head down to the crypt (where a new 270° projector, the Oculus, runs a film on the cathedral's history) to see Nelson's grand tomb and the small tombstone of Sir Christopher Wren himself, inscribed: 'Reader, if you seek a monument, look around you.'

30 St Mary Axe (Gherkin)

www.30stmaryaxe.com. Liverpool Street tube/rail. **Map** p151 F4 **39**

Completed only in 2004, Lord Foster's distinctively curved skyscraper has already become a cherished icon of modern London, its 'Gherkin' nickname plainly apt. Unfortunately, there's no public access.

Tower Bridge Exhibition

Tower Bridge, SE1 2UP (7403 3761, www.towerbridge.org.uk). Tower Hill tube or Tower Gateway DLR. **Open** *Apr-Sept* 10am-6.30pm daily. *Oct-Mar* 9.30am-6pm daily. **Admission** £8; free-£5.60 reductions; £11 family. **Map** p151 F5 **40**

Opened in 1894, this is the 'London Bridge' that wasn't sold to America. Originally powered by steam, the drawbridge is now opened by electric rams when big ships need to venture this far upstream (check when the bridge is next due to be raised on the website). An entertaining exhibition on the history of the bridge is displayed in the old steamrooms and on the west walkway, which provides a crow's-nest view along the Thames. The bridge is looking particularly splendid after a restoration was completed in 2011.

Tower of London

Tower Hill, EC3N 4AB (0844 482 7777, www.hrp.org.uk). Tower Hill tube or Tower Gateway DLR. **Open** *Mar-Oct* 10am-5.30pm Mon, Sun; 9am-5.30pm Tue-Sat. *Nov-Feb* 10am-4.30pm Mon, Sun; 9am-4.30pm Tue-Sat. **Admission** £18; free-£15.50 reductions; £47 family. **Map** p151 F5 **41**

Despite exhausting crowds and long climbs up narrow stairways, this is one of Britain's finest historical sites. Who wouldn't be fascinated by a close-up look at the crown of Queen Victoria or the armour (and mighty codpiece) of Henry VIII? The buildings of the Tower span 900 years of history and the bastions and battlements house a series of interactive displays on the lives of monarchs – and excruciatingly painful deaths of traitors. The highlight has to be the Crown Jewels, viewed from a slow-moving travelator (get there early to minimise queuing), but the other big draw is the Royal Armoury in the White Tower: four floors of swords, armour, pole-axes, halberds and other gruesome tools for chopping people up. Executions of noble prisoners were carried out on the green in front of the Tower – the site is marked by a glass pillow sculpture.

Tickets are sold in the kiosk just west of the palace and visitors enter

Bodean's p165

Room at the Top

Eat and drink in the city's tallest buildings.

Vertigo 42

We love the Gherkin (30 St Mary Axe, p162) and the Lloyd's building (p161), but we can't help thinking they missed a trick. Each year, locals scour the brochure for the Open-City London architecture festival (p36) to see which iconic skyscrapers will be open to the public. But for many of the city's most distinctive modern buildings, there's no way in unless you're lucky enough to work there.

For the new breed of London skyscrapers, this isn't going to be a problem. Perhaps taking note of **Vertigo 42** (right), the champagne bar high in the City skyscraper you'd most like to be looking out of rather than at, a new breed of behemoth is courting the public.

The City's new tallest building, **Heron Tower** (p161), leads the charge in the financial centre. A restaurant and cocktail bar, The Drift, is already open and Sushi Samba, a restaurant offering 'a unique blend of Japanese, Brazilian and Peruvian cuisine, culture and striking design' is set to open in summer 2012. We'll have to wait to see what the food is like, but we can confidently say that the views, 570ft up, are stupendous.

Across the river, Renzo Piano's **Shard** (p66) is also offering public access. It not only has restaurants (floors 31-33) and a Shangri-La hotel (floors 34-52), but a public observatory – above even the hotel, on floors 68-72. The Shard opens in July 2012.

Before the arrival of these attention-grabbing newcomers it was still possible to enjoy a cocktail with a view. **Galvin at Windows** (p116) on the 28th floor of the Park Lane Hilton offers excellent views of the west of town, but architecture fans will be more interested in **Paramount** (p144), the fine restaurant atop the landmark Centre Point tower.

LONDON BY AREA

through the Middle Tower, but there's a free audio-visual display in the Welcome Centre outside the walls. There's plenty enough to do to fill a day, but skip to the highlights using the audio tour (which takes an hour), or by joining the highly entertaining free tours led by the Yeoman Warders (Beefeaters), who also care for the Tower's ravens.

Eating & drinking

Cinnamon Club (p80) has a sibling in the City: **Cinnamon Kitchen** (9 Devonshire Square, EC2M 4YL, 7626 5000, www.cinnamon-kitchen. co.uk); for a cheap lunch, the Cheapside branch of **Hummus Bros** (p130) is well located for St Paul's Cathedral (but closed at weekends). For drinks and eats with a view, see box (left).

Black Friar

174 Queen Victoria Street, EC4V 4EG (7236 5474). Mansion House tube or Blackfriars tube/rail. **Open** 10am-11pm Mon-Sat; noon-10.30pm Sun. **Pub.** **Map** p150 C4 **42**
This wedge-shaped pub at the north end of Blackfriars Bridge offers a handful of real ales, wine by the glass, standard lagers and decent pub nosh, but it's the extraordinary Arts & Crafts interior, resplendent with carvings of monks and odd mottos, that makes the place worth a visit.

Bodean's

16 Byward Street, EC3R 5BA (7488 3883, www.bodeansbbq.com). Tower Hill tube. **Open** noon-11pm Mon-Fri; noon-10.30pm Sat. **££. American.** **Map** p151 E5 **43**
Across Bodean's five branches – also in Soho, Westbourne Grove, Fulham and Clapham – the shtick remains unchanged: generous portions of Kansas City barbecued meat, served in an informal upstairs or smarter downstairs where US sport is on TV.

Restaurant at St Paul's

St Paul's Cathedral, St Paul's Churchyard, EC4M 8AD (7248 2469, www.restaurantatstpauls.co.uk). St Paul's tube. **Open** noon-4.30pm daily. **£££. British.** **Map** p150 C4 **44**
This is a handsome, light-filled space in the cathedral crypt, with sensuous and textural decor – great for a restaurant, surprising in a place of worship. The food is excellent – along the lines of asparagus and poached duck egg, prettily pink barnsley chop, portobello mushroom wellington and a gooseberry cobbler for pudding – and well-priced. There's also a cafe; both are closed in the evening.

Sweetings

39 Queen Victoria Street, EC4N 4SA (7248 3062). Mansion House tube. **Open** 11.30am-3pm Mon-Fri. **£££. Fish & seafood.** **Map** p151 D4 **45**
In these days of makeovers and global menus, Sweetings is that rare thing – a traditional British restaurant that clings to its traditions as if the Empire depended on it. It opens only for lunch, takes no bookings, and is full soon after noon with City gents, so order a silver pewter mug of Guinness and enjoy the wait.

Vertigo 42

Tower 42, 25 Old Broad Street, EC2N 1HQ (7877 7842, www. vertigo42.co.uk). Bank tube/DLR or Liverpool Street tube/rail. **Open** noon-4.30pm, 5-11pm Mon-Fri; 5-11pm Sat. **££££. Champagne bar.** **Map** p151 E4 **46**
Short of introducing iris-recognition scanning, the process of going for a drink in Tower 42 could scarcely be more MI5. (You'll need to book in advance, promise a £10 spend and then get X-rayed and metal-detected on arrival). But it's all worth it: the 42nd floor location delivers stupendous views. There are nibbles and the champagne list offers five labels by the flute.

One New Change

Shopping

The City's strategy for improving the area's shopping is spearheaded by new mall **One New Change** (below). In addition, check out **Daunt Books** (61 Cheapside, EC2V 6AX, 7248 1117, www.daunt books.co.uk), a short walk east of the mall; the first Daunt is on Marylebone High Street (p105).

One New Change

1 New Change, EC4M 9AF (www.onenewchange.com). St Paul's tube. **Map** p150 C4 **㊼**
Designed by Pritzker Prize-winning French starchitect Jean Nouvel, and known as the 'stealth building' for its resemblance to a stealth bomber, this dark, low-slung 'groundscraper' mall isn't an immediately lovable building – and even the shops (Reiss, Topshop, Swarovski) and eateries (Eat, Nando's, a Searcys champagne bar) feel a little predictable. But take the glass elevators up to the top floor and you'll be rewarded with superb views on a level with the dome of St Paul's.

Arts & leisure

Barbican Centre

Silk Street, EC2Y 8DS (7638 4141, 7638 8891 box office, www.barbican. org.uk). Barbican tube or Moorgate tube/rail. **Map** p151 D3 **㊾**
The Barbican is a prime example of 1970s brutalism, softened by square ponds of friendly resident ducks. The complex has a concert hall, theatre, cinema and art galleries, a labyrinthine array of spaces that isn't at all easy to navigate. Programming, however, is first class. At the core of the classical music roster, performing 90 concerts a year, is the brilliant London Symphony Orchestra (LSO), supplemented by top rock, jazz and world-music gigs. The annual BITE season cherry-picks exciting theatre and dance from around the globe, and the cinema shows a good mixture of mainstream, art-house and international films.
Event highlights Architecture Tour 2012. Meet at Advance Ticket Desk on Level G Wed-Sun, see website for details.

LSO St Luke's

161 Old Street, EC1V 9NG (7490 3939, 7638 8891 box office, www.lso. co.uk/lsostlukes). Old Street tube/rail. **Map** p151 D2 **㊿**
The London Symphony Orchestra's conversion of this Grade I-listed Hawksmoor church into a 370-seat concert hall some years ago cost £20m, but the classical concerts and sheer variety of pop/rock gigs prove it was worth every penny.

Shoreditch

Just north-east of the City proper, the pleasure zones of Shoreditch soak up bankers' loose change. The area's edginess and artiness have begun to follow cheaper rents north and east into Dalston and Hackney (pp175-76), but in and around the triangle made by Shoreditch High Street, Great Eastern Street and Old Street the many bars and clubs remain lively – on a Friday or a Saturday night, often unpleasantly so. It's still a scruffy bit of town, though, notwithstanding the fashion kids traipsing around.

Eating & drinking

Book Club

100-106 Leonard Street, EC2A 4RH (7684 8618, www.wearetbc.com). Old Street tube/rail. **Open** 8am-midnight Mon-Thur; 10am-2am Fri, Sat; noon-midnight Sun. **Admission** free-£5. **Bar/café**. **Map** p151 E2 **㉛**
The lovely-looking, open and airy Book Club fuses lively creative events with late-night drinking seven nights of the week. Locally themed cocktails include the Shoreditch Twat (a mix of tequila,

Jagermeister, vermouth, vanilla sugar and egg), and food is served all day. There's also free Wi-Fi, a pool table, ping pong and lots of comfy seats. The programme might include Scroobius Pip's We.Are.Lizards or perhaps a Thinking & Drinking lecture.

Callooh Callay

65 Rivington Street, Shoreditch, EC2A 3AY (7739 4781, www.calloohcallay bar.com). Old Street tube/rail or Shoreditch High Street rail. **Open/food** served 6pm-midnight Mon-Wed, Sun; 6pm-1am Thur-Sat. **Bar**. **Map** p151 F1 ⑤

Only a pair of intertwined Cs divulges Callooh Callay's location. Inside, it's warm and whimsical; the neo-Victorian decor is as eclectic as 'Jabberwocky', the poem by Lewis Carroll from which the bar gets its name. A laid-back lounge, a mirrored bar and loos tiled in old cassettes lie behind an oak Narnia wardrobe. Stake out seats here to people-watch: lots of vintage fabrics and fixed-gear cyclists.

Eyre Brothers

70 Leonard Street, EC2A 4QX (7613 5346, www.eyrebrothers.co.uk). Old Street tube/rail. **Open** noon-2.45pm, 6.30-10.45pm Mon-Fri; 7-11pm Sat. **££**. **International**. **Map** p151 E2 ⑤

News has got around: Eyre Brothers does everything exceptionally well, thus it can be hard to book a table. Brothers David and Robert clearly spend as much time crafting the changing menu as they must have fashioning the clean-lined decor – all chic leather furniture, designer lamps and divided dining areas. Authentic Portuguese dishes reflect their upbringing in Mozambique, while Spanish and French flavours add range and luxury to the offerings.

Pizza East

56 Shoreditch High Street, E16JJ (7729 1888, www.pizzaeast.com). Shoreditch High Street rail. **Open** noon-11pm

Mon-Wed, Sun; noon-midnight Thur; noon-1am Fri, Sat. **£**. **Pizza**. **Map** p151 F2 ⑤

Pizza East is in a big space that used to be a club and still looks like one floor of an old factory. There's more than pizza on the Italian-American menu (calamari with caper aioli, polenta with deep-fried chicken livers), but the pizzas are well-made and adventurous (witness clam pizza, a New England speciality, which comes garnished with cherry tomatoes). This place is noisy, but the welcome friendly.

Shopping

Just south of Shoreditch is one of the city's best shopping areas. We've listed key boutiques around **Old Spitalfields Market** and **Brick Lane** on pp178-180.

A Child of the Jago

10 Great Eastern Street, EC2A 3NT (7377 8694, www.achildofthejago.com). Shoreditch High Street rail. **Open** 11am-7pm Mon-Sat; noon-5pm Sun. **Map** p151 E2 ⑤

Joe Corre (Vivienne Westwood's son) and fashion designer Simon 'Barnzley' Armitage's eclectic shop is about as far from 'high street' as it gets, with its deft and very Shoreditch combination of modern and vintage clothes. You'll find the likes of Barnzley's cashmere hooded tops (they're handmade in Scotland) and Westwood's World's End collection.

Goodhood

🆕 *41 Coronet Street N1 6HD (7729 3600, http://goodhoodstore.com). Old Street tube/rail.* **Open** 11am-7pm Mon-Fri; 11am-6.30pm Sat. **Map** p151 E1 ⑤

Stock for this boutique-like store is selected by streetwear obsessives/owners Kyle and Jo, with items weighted towards Japanese independent labels. There are also knits and T-shirts from Australia's Rittenhouse, shirts and tops for men from Norse Projects, womenswear from APC Madras, and covetable pieces for both men and women from Peter Jensen and Wood Wood. A cabinet full of watches, sunglasses and jewellery makes this a great place for pressies for hard-to-please boyfriends and girlfriends.

Nightlife

Book Club (p167) offers a terrific range of unusual night-time events, from music to spoken word.

Comedy Café
66-68 Rivington Street, EC2A 3AY (7739 5706, www.comedycafe.co.uk). Old Street tube/rail or Shoreditch High Street rail. **Map** p151 F2 ⑤⑦
Comedy Café is a purpose-built club, with a fun atmosphere and food is an integral part of the experience.

East Village
89 Great Eastern Street, EC2A 3HX (7739 5173, www.eastvillageclub.com). Old Street tube/rail. **Open** 5pm-midnight Tue, Wed; 5pm-1am Thur; 5pm-1am Fri; 9pm-4am Sat; 2-11pm Sun.* **Map** p151 E2 ⑤⑧
Stuart Patterson, one of the Faith crew who have been behind all-day house-music parties across London for more than a decade, created this two-floor, 'real house' bar-club – and it's still punching above its weight. The top-notch DJs should suit any sophisticated clubber; you can expect the likes of Chicago house don Derrick Carter and London's own Mr C. It also hosts Rootikal, House Not House and our very own bimonthly Nite Sessions.

Horse & Groom
28 Curtain Road, EC2A 3NZ (7503 9421, www.thehorseandgroom.net). Old Street tube/rail. **Open** 6pm-1am Tue-Thur, Sun; 6pm-2am Fri, Sat. **Map** p151 F2 ⑤⑨
This two-floor, self-proclaimed 'disco pub' hosts nights ranging from house and electro to contemporary classical and pub quizzes.

Old Blue Last
38 Great Eastern Street, EC2A 3ES (7739 7033, www.theoldbluelast.com). Old Street tube/rail or Shoreditch High Street rail. **Open** noon-midnight Mon-Wed; noon-12.30am Thur, Sun; noon-1.30am Fri, Sat. **Map** p151 F2 ⑥⓪
Klaxons, Arctic Monkeys and Lily Allen have all played secret shows to the high-fashion rock 'n' rollers in the sauna-like upper room at this shabby two-floor Victorian boozer. The Old Blue Last's programme was recently revamped, and regular club nights might include the pop-punk favourite What's My Age Again, Skill Wizard, Bounty and electro night Dollop.

Plastic People
147-149 Curtain Road, EC2A 3QE (7739 6471, www.plasticpeople.co.uk). Old Street tube/rail or Shoreditch High Street rail. **Open** 10pm-2am Thur; 10pm-4am Fri, Sat; 7-11pm Sun. **Map** p151 F1 ⑥①
The long-established, long-popular Plastic People subscribed to the old-school line that all you need for a party is a dark basement and a kicking sound system – then to everybody's surprise closed for a refurb. The programming remains true to form: from deep techno to house, with all-girl DJ line-ups and many a star arriving to play a secret gig on the exemplary sound system.

XOYO
32-37 Cowper Street, EC2A 4AP (7729 5959, www.xoyo.co.uk). Old Street tube/rail. **Map** p151 E2 ⑥②
XOYO stands out from its competitors because of its size (its 900-person capacity is big for the area), but also because it functions as a club, a gig hub and an exhibition space, with a stark white gallery-like room upstairs and a dance basement below (offset by an unusually high ceiling). One of the founders, Cymon Eckel, describes it as 'essentially… a disco loft-club', but it has a pleasingly open attitude to all tribes of clubber.

LONDON BY AREA

Old Spitalfields Market p179

Neighbourhood London

Like many modern cities, London is really two different kinds of metropolis: the centre, for work, play and lucky tourists, and the periphery, where rent is cheaper and most locals live. Restaurants and bars are often more vital in these neighbourhoods – and cool scenes are more apt to develop.

To the north are **Camden** and **Islington** (p174). In the east, **Spitalfields to Dalston** (p175) is the city's hippest zone, but do also visit **Docklands** (p182) and the area around **Olympic Park** (p183). Head south of the Thames for spectacular **Greenwich** (p185) and lively **Brixton & Vauxhall** (p187), or shop in **Notting Hill** (p188) to the west of town.

London is a huge city, which means some sights are a day trip in themselves. We've included these in their own chapter: **Worth the Trip** is on pp190-192.

Camden

The key north London destination is the partly gentrified Camden. Famous for its **market** and close to Regent's Park and **London Zoo**, it's one of London's liveliest nightlife areas. West of Camden, snooty **St John's Wood** is the spiritual home of cricket.

Sights & museums

Jewish Museum
Raymond Burton House, 129-131 Albert Street, NW1 7NB (7284 7384, www.jewishmuseum.org.uk). Camden Town tube. **Open** 10am-5pm Mon-Thur, Sun; 10am-2pm Fri. **Admission** £7.50; free-£6.50 reductions; £18 family. This expanded museum reopened in 2010, and it's a brilliant exploration of Jewish life since 1066. Access is free to the downstairs café, beside an ancient ritual bath, and shop. You must pay to

go upstairs, but there you can wield the iron in a tailor's sweatshop, sniff chicken soup and pose for a wedding photo. There's a powerful Holocaust section, focused on a single survivor, Leon Greenman. Opposite, a beautiful room of religious artefacts, including a 17th-century synagogue ark and centrepiece chandelier of Hanukkah lamps, introduces Jewish ritual.

Lord's & MCC Museum

St John's Wood Road, NW8 8QN (7616 8595, www.lords.org). St John's Wood tube. **Tours** phone or see website for details. **Admission** £15; free-£9 reductions; £37 family.
The opposite side of Regent's Park from Camden, Lord's is more than just a famous cricket ground – as the headquarters of the Marylebone Cricket Club (MCC), it is official guardian of the rules of cricket. As well as staging test matches and internationals, the ground is home to the Middlesex County Cricket Club (MCCC). Visitors can take an organised tour round the futuristic, pod-like NatWest Media Centre and august, portrait-bedecked Long Room.

ZSL London Zoo

Regent's Park, NW1 4RY (7722 3333, www.zsl.org/london-zoo). Baker Street or Camden Town tube then 274, C2 bus. **Open** 10am-6pm daily. **Admission** £18.60; free-£17.10 reductions.
London Zoo has been open in one form or another since 1826. Spread over 36 acres and containing more than 600 species, it cares for many of the endangered variety – as well as your nippers at the children's zoo. The emphasis throughout is on upbeat education. Exhibits are always entertaining – we especially like the recreation of a kitchen overrun with cockroaches – but sometimes the zoo sensibly just lets the animals be the stars: witness the much expanded Penguin Beach, which opened in spring 2011.

Eating & drinking

Proud (p172) is great for rock 'n' roll boozing, while the original **Haché** (24 Inverness Street, 7485 9100, www.hacheburgers.com) provides sustenance.

Chin Chin Laboratorists

49-50 Camden Lock Place, NW1 8AF (www.chinchinlabs.com). Camden Town tube. **Open** noon-7pm Tue-Sun. No credit cards. **£. Ice-cream**.
The 'laboratorists' are husband-and-wife duo Ahrash Akbari-Kalhur and Nyisha Weber. In their ice-cream parlour, which looks like a mad scientist's lab, they use liquid nitrogen to make ice-cream on demand. The ice-cream, frozen so fast no coarse ice-crystals can form, is wonderfully smooth. The practical application of science has never been cooler, tastier or more fun.

Market

43 Parkway, NW1 7PN (7267 9700, www.marketrestaurant.co.uk). Camden Town tube. **Open** noon-2.30pm, 6-10.30pm Mon-Sat; 1-3.30pm Sun. **££. British**.
Stripped-back hardly covers the decor here: brick walls are ragged and raw; zinc-topped tables are scuffed; wooden chairs look as if they were once used in a classroom. Food is similarly pared down, reliant on the flavours of high-quality seasonal produce.

Masala Zone

25 Parkway, NW1 7PG (7267 4422, www.masalazone.com). Camden Town tube. **Open** 12.30-3pm, 5.30-11pm Mon-Fri; 12.30-11pm Sat; 12.30-10.30pm Sun. **££. Indian**.
This branch of the Masala Zone chain is popular with hip youngsters who come for the buzzy vibe, reasonable prices and decent pan-Indian food: earthy curries, thalis and zesty street snacks. The eye-catching decor is themed round colourful 1930s-style posters and retro artefacts.

LONDON BY AREA

Shopping

Alfie's Antique Market

13-25 Church Street, NW8 8DT (7723 6066, www.alfiesantiques.com). Edgware Road tube or Marylebone tube/rail. **Open** 10am-6pm Tue-Sat. No credit cards.

To the south-east of Regent's Park, Church Street is probably London's most important area for antiques shops, with a cluster centred on estimable Alfie's. The market itself has more than 100 dealers in vintage furniture and fashion, art, books and maps.

Camden Market

Camden Lock *Camden Lock Place, off Chalk Farm Road, NW1 8AF (www.camdenlockmarket.com).* **Open** 10am-6pm daily (reduced stalls Mon-Fri).
Camden Lock Village *east of Chalk Farm Road, NW1 (www.camdenlock.net).* **Open** 10am-8.30pm daily.
Camden Market *Camden High Street, at Buck Street, NW1 (www.camdenmarkets.org).* **Open** 9.30am-5.30pm daily.
Inverness Street Market *Inverness Street, NW1 (www.camdenlock.net).* **Open** 8.30am-5.30pm daily.
Stables Market *off Chalk Farm Road, opposite Hartland Road, NW1 8AH (7485 5511, www.stablesmarket.com).* **Open** 10.30am-6pm Mon-Fri (reduced stalls); 10am-6pm Sat, Sun.
All *Camden Town or Chalk Farm tube.* 'Camden Market' can refer to several markets in Camden; weekends are by far the busiest time to visit, although some stalls are open all week.

Camden Market is the place for neon sunglasses and pseudo-witty slogan garments. Almost next door is the Electric Ballroom, which sells vinyl and CDs at weekends and is also a music venue. Inverness Street market oppostie sells similar garb to Camden Market, as well as a diminishing supply of fruit and veg. North, next to the railway bridge, is Camden Lock, with numerous stalls selling crafts, home furnishings, jewellery, toys an gifts; West Yard has some tasty food stalls. Camden Lock Village which runs along the towpath, opened after major fire damage in 2009. North along Chalk Farm Road is the Stables Market, noted for its new and vintage fashion. The Horse Hospital area is good for second-hand clothing, food stands and designer furniture.

Nightlife

Koko

1A Camden High Street, NW1 7JE (0870 432 5527, 0844 847 2258 box office, www.koko.uk.com). Mornington Crescent tube.

Avoid standing beneath the sound-muffling overhang downstairs and you may find that this one-time music hall is one of London's finest venues. The 1,500-capacity hall stages weekend club nights and gigs by indie rockers, from cultish to those on the up.

Lock Tavern

35 Chalk Farm Road, NW1 8AJ (7482 7163, www.lock-tavern.co.uk). Chalk Farm tube. **Open** noon-midnight Mon-Thur; noon-1am Fri, Sat; noon-11pm Sun.

A tough place to get into at weekends, with queues of artfully distressed rock urchins and one of Camden's most arbitrary door policies. It teems with aesthetic niceties inside (cosy black couches and warm wood panels downstairs; open-air terrace on the first floor), but it's the unpredictable after-party vibe that packs in the punters.

Proud

Horse Hospital, Stables Market, Chalk Farm Road, NW1 8AH (7482 3867, www.proudcamden.com). Chalk Farm tube. **Open** 11am-1.30am Mon-Wed; 11am-2.30am Thur-Sat; 11am-12.30pm Sun.

North London guitar slingers do rock-star debauchery at this former Horse Hospital, whether draping themselves – cocktail in hand – over the luxurious

textiles in the stable-style booths, sinking into deck chairs on the terrace, or spinning round in the main band room to trendonista alt-sounds.

Roundhouse

Chalk Farm Road, NW1 8EH (7424 9991 information, 0844 482 8008 box office, www.roundhouse.org.uk). Chalk Farm tube.

A one-time railway turntable shed, the Roundhouse was used for experimental theatre and hippie happenings in the 1960s before becoming a rock venue in the '70s. The venue reopened a few years ago, and now mixes arty rock gigs with dance, quality theatre and multimedia events. Sightlines can be poor, but acoustics are good.

Islington

Camden's north London neighbour Islington combines bars, boutiques and small arts venues.

Eating & drinking

For great weekend vibes, get down to the **Old Queen's Head** (below).

Ottolenghi

287 Upper Street, N1 2TZ (7288 1454, www.ottolenghi.co.uk). Angel tube or Highbury & Islington tube/rail. **Open** 8am-10pm Mon-Wed; 8am-10.30pm Thur-Sat; 9am-7pm Sun. **££. Bakery-café.**

This is more than an inviting bakery. Behind the pastries piled in the window is a slightly prim deli counter with lush salads, available day and evening, eat-in or take away. As a daytime café, it's brilliant, but people also flock here for fine fusion food at dinner.

69 Colebrooke Row

69 Colebrooke Row, N1 8AA (07540 528593 mobile, www.69colebrooke row.com). Angel tube. **Open** 5pm-midnight Mon-Wed, Sun; 5pm-1am Thur; 5pm-2am Fri, Sat. **Bar.**

With just a handful of tables plus a few stools at the bar, 69 may be smaller than your front room, but the understated, intimate space proves a fine environment in which to enjoy pristine cocktails (liquorice whisky sours, perhaps), mixed with quiet ceremony. Impeccably attired staff, handwritten bills and tall glasses of water poured from a cocktail shaker mark out this lovely enterprise.

Shopping

Just off Upper Street near Angel tube, **Camden Passage** (7359 0190, www.camdenpassage antiques.com) retains some of the quirky antiques dealers who first brought shoppers here, as well as wonderful boutiques.

Paul A Young Fine Chocolates

33 Camden Passage, N1 8EA (7424 5750), www.payoung.net). Angel tube. **Open** 10am-6.30pm Tue-Sat; 10am-7pm Fri; noon-5pm Sun.

A gorgeous boutique with almost everything – chocolates, ice-cream, cakes – made in the downstairs kitchen and finished in front of customers. The white chocolate with rose masala is divine, as are the salted caramels.

Smug

13 Camden Passage, N1 8EA (7354 0253, www.ifeelsmug.com). Angel tube. **Open** 11am-6pm Wed, Fri, Sat; noon-7pm Thur; noon-5pm Sun.

Graphic designer Lizzie Evans has decked out this cute lifestyle boutique with rainbow kitchen accessories, Lisa Stickley wash bags, vintage-inspired soft toys and 1950s and '60s furniture.

Nightlife

Old Queen's Head

44 Essex Road, N1 8LN (7354 9993, www.theoldqueenshead.com). Angel tube. **Open** noon-midnight Mon-Wed, Sun; noon-1am Thur; noon-2am Fri, Sat.

Another place with long weekend queues – no wonder, when DJs such as Freestylers, Eno and Mr Thing are on the roster. There are two floors and outside seating, and during the week you can lounge on the sofas. Weekends are for dancing and minor celeb-spotting.

Arts & leisure

Almeida

Almeida Street, N1 1TA (7359 4404, www.almeida.co.uk). Angel tube.
A well-groomed 325-seat venue with a funky bar attached, the Almeida turns out thoughtfully crafted theatre directed by such star directors as Thea Sharrock and Rupert Goold.

Arsenal Football Club

Emirates Stadium, Ashburton Grove, Highbury, N7 7AF (0844 277 3625, www.arsenal.com). Arsenal tube.
The Premier League team's new stadium – north of Islington – is one of the country's best, and has a club museum.

Sadler's Wells

Rosebery Avenue, EC1R 4TN (0844 412 4300, www.sadlerswells.com). Angel tube.
This dazzling complex is home to an impressive line-up of local and international contemporary dance. Perhaps the key London venue for dance.

Screen on the Green

83 Upper Street, N1 0NP (0871 906 9060, www.everymancinema.com). Angel tube.
Boutique cinema chain Everyman now owns three former Screen cinemas, of which this is the best – refurbished a few years back, it lost seats to make space for the more comfortable kind, gained an auditorium bar and stage for live events, but kept its retro neon sign.

Spitalfields to Dalston

On the doorstep of the City, **Spitalfields** is known for its covered market, around which spread restaurants and bars. To the east, **Brick Lane** may be world-famous for its curries, but it is increasingly home to hip bars and boutiques. Slightly north, **Hoxton** begins where the City overspill into Shoreditch comes to an end: it's a good bet for late drinking and clubbing. Eastwards, **Bethnal Green** has the Museum of Childhood; to the north, unheralded **Dalston** has stealthily become a fine cluster of out-there music and arts venues, with the London Overground line (p214) having made them all more accessible.

Sights & museums

Dennis Severs' House

18 Folgate Street, E1 6BX (7247 4013, www.dennissevershouse.co.uk). Liverpool Street tube/rail or Shoreditch High Street rail. **Open** noon-4pm Sun; noon-2pm Mon following 1st & 3rd Sun of mth; times vary Mon evenings. **Admission** £10 Sun; £7 noon-2pm Mon; £14 Mon evenings.
The ten rooms of this original Huguenot house have been decked out to recreate vivid snapshots of daily life in Spitalfields between 1724 and 1914. A tour through the compelling 'still-life drama', as American creator Dennis Severs dubbed it, takes you through the cellar, kitchen, dining room, smoking room and upstairs to the bedrooms. With hearth and candles burning, smells lingering and objects scattered apparently haphazardly, it feels as though the inhabitants have deserted the building only moments before you arrived.

Geffrye Museum

136 Kingsland Road, E2 8EA (7739 8543, www.geffrye-museum.org.uk). Hoxton rail. **Open** 10am-5pm Tue-Sat; noon-5pm Sun. **Admission** free; donations appreciated.
In a set of 18th-century almshouses, the Geffrye offers a vivid physical history of the English interior. Displaying

original furniture, paintings, textiles and decorative arts, the museum recreates a sequence of typical middle-class living rooms from 1600 to the present – a fascinating take on domestic history.

V&A Museum of Childhood

Cambridge Heath Road, E2 9PA (8983 5235, www.museumofchildhood.org.uk). Bethnal Green tube/rail or Cambridge Heath rail. **Open** 10am-5.45pm daily. **Admission** free; donations appreciated.
Home to one of the world's finest collections of kids' toys, dolls' houses, games and costumes, the Museum of Childhood shines brighter than ever after extensive refurbishment, which has given it an impressive entrance. Part of the Victoria & Albert (p88), the museum has been amassing child-related objects since 1872, with Barbie Dolls complementing Victorian praxinoscopes. There are plenty of interactive exhibits and a decent café too.

Eating & drinking

Beside Old Spitalfields Market, **St John Bread & Wine** (7251 0848, www.stjohnbreadandwine.com) is the fine offshoot of St John (p157).

Albion

Boundary, 2-4 Boundary Street, E2 7DD (7729 1051, www.albioncaff.co.uk). Old Street tube/rail or Shoreditch High Street rail. **Open** 8am-midnight daily. **£. Café.**
Almost every new London restaurant seems to be mining the vein of nostalgia for traditional British cuisine these days, but few have pulled it off as well as Terence Conran's stand-out 'caff', shop and bakery in the Boundary hotel, with its platters of cupcakes and doorstop-thick slices of battenberg baked on-site, and mains such as toad in the hole or devilled kidneys.

Brick Lane Beigel Bake

159 Brick Lane, E1 6SB (7729 0616). Liverpool Street tube/rail, Shoreditch
High Street rail or bus 8. **Open** 24hrs daily. **£.** No credit cards. **Bagel bakery.**
This little East End institution produces perfect bagels both plain and filled (cream cheese, brilliant salt beef), superb bread and moreish cakes. Even at 3am, fresh baked goods are being pulled from the ovens; no wonder the queue trails out the door when local bars and clubs begin to close.

Dreambagsjaguarshoes

34-36 Kingsland Road, E2 8DA (7729 5830, www.jaguarshoes.com). Hoxton rail. **Open** noon-1am daily. **Bar.**
Still as trendy as the day it first opened, this bar offers a fast-track education in what makes Shoreditch cool. Grungey but glam scruffs lounge in decor that changes, regularly and completely, with artists commissioned at intervals to give the place a makeover. The background music is self-consciously edgy and good pizzas roll in from next door.

Poppies

6-8 Hanbury Street, E1 6QR (7247 0892, www.poppiesfishandchips. co.uk). Liverpool Street tube/rail or Aldgate East tube. **Open** 11am-11pm daily. **££. Fish & chips.**
A worthy replacement for the East End caff that preceded it, Poppies serves perfectly fried fish from Billingsgate Market (cod, haddock, rock, scampi, halibut) with hand-cut chips, home-made tartare sauce and mushy peas. You can sit in – service is by sharply dressed, authentically amiable Italian chaps. The location between Brick Lane and Spitalfields (p179) is handy.

Song Que

134 Kingsland Road, E2 8DY (7613 3222). Hoxton rail or Old Street tube/ rail then bus 243. **Open** noon-3pm, 5.30-11pm Mon-Sat; 12.30pm-11pm Sun. **£. Vietnamese.**
North-east London holds its monopoly on the best Vietnamese restaurants in the city, with Song Que the benchmark. It's a canteen-like operation to which

Dalston Nights

Hot clubbing, cool prices.

Dalston is the sparkling new pearl of London's clubbing scene. It used to all happen in Shoreditch, but as the area became more like a true sister to Soho, with troupes of hen dos storming the streets, so the real partiers migrated north up Kingsland Road. It's here that the party scene is really taking off, where basement dives line the streets and a sense of unbridled, anti-commerical hedonism rules.

Take the **Shacklewell Arms** (71 Shacklewell Lane, 7249 0810, www.shacklewellarms.com). A longtime Dalston dive and pub, it has retained its original decor – dodgy tropical-themed murals, signs for 'the dancehall' inside – and edgy programming. Music falls on the experimental side of electronic, with parties such as Feeding Time, Beach Creep and Lanzarote, while the odd mixed and gay night (Homoelectric and Hot Boy Dancing Spot) and girly electro-disco rave-up (Lovesick and Club Motherfucker) have been added to the mix.

Equally exciting is the **Nest** (p180). The basement club (they all are around here) is in what used to be Bardens Boudoir, but has taken the hallowed space's sound in a fresher direction. Its weekly Saturday party Lemonade is crammed with cool electro, disco, house and rock 'n' rave tunes, while its in-house Friday nighter attracts the cream of the DJ crop from across the electronic spectrum. Over the road, the **Alibi** (91 Kingsland High Street, 7249 2733, www.thealibilondon.co.uk) is an underground labyrinth of

Dalston Superstore

mirrors, booths and dancefloors, loved for its nightly free entry and roll call of hip bassline-driven nights such as Wifey, Yeah Maybe and Get Me!.

Next door is where it all started, though: **Dalston Superstore** (p180) spearheaded Dalston's creative renaissance in 2009 and still pulls huge crowds into its intense and pitch-black dancefloor. Upstairs, alternative drag cabaret stars line the bar and whip revellers into shape with their sharp one-liners, while downstairs goes for a typically east London mix of classic and cutting-edge music – mainly house – which could be anything from vogueing stompers (at the bi-monthly Paris Acid Ball) to acid (at monthly session Society).

Further up the road, the polysexual fashion elite assemble for no-frills nights at Stoke Newington speakeasy **Vogue Fabrics** (66 Stoke Newington Road, www.voguefabricsdalston.com), or cram into new venue the **Waiting Room** (175 Stoke Newington High Street, no phone/web).

diners of all types are attracted – be prepared to share tables at busy times. Beef pho and barbecued quail with citrus dipping sauce are superb.

Tayyabs

83 Fieldgate Street, E1 1JU (7247 9543, www.tayyabs.co.uk). Aldgate East or Whitechapel tube. **Open** noon-11.30pm daily. **£. Pakistani**.

A bit of a walk south-east of Brick Lane, Tayyabs is the East End equivalent of the caffs favoured by truckers in South Asia. It has been around since the 1970s, and although the interior has been extended, it's a challenge to bag a table. Cooking is big, bold and sassy. When it's just too busy, try Needoo Grill, round the corner (87 New Road).

Viajante/Corner Room

Town Hall Hotel, Patriot Square, E2 9NF (7871 0461, www.viajante.co.uk). Bethnal Green tube/rail or Cambridge Heath rail. **Open** 6-9.30pm Mon, Tue; noon-2pm, 6-9.30pm Wed-Sun. **££££**. **Modern European**.

In nowhere-land north of Bethnal Green station, fêted young chef Nuno Mendes has opened his own restaurant in a posh new hotel (p210). A stint at El Bulli informs his cooking: the six-, nine- or 12-course tasting menus are firmly in the 'experimental' camp. Expect culinary fireworks. Inventive tapas are served at the bar and there's a more affordable three-course lunch. In the same building, the Corner Room has received plaudits for its adventurous cooking and reasonable prices; no bookings are taken here.

Shopping

On Sundays, the whole area from **Old Spitalfields Market** (p179) east to Brick Lane is hectic with shoppers. Watch out for the new **Box Park** (www.boxpark.co.uk) at Shoreditch High Street station – a 'shopping mall' in 40 recycled shipping containers.

Beyond Retro

NEW *92-100 Stoke Newington Road, N16 7XB (7923 2277, www.beyond retro.com). Dalston Kingsland rail.* **Open** 10am-7pm Mon-Wed, Fri, Sat; 10am-8pm Thur; 10am-6pm Sun.

This enormous palace of secondhand clothing and accessories is the starting point of many an expert stylist, thrifter or fashion designer on the hunt for inspiration. Items include 1950s dresses, cowboy boots and denim hotpants, and there's plenty under £20. There are other branches in Shoreditch (112 Cheshire Street, E2 6EJ) and Soho (57-59 Great Marlborough Street, W1F 7JY).

Broadway Market

www.broadwaymarket.co.uk. London Fields rail or bus 236, 394.

Broadway Market has huge fashion kudos, but it's high-quality produce (this is primarily a specialist food market), well-edited vintage clothing and independent boutiques (Artworks, Black Truffle) that make it really worth a visit. The market wasn't always like this: after years of decline, in 2004 the local traders' and residents' association set about transforming their ailing fruit and veg market. Now, it's one of the city's most successful local markets.

Columbia Road Market

Columbia Road, E2. Hoxton rail or bus 26, 48, 55. **Open** 8am-2pm Sun.

On Sunday mornings, this unassuming East End street is transformed into a swathe of fabulous plant life and the air is fragrant with blooms. But it's not just about flora: alongside the market is a growing number of shops selling everything from pottery and Mexican glassware to cupcakes and perfume. Get there early for the pick of the crop, or around 2pm for the bargains; refuel at Jones Dairy (23 Ezra Street).

Dray Walk

Liverpool Street tube/rail or Shoreditch High Street rail.

The great brick buildings of the Old

Truman Brewery, about halfway up Brick Lane, are home to a formidable array of funky retailers: Junky Styling (no.12) for innovative reworkings of second-hand clothes; Folk (no.11) for cutting-edge brands such as Hillside; Traffic People (no.10) for classic polos and girly flower-print designs; Number 6 (no.6) for hip new casual attire; and, of course, Rough Trade East (below). Open only one day a week, the buzzy Sunday (Up)Market (7770 6100, www.sundayupmarket.co.uk) collects 140 stalls selling edgy fashion from fresh young designers, vintage gear and well-priced jewellery. It's more relaxed, cheaper and hipper than Old Spitalfields Market (below).

LN-CC

18-24 Shacklewell Lane, E8 2EZ (3174 0726, www.ln-cc.com). Dalston Kingsland rail. **Open** by appointment.
The various rooms in this 5,000sq ft basement have been transformed by in-demand set designer Gary Card to play host to myriad designer labels: for men, New Power Studio, Rick Owens, Maison Martin Margiela and archive Raf Simons; for women, archive Yohji Yamamoto, Comme des Garçons and Issey Miyake. There are also rare books and even an events space.

Old Spitalfields Market

Commercial Street, between Lamb Street & Brushfield Street, E1 6AA (7247 8556, www.spitalfieldsoldmarket. com). Liverpool Street tube/rail or Shoreditch High Street rail. **Open** 9.30am-5pm Thur, Fri, Sun. *Antiques* 8.30am-4.30pm Thur. *Food* 10am-5pm Fri-Sun. *Fashion* 9.30am-5pm Fri. *Records & books* 10am-4pm 1st & 3rd Fri of the mth. No credit cards.
Since the 2003 renovation and total overhaul of the much-loved Spitalfields Market, it's a leaner, cleaner affair, bulked out with slightly soulless boutiques. A pitch here is expensive, so expect gastro-nibbles, wittily sloganed baby T-shirts and leather bags. If you want to avoid the crowds and make more idiosyncratic finds, forget the busy Sunday market and come on a Thursday for heaps of vintage fashion.

Redchurch Street

Shoreditch High Street rail.
A shabby Shoreditch cut-through, Redchurch is suddenly a strong contender for London's best shopping street. Aussie botanical beauty shop Aesop (no.5A) and classic menswear brand Sunspel (no.7) can be found at one end. Further up are darkly lit menswear store Hostem (nos.41-43), decadent interiors at Maison Trois Garçons (no.45), vintage-style up-dos and manicures at hair salon the Painted Lady (no.65) and even a grungy thrift shop, Sick (no.105), that specialises in 1990s, er, vintage. Two key arrivals are concept store Aubin & Wills (nos.64-66), where you can buy men's, women's and homeware lines, or catch a film in the small cinema, and expansive new premises for long-term favourite Labour & Wait (no.85), selling its aesthetically pleasing mops, enamel bread bins and stylish ladles. The buzz surrounding Redchurch Street was intensified with the hullaballo that greeted Boundary (p207) and nearby members' club Shoreditch House, which houses an open-to-all branch of Cowshed spa.

Rough Trade East

Dray Walk, Old Truman Brewery, 91 Brick Lane, E1 6QL (7392 7788, www. roughtrade.com). Liverpool Street tube/ rail. **Open** 8am-9pm Mon-Thur; 8am-8pm Fri; 10am-8pm Sat; 11am-7pm Sun.
Since opening on Dray Walk (p178) in 2007, the indie music store has never looked more upbeat. This 5,000sq ft record store, café and gig space offers a dizzying range of vinyl and CDs, spanning punk, indie, dub, soul, electronica and more. With 16 listening posts and a stage for live sets, this is close to musical nirvana.

Vintage Emporium

*14 Bacon Street, E1 6LF (7739 0799,
www.thevintageemporiumcafe.com).
Shoreditch High Street rail.* **Open**
10am-7pm daily.

We love this relaxed vintage store and
café (complete with bright yellow
1960s coffee machine). Partners Jess
Collins and Oli Stanion opened it on a
shoestring on a Brick Lane back alley,
selling clothes from the Victorian era
through to the 1950s. Oh, and it hosts
naked life-drawing classes – a sight to
behold as you sip your herbal tea.

Nightlife

Bethnal Green Working Men's Club

*42-44 Pollard Row, E2 6NB (7739
7170, www.workersplaytime.net).
Bethnal Green tube/rail.* **Open** hrs
vary; check website for details.

The sticky red carpet and broken lamp-
shades perfectly suit the programme of
quirky lounge, retro rock 'n' roll and
fancy-dress burlesque parties from
spandex-lovin' dance husband-and-
wife duos and the like. The mood is
friendly, the playlist upbeat and the air
always full of artful, playful mischief.

Café Oto

*18-22 Ashwin Street, E8 3DL (7923
1231, www.cafeoto.co.uk). Dalston
Junction or Dalston Kingsland rail.*
No credit cards. **Open** 9.30am-1am
Mon-Fri; 10.30am-midnight Sat, Sun.

This 150-capacity Dalston café and
music venue can't easily be cate-
gorised, though it offers the tidy definition: 'creative new music that exists
outside of the mainstream'. That
means Japanese noise rockers, electronica pioneers, improvising noiseniks
and artists from the strange ends of the
rock, folk and classical spectrums.

Dalston Superstore

*117 Kingland High Street, E8 2PB (7254
2273). Dalston Kingsland rail.* **Open**
noon-2am Mon-Fri; 11am-2am Sat, Sun.

The opening of this gay arts-space-
cum-bar cemented Dalston's status as
the final frontier of east London's gay
scene. It's a confidently cool, New
York-style dive bar split between two
floors, clad in cement, brick and steel
vents, but enlivened with fluoro flashes, graffiti and art installations. During
the day there's café grub and Wi-Fi; at
night, expect queues for the impressive
and eclectic guest DJs.

Nest

*36 Stoke Newington Road, N16 7XJ
(7354 9993, www.ilovethenest.com).
Dalston Kingsland rail.* **Open** 9pm-4am
Fri, Sat.

Cult venue Bardens Boudoir – a 350-
capacity basement under a disused furniture store in the heart of Turkish
Dalston – reopened as a brighter and
chirpier version last year, controlled by
pub-club pros from the Old Queen's
Head (p174) and Paradise (p189). It programmes out-there line-ups nightly for
the hipsters that love them.

Vortex Jazz Club

*Dalston Culture House, 11 Gillet Street,
N16 8JN (7254 4097, www.vortexjazz.
co.uk). Dalston Kingsland rail.*

The Vortex is on the first floor of a
handsome new-build, with a restaurant
on the ground floor. The space can feel
a bit sterile, but the programming is
superb, packed with left-field talent
from Britain, Europe and the US.
London's most exciting jazz venue.

Arts & Leisure

Rivington Place

*Rivington Place, EC2A 3BA (7729
9616, www.rivingtonplace.org). Old
Street tube/rail or Shoreditch High
Street rail.* **Open** 11am-6pm Tue, Wed-
Fri; 11am-9pm Thur; noon-6pm Sat.
Admission free.

Designed by David Adjaye and one of
Shoreditch's more exciting recent addi-
tions, this was London's first new-built
gallery since the opening of the

Museum of London Docklands
p182

Hayward in 1968. The programme champions culturally diverse visual arts. Two project spaces provide a platform for British and international work, and there's a ground-floor café.

Whitechapel Gallery

77-82 Whitechapel High Street, E1 7QX (7522 7888, www.whitechapelgallery. org). Aldgate East tube. **Open** 11am-6pm Tue, Wed, Fri-Sun; 11am-9pm Thur. **Admission** free.

This East End stalwart has enjoyed a major redesign that saw the Grade II-listed building expand into the equally historic former library right next door – cleverly, the architects left the two buildings stylistically distinct rather than smoothing out their differences. The gallery gave itself an archive centre, restaurant and café, and tripled its exhibition space, improving a reputation as an art pioneer that was built on shows of Picasso (in 1939, his *Guernica* was shown here), Pollock and Kahlo.

Docklands

The flagship for finance-led urban redevelopment under the last Tory government in an area that had once been thriving docks, Docklands was for many years a chunk of barely populated tower blocks awaiting economic revival. Nowadays, the northern end of the Thames peninsula known as the Isle of Dogs is all shiny megabanks, and **One Canada Square** has become known as a London landmark.

Sights & museums

Museum of London Docklands

No.1 Warehouse, West India Quay, Hertsmere Road, E14 4AL (7001 9844, www.museumindocklands.org. uk). Canary Wharf tube or West India Quay DLR. **Open** 10am-6pm daily. **Admission** free.

Housed in a 19th-century warehouse (itself a Grade I-listed building), this huge sibling of the Museum of London (p161) provides an excellent introduction to the complex history of London's docks and the river. Displays over three storeys take you from the arrival of the Romans all the way to the docks' 1980s closure and the area's redevelopment. There are temporary exhibitions on the ground floor, along with a café and play area.

One Canada Square

Canary Wharf tube/DLR.

Cesar Pelli's dramatic office block – sometimes known as Canary Wharf – was the country's tallest building from 1991 to 2010, when it was finally overtaken by the Shard (see box p66). It remains a blank-faced icon of financial over-confidence, its pyramid roof instantly recognisable across London.

Thames Barrier Park

North Woolwich Road, E16 2HP (www.thamesbarrierpark.org.uk). Pontoon Dock DLR.

Crisply beautiful, this was London's first new park in half a century when it opened in 2001. It has a lush sunken garden of waggly hedges and offers perhaps the best views from land of the shiny metal fins of the massive Thames Barrier. A white footbridge, high above Royal Victoria Dock, brings you here from the ExCeL centre.

Trinity Buoy Wharf

64 Orchard Place, E14 0JW (7515 7153, www.trinitybuoywharf.com). East India DLR. **Open** *Long Player* 11am-5pm Sat, Sun.

In the 1860s, London's only lighthouse was built here to train lighthouse keepers and trial new light technology. The former repairs yard – which has great views of the O2 Arena (p186) on the far bank – now hosts regular art events, and the lighthouse is a permanent home for the meditative sounds of the *Long Player* art installation. There's

also a 1940s diner car (7987 4334, www.
fatboysdiner.co.uk, 10am-5pm Tue-
Sun) and café (8am-3pm Mon-Fri).

Eating & drinking

Yi-Ban
*London Regatta Centre, Dockside Road,
E16 2QT (7473 6699, www.yi-ban.
co.uk). Royal Albert DLR.* **Open** noon-
11pm Mon-Sat; 11am-10.30pm Sun.
££. Chinese.
Yi-Ban has a fun view across Royal
Albert Dock to London City Airport
(p211). The room takes cues from hotel
dining areas, but the food doesn't have
to follow sweet-and-sour clichés.
Instead diners can experiment with the
daytime dim sum, west lake soup or
Cantonese-style crispy roast pork belly.
The staff are charming, serving the terrific food with style and efficiency.

Olympic Park & around

The Olympic Park, scene of the
2012 Games, is an area of around
a square mile located in the
Lower Lee Valley in east London,
extending into the boroughs of
Hackney, Newham, Tower Hamlets
and Waltham Forest. Following the
Games, the park closed to allow
work on developing its legacy:
transforming it from a major events
arena into a viable area for work,
living, sport, culture and leisure.

Sights & museums

Olympic Park
*Stratford tube/rail/DLR, West Ham
tube/rail.* Park will begin to reopen
summer 2013.
The post-Games Olympic Park – to be
officially renamed the Queen Elizabeth
Olympic Park in January 2013– will
have two distinct areas: the South Park
will retain the Stadium, the Aquatics
Centre and the ArcelorMittal Orbit

sculpture, and will be a hub for sports
and other events. The area to the north
of the river, in contrast, will be home to
parklands, five new residential neighbourhoods and a business campus centred around what was the Press Centre
and the Broadcast Centre. The VeloPark
will reopen for local use and Eton
Manor, used for aquatics training and
wheelchair tennis during the Games,
will become the Lee Valley Hockey and
Tennis Centre. The Park will reopen to
the public in stages, beginning with part
of the North Park in July 2013.

Three Mills
*Three Mill Lane, E3 3DU (8980 4626,
www.housemill.org.uk). Bromley-by-Bow
tube.* **Tours** May-Oct 1-4pm Sun. *Mar,
Apr, Dec* 11am-4pm 1st Sun of mth.
Admission £3; £1.50 reductions;
free under-16s. No credit cards.
Just south of the Olympic Park, this
pretty island on the River Lea takes its
name from the three mills that ground
flour and gunpowder here. The House
Mill, built in 1776, is the oldest and
largest tidal mill in Britain and it is
occasionally opened to the public. Even
when the House Mill is closed, the
island provides pleasant walks that
can feel surprisingly rural. Victorian
sewer engineer Sir Joseph Bazalgette's
extraordinary, Byzantine Abbey Mills
Pumping Station can be seen nearby.

Eating & drinking

Forman's Restaurant
*Stour Road, Fish Island, E3 2PA (8525
2365, www.formans.co.uk/restaurant).
Pudding Mill Lane DLR or Hackney
Wick rail.* **Open** *Restaurant* 7-11pm
Thur, Fri; 10am-2pm, 7-11pm Sat; noon-
5pm Sun. *Gallery Bar* 5-9pm Thur, Fri;
noon-5pm, 7-11pm Sat; noon-5pm Sun.
££-£££. British.
Come here to enjoy a truly local special-
ity in a truly amazing setting: London-
cured smoked salmon, made in the East
End in the same way since 1905, scoffed
in plain view of the Olympic Park. The

Cutty Sark Reborn

The tea clipper has been restored to her former glory.

When the *Cutty Sark* went up in flames in May 2007, it looked like the end of an adventurous life for one of London's best-loved landmarks. She'd been enjoying retirement as a tourist attraction after a working life that began in 1870, crossing the world's oceans with cargoes of tea, wine spirits, beer, coal, jute, wool and castor oil. Built in Scotland, the *Cutty Sark* had been the fastest in the business, but steam quickly overtook sail in the 19th century, and the old clipper eventually found in a home in this dry dock in the 1950s.

The damage caused by the fire could have been worse: the vessel was closed for conservation at the time of the disaster, so many parts had already been removed and put in storage. And there was another silver lining – the post-fire £50 million restoration has been far more extensive than what had been originally planned. As well as preserving a substantial portion of the ship's original fabric, the scheme has raised the *Cutty Sark* off the ground and surrounded her with a dramatic glass 'skirt'. Critics have complained that the glazed canopy obscures the elegant go-faster ines of her hull, but it does allow visitors to admire the hull from underneath for the first time.

The creation of a space beneath the ship has also made it possible to display the ship's collection of more than 80 merchant navy figureheads in its entirety for the first time. The carved figures – representing figures including Florence Nightingale, William Wilberforce and Hiawatha, among others – were positioned on the prow of sailing ships for decoration and to aid identification.

restaurant serves buckwheat blinis with the salmon, as well as other seasonal produce such as smoked eel and Hampshire buffalo mozzarella.

Hackney Pearl
11 Prince Edward Road, E9 5LX (8510 3605, www.thehackneypearl. com). Hackney Wick rail. **Open** 8am-11pm Tue-Fri; 10am-11pm Sat, Sun. **££. Café-bar.**
Hackney Pearl is a friendly neighbourhood hangout, with the owners having made something special out of not very much. Two shop units in a post-industrial enclave between Victoria Park and the Lea Navigation have been enlivened by furniture that seems salvaged from a groovy thrift shop – colourful rugs, Formica tables and old dressers – and a compact menu that lists simple but imaginative food.

Shopping

Westfield Stratford City
NEW *http://uk.westfield.com/stratford city. Stratford tube/DLR/rail.*
Westfield's £1.45bn retail behemoth snakes through what was the London Olympic site, with 300 retail units – the cornerstones of which are gigantic versions of high-street brands John Lewis, Marks & Spencer and Waitrose – 70 restaurants, bars and cafés, and a 17-screen digital cinema.

Arts & leisure

Just east of Stratford International station, **Theatre Square** has a little cluster of entertainment venues: a multiplex, the Stratford Circus arts venue (0844 357 2625, www.stratford-circus.com) and the Theatre Royal Stratford East.

Theatre Royal Stratford East
Gerry Raffles Square, E15 1BN (8534 0310, www.stratfordeast.com). Stratford tube/rail/DLR.

The Theatre Royal is a community theatre, with many shows written, directed and performed by black or Asian artists. Musicals are big here – *The Harder They Come* went on to West End success – but there's also a fine comedy night, the Christmas pantomime and some harder-hitting fare.

Greenwich

Greenwich is laden with centuries of royal and maritime heritage. The most easterly of London's UNESCO World Heritage Sites – and with the shimmering riverside colonnades of the Old Royal Naval College one of the most breathtaking – it merits a day's exploration by itself.

From summer 2012, a cross-river **cable car**, the Emirates Air Line, will allow pedestrians and cyclists to cross the Thames within five minutes, from terminals at Emirates Greenwich Peninsula and Emirates Royal Docks.

Sights & museums

Cutty Sark
King William Walk, SE10 9HT (www.cuttysark.org.uk). Cutty Sark DLR or Greenwich DLR/rail.
See box left.

Discover Greenwich & Old Royal Naval College
2 Cutty Sark Gardens, SE10 9LW (8269 4799, www.oldroyalnavalcollege. org.uk). Cutty Sark DLR. **Open** 10am-5pm daily. **Admission** free.
Designed by Wren in 1694, with Hawksmoor and Vanbrugh helping to complete it, the Old Royal Naval College was originally a hospital for seamen, with pensioners living here from 1705 to 1869, when the complex became the Royal Naval College. The public are allowed into the impressive rococo chapel, where there are free organ recitals, and the Painted Hall, a tribute to William and Mary that took

LONDON BY AREA

Sir James Thornhill 19 years to complete. In 2010, the Pepys Building (the block of the Naval College nearest the *Cutty Sark*, the pier and Cutty Sark DLR) reopened as the excellent Discover Greenwich. It's full of focused, informative exhibits on the surrounding buildings, the life of the pensioners, Tudor royalty and so forth, delivered with a real sense of fun: while grown-ups read about scagliola (a fake stone building material), the kids can try on a knight's helmet.

National Maritime Museum

Romney Road, SE10 9NF (8858 4422, 8312 6565 information, www.nmm.ac.uk). Cutty Sark DLR or Greenwich DLR/rail. **Open** 10am-5pm daily. **Admission** free; donations appreciated.

The world's largest maritime museum contains a huge store of creatively organised maritime art, cartography, models and regalia. Ground-level galleries include Explorers, which covers great sea expeditions back to medieval times, and Maritime London, which concentrates on the city as a port. The new Sammy Ofer wing contains Nelson's uniform, complete with fatal bullet-hole, as well as the introductory Voyages gallery, temporary exhibitions, a café, brasserie and shop. Upstairs are Your Ocean, which reveals our dependence on the health of the world's oceans. Level two holds the interactives: the Bridge has a ship simulator, and All Hands lets children load cargo, and you can even try your hand as a ship's gunner. The Ship of War is the museum's collection of models; Oceans of Discovery commemorates the history of world exploration; and the Atlantic World gallery looks at the relationship between Britain, Africa and the Americas.

From the museum a colonnaded walkway leads to the Queen's House (8312 6565, open 10am-5pm daily, free admission), designed by Inigo Jones and holding art by Hogarth and Gainsborough. At the top of the hill in the park, the Royal Observatory and Planetarium (8312 6565, www.rog.nmm.ac.uk; £10, admission varies) are also part of the museum – take some time to straddle the Prime Meridian Line.

Eating & drinking

Old Brewery

Pepys Building, Old Royal Naval College, SE10 9LW (3327 1280, www.oldbrewerygreenwich.com). Cutty Sark DLR. **Open** 11am-11pm daily. **££. Modern British/microbrewery.**

By day, the Old Brewery is a café; by night, a restaurant. There's a small bar, with tables outside in a large walled courtyard – a lovely spot in which to test the 50-strong beer list – but most of the action is in the vast, high-ceilinged main space, beneath a wave-like structure of empty bottles and a wall of shiny copper vats – handsome enough to net our award for Best Design in 2010. The short menu highlights provenance and seasonality, with matching beers suggested for each dish.

Nightlife

O2 Arena & IndigO2

Millennium Way, SE10 0BB (8463 2000 information, 0844 856 0202 box office, www.theo2.co.uk). North Greenwich tube.

Since its launch in 2007, this conversion of the Millennium Dome has been a huge success. The O2 Arena – a state-of-the-art, 23,000-capacity enormo-dome with good acoustics and sightlines – hosts the headline rock and pop acts. Its little brother, IndigO2, isn't actually that little (capacity 2,350) but is a good fit for big soul, funk and pop-jazz acts (Roy Ayers, Stacey Kent), old pop stars (Gary Numan, Ultravox) and all points between. Thames Clippers (p214) run half hourly back into town.

Proud2

O2 Arena, Peninsula Square, SE10 ODX (8463 3070, www.proud2. com). North Greenwich tube.
The most ambitious of the growing network of Proud nightlife venues, Proud2 has had a blinding kaleidoscopic paint job, laid on £2 shuttle buses to central London and created a Vegas-style night out. From plush seating to the multisensory carnival within, few London clubs have been this bold on this scale.

Brixton & Vauxhall

The key hub in south London, **Brixton** has been through its troubles, scarred by the 1981 riots, but is now a vibrant area. **Brixton Village Market**, near Brixton tube, is hoime to 20 or so new cafés and restaurants. Right on the river to the north of Brixton, anonymous **Vauxhall** – central, but pretty much off the radar on the wrong side of the river from Westminster (p74) – has some of the fiercest gay nightlife in the city: Fire (right) never seems to close, and RVT (right) is an iconic alt-cabaret venue. To the west in **Battersea**, the BAC (right) is a hotbed of exciting new theatre.

Eating & drinking

Franco Manca

4 Market Row, Electric Lane, SW9 8LD (7738 3021, www.francomanca.co.uk). Brixton tube/rail. Open noon-5pm Mon-Wed; noon-9pm Thur-Sat; noon-4pm Sun. £. Pizza.
Franco Manca is the sort of discreet place you might walk past while ogling the Afro-Caribbean goodies in the surrounding market. Don't. It uses well-sourced, quality ingredients (many organic), top-notch equipment and good sourdough bases, quickly baked at high temperatures in the Neopolitan manner to seal in the flavour and lock in the moisture of the crust.

Nightlife

Fire

South Lambeth Road, SW8 1UQ (3242 0040, www.fireclub.co.uk). Vauxhall tube/rail. Open varies, check website.
Craving clubs full of shirts-off muscle boys going at night-and-day techno? For a number of years the 'Vauxhall Village' has been destination of choice for hardcore gay clubbers, the sort who think nothing of starting on Friday and finding themselves still dancing on Monday, but key venues such as Fire now host dance nights for hedonists of any sexual persuasion. The Lightbox here is an all-round LED sensation.

Plan B

418 Brixton Road, SW9 7AY (7733 0926, www.plan-brixton.co.uk). Brixton tube/rail. Open varies, check website.
It may be small, but Plan B is very cool. Since reopening after a fire a few years back, packing a delicious Funktion 1 Soundsystem, the flow of top-notch hip hop and funk stars just hasn't stopped. Community, Plan B's Saturday night shindig, is an absolute beauty.

RVT

372 Kennington Lane, SE11 5HY (7820 1222, www.rvt.org.uk). Vauxhall tube/rail. Open 7pm-midnight Mon, Wed, Thur; 6pm-midnight Tue; 7pm-2am Fri; 9pm-2am Sat; 2pm-midnight Sun.
If you're seeking a very London gay experience, the Royal Vauxhall Tavern is where to start. It operates a famously broad, anything-goes booking policy, but there are some fixtures: Saturday's alt-cabaret performance night Duckie (www.duckie.co.uk) might range from strip cabaret to rude puppets.

Arts & leisure

BAC

Lavender Hill, SW11 5TN (7223 2223, www.bac.org.uk). Clapham Common tube, Clapham Junction rail or bus 77, 77A, 345.

Housed in the old town hall, the forward-thinking Battersea Arts Centre hosts young theatre troupes – increasingly literally, with bedrooms installed to facilitate artist collaboration. Expect quirky, fun and physical theatre from the likes of cult companies Kneehigh and 1927. There are also exciting festivals that combine theatre and performance art, or showcase stand-up comedy and spoken word.

Notting Hill

Notting Hill Gate, Ladbroke Grove and Westbourne Park tube stations form a triangle that contains lovely squares, grand houses and fine gardens, along with shops, bars and restaurants that serve the kind of bohemian who can afford to live here. Off Portobello Road are the boutiques of Westbourne Grove and Ledbury Road.

Sights & museums

Museum of Brands, Packaging & Advertising

Colville Mews, Lonsdale Road, W11 2AR (7908 0880, www.museumof brands.com). Notting Hill Gate tube. **Open** 10am-6pm Tue-Sat; 11am-5pm Sun. **Admission** £6.50; free-£4 reductions.

Robert Opie began collecting the things others throw away when he was 16. Over the years the collection has grown to include milk bottles, vacuum cleaners and cereal packets. The emphasis is on British consumerism through the last century, though there are items as old as an ancient Egyptian doll.

Eating & drinking

Hereford Road

3 Hereford Road, W2 4AB (7727 1144, www.herefordroad.org). Bayswater tube. **Open** noon-3pm, 6-10.30pm Mon-Fri; noon-3.30pm, 6-10.30pm Sat; noon-4pm, 6-10pm Sun. **££. British**.

Hereford Road has real self-assurance, even though it's only been around a few years. It's an easy place in which to relax, with a mixed crowd and a happy buzz. Starters include the likes of (undyed) smoked haddock with white beans and leeks, while mains might feature mallard cooked with braised chicory and lentils.

Ledbury

127 Ledbury Road, W11 2AQ (7792 9090, www.theledbury.com). Westbourne Park tube. **Open** 6.30-10.30pm Mon; noon-2.30pm, 6.30-10.30pm Sun. **£££. French.**

Notting Hillites flock to this elegant gastronomic masterpiece, where the food is as adventurous and accomplished as any, but less expensive than many. Flavours are delicate but intense, often powerfully earthy. A well-priced, top-quality wine list too.

Portobello Star

171 Portobello Road, W11 2DY (7229 8016). Ladbroke Grove tube. **Open** 11am-11pm Mon-Thur; 11am-12.30am Fri; 10am-12.30am Sat; 11am-11.30pm Sun. **Cocktail bar.**

Portobello Star is just a long, thin room, but it's a handsome space, more appealing than it seems at first. The USPs are the likeable bartenders' convincing renditions of cocktails both traditional (a richly flavourful mint julep, a margarita modified by agave) and modern (Dick Bradsell's Bramble). You may have to shout to make yourself heard when the DJs crank it up – the music policy bounces from generic indie to more danceable tunes.

Shopping

The strip of boutiques along **Ledbury Road** is shopping catnip for yummy mummies – but Wolf & Badger (right) is our current favourite. Due west of Notting Hill is the huge **Westfield London** shopping mall (Ariel Way, W12 7GF,

7333 8118, www.westfield.com/
london), predecessor to the new
Westfield Stratford City (p185) and
packed with shops and restaurants.

Mary's Living & Giving Shop

*177 Westbourne Grove, W11 2SB
(7727 6166, www.maryportas.com/
livingandgiving). Notting Hill Gate
tube.* **Open** 11am-6pm Mon-Sat;
noon-5pm Sun.
Part of an ongoing project with Save
the Children, TV star shopper Mary
Portas has rebranded one of the organisation's west London sites to create an
extraordinarily popular shop that's
more boutique than bargain basement.
It's had donations from labels Acne,
Stella McCartney, Agent Provocateur
and Paul Smith. The vintage Chanel
bag collection is a cult favourite.

Portobello Road Market

*Portobello Road, Notting Hill, W10
(www.portobelloroad.co.uk). Ladbroke
Grove or Notting Hill Gate tube.* **Open**
8am-6.30pm Mon-Wed, Fri, Sat; 8am-
1pm Thur. *Antiques* 4am-4pm Fri, Sat.
No credit cards.
Portobello is always busy, but fun.
Antiques start at the Notting Hill end,
further down are food stalls, and
emerging designer and vintage clothes
congregate under the Westway and
along the walkway to Ladbroke Grove
on Fridays (usually marginally quieter)
and Saturdays (invariably manic).
Portobello also has fine shops, such as
Honest Jon's record emporium (no.278),
approaching 40 years in the business.

Wolf & Badger

*Wolf & Badger, 46 Ledbury Road,
W11 2AB (7229 5698, www.wolfand
badger.com). Notting Hill Gate tube.* **Open**
10am-6pm Mon-Sat; 11am-5pm Sun.
This concept boutique has a somewhat
rare philosophy – to bypass well-
known luxury labels and showcase
young designers instead. Retail space
is rented out to fledgling labels, who

gain business advice on how to grow
their brand while being snapped up by
style-savvy west Londoners. Owners
Samir Ceric and Zoë Knight have excellent style credentials – one is a gallery
owner, the other designs accessories.

Nightlife

Notting Hill Arts Club

*21 Notting Hill Gate, Notting Hill, W11
3JQ (7460 4459, www.nottinghillarts
club.com). Notting Hill Gate tube.* **Open**
hrs vary, but around 7pm-2am Wed-Fri;
4pm-2am Sat; 6pm-1am Sun.
Notting Hill Arts Club almost single-
handedly keeps this side of town on the
radar thanks to its mid-weekers YoYo!
and Death2Disco, plus new nights such
as heavy rocker Raw Power and future-
thinking electronic bash Talking At Me.

Paradise

*19 Kilburn Lane, W10 4AE (8969
0098, www.theparadise.co.uk).
Kensal Green tube or Kensal Rise
rail.* **Open** 4pm-midnight Mon-Wed;
noon-1am Thur; 4pm-2am Fri; noon-
2am Sat; noon-midnight Sun.
This is a star among the legion of pub-
clubs, thanks to its alternative programme of art auctions, burlesque life
drawing and late-night club nights, making it more than just a good local spot.

Arts & leisure

Lyric Hammersmith

*Lyric Square, King Street, W6 0QL
(0871 221 1722, www.lyric.co.uk).
Hammersmith tube.*
Hammersmith, south-west of Notting
Hill, is not a glamorous part of town,
but the Lyric is a theatre people will
cross the city for. Artistic director Sean
Holmes has brought writers back to the
Lyric, making space for neglected modern classics and new plays alongside
the cutting-edge physical and devised
work for which the theatre had become
known. The roof terrace bar is a real
attraction in good weather.

Hampton Court Palace

Worth the Trip

North

Hampstead Heath
Hampstead tube or Hampstead Heath rail.
The trees and grassy hills of the heath make it a surprisingly wild patch of the metropolis. Aside from the pleasure of walking, sitting and even swimming in the ponds, there's Kenwood House/ Iveagh Bequest (Hampstead Lane, 8348 1286, www.english-heritage.org.uk), every inch the stately pile. Built in 1616, it was bought by brewing magnate Edward Guinness, who donated his brilliant art collection in 1927. Highlights include a Rembrandt self-portrait.

Lee Valley White Water Centre
Station Road, Waltham Cross, Herts EN9 1AB (0845 677 0606, www.gowhitewater.co.uk). Liverpool Street tube/rail to Waltham Cross rail (25min journey).
See box p192.

North-west

Wembley Stadium
Stadium Way, Wembley, Middx HA9 0WS (0844 980 8001, www.wembley stadium.com). Wembley Park tube or Wembley Stadium rail.
Reopened in 2007, this 90,000-seater stadium is impressive, its steel arch an imposing feature on the skyline. It was an appropriate venue for London 2012 – get a flavour of the heritage on one of the stadium guided tours.

South-west

Hampton Court Palace
East Molesey, Surrey KT8 9AU (0844 482 7777, www.hrp.org.uk). Hampton Court rail, or riverboat from Richmond or Westminster to Hampton Court Pier (Apr-Oct). **Open Palace** Apr-Oct 10am-6pm daily; Nov-Mar 10am-4.30pm daily. **Admission Palace, courtyard, cloister & maze** £14; free-£11.50 reductions; £38 family.

Maze £3.50; free-£2.50 reductions. *Gardens* Apr-Oct £4.60; free-£4 reductions; Nov-Mar free.

A half-hour train ride from central London, this is a spectacular palace, once owned by Henry VIII. It was built in 1514 and for 200 years was a focal point of English history: Shakespeare gave his first performance to James I here in 1604; and, after the Civil War, Oliver Cromwell was so besotted by the building he moved in. Centuries later, the rosy walls of the palace still dazzle. Its vast size can be daunting, so take advantage of the costumed guided tours. The Tudor Kitchens are great fun, with their giant cauldrons and fake pies, and the exquisitely landscaped gardens contain fine topiary and the famous maze. One of the free events for London 2012, the Cycling Road Time Trial, starts and finishes here.

Royal Botanic Gardens (Kew Gardens)

Kew, Richmond, Surrey TW9 3AB (8332 5655, www.kew.org). Kew Gardens tube/rail, Kew Bridge rail or riverboat to Kew Pier. **Open** *Apr-Aug* 9.30am-6.30pm Mon-Fri; 9.30am-7.30pm Sat, Sun. *Sept, Oct* 9.30am-6pm daily. *Nov-Jan* 9.30am-4.15pm daily. *Feb, Mar* 9.30am-5.30pm daily. **Admission** £13.50; free-£11.50 reductions.

The unparalleled collection of plants at Kew was begun by Queen Caroline, wife of George II, with exotic plants brought back by voyaging botanists (Charles Darwin among them). In 1759, 'Capability' Brown was employed by George III to improve on the work of his predecessors, setting the template for a garden that attracts thousands of visitors each year. Head straight for the 19th-century greenhouses, filled to the roof with tropical plants, and next door the Waterlily House's quiet and pretty indoor pond (closed in winter). Brown's Rhododendron Dell is at its best in spring, while the Xstrata Treetop Walkway, some 60ft above the ground, is terrific fun among autumn leaves.

Wimbledon Lawn Tennis Museum

Museum Building, All England Lawn Tennis Club, Church Road, SW19 5AE (8946 6131, www.wimbledon.org/ museum). Southfields tube or bus 39, 493. **Open** 10am-5pm daily; ticket holders only during championships. **Admission** £18; free-£15.75 reductions.

This museum on the history of tennis has a 200° screen that simulates playing on Centre Court and a re-creation of a 1980s men's dressing room, complete with 'ghost' of John McEnroe. The ticket price includes a behind-the-scenes tour: you can admire Centre Court's new retractable roof, which will permit extended evening play – as well as preventing rain delays – for both the annual Wimbledon tournament and the London 2012 Tennis competition.

WWT Wetland Centre

Queen Elizabeth's Walk, Barnes, SW13 9WT (8409 4400, www.wwt. org.uk/london). Hammersmith tube then 33, 72, 209 or 283 bus. **Open** *Summer* 9.30am-6pm daily. *Winter* 9.30am-5pm daily. *Tours* 11am, 2pm daily. *Feeding tours* 3pm daily. **Admission** £9.95; free-£7.40 reductions; £27.75 family.

Reclaimed from industrial reservoirs a decade ago, the 43-acre wetland reserve is four miles from central London, but feels a world away. Quiet ponds, rushes, rustling reeds and wildflower gardens all teem with bird life – some 150 species – as well as the now very rare water vole. Naturalists ponder its 27,000 trees and 300,000 aquatic plants and swoon over 300 varieties of butterfly, 20 types of dragonfly and four species of bat (now sleeping in a stylish new house designed by Turner Prize-winning artist Jeremy Deller). You can explore water-recycling initiatives in the RBC Rain Garden or check out the new interactive Pond Safari and Down the Plughole exhibits. Traditionalists needn't be scared – plain old pairs of binoculars can be hired.

LONDON BY AREA

Ride the White Waves

White water rafting? In London? Yes.

Think of a challenging white water rafting or kayaking course and Zambia's Zambezi or the Whataroa in New Zealand might spring to mind. But London's Lee Valley Park? We spoke to GB Slalom kayaker and 2012 competitor Huw Swetnam, who helped to develop London's own white water course, the Lee Valley White Water Centre (p190). 'The centre's the best [artificial] white water facility in Britain and one of the best in the world,' he told us. 'It imitates some of the best natural white water rivers, such as the Etive in Scotland, the Grandtully course on the Tay, and the Tryweryn in Wales.' Swetnam explained that the course is special because you can change the features to make it harder or easier to negotiate.

The site of the London 2012 Canoe Slalom contests was the only new venue open to the public in the run-up to the Games, and is scheduled to reopen to the public on 8 September, after the Games. It offers exhilarating half-day sessions of rafting for £49. Booking ahead is essential.

The centre, which cost £35m to build, looks impressive. As well as the two water courses, there's a roomy wood-decked viewing terrace that traps sunlight all day.

The course used for the Games is 300m from start to finish, with a 5.5m drop. Five powerful machines pump up to 15,000 litres of water per second, so there's plenty of white froth. The rapids are equivalent to a grade three or four river, but because the course isn't as long as a river, public rafting sessions involve four or five runs that take about an hour and a half. And there's no hauling the boat up a steep bank – one of the best bits is the giant conveyer that takes you and your canoe or raft to the starting pool.

Essentials

W London Leicester Square p206

Hotels

London was short on hotel rooms when it was named Olympic host city and the building frenzy that ensued led to dozens of new hotels opening at all points on the price spectrum, with many more being restored, revamped or extended.

Of the prestige hotels, the reopening of a glamorously refitted **Savoy** (p206) in late 2010 was a major event – trumped by the Dorchester in 2011 with the opening of the all-new and très chic **45 Park Lane** (p199). The W empire – which aims for urban hip and usually achieves it – has finally come to town in the form of **W London Leicester Square** (p206). It's an impressive UK debut for the chain, but its boutique aspirations are better realised by the nearby **St John Hotel** (p204), a 'with rooms' version of the landmark restaurant.

Catching a lot of buzz is the reopened hotel behind the Grade I-listed frontage of St Pancras Station, the **St Pancras Renaissance** (p204). The restored historic grandeur is breathtaking, and open to all in the Booking Office bar (p124).

Room prices remain high. Significantly, **Dean Street Townhouse** (p202), its slightly younger sibling **Shoreditch Rooms** (p208) and St John Hotel offer 'tiny' or 'post-supper' rooms at lower-than-you-might-fear rates. The popularity of hip new B&Bs (**Rough Luxe**, p204; **40 Winks**, p209) and no-frills hotel concepts speaks to the same need.

Still, you can't expect bargains in London: there is good value to be found, but to get a room that's genuinely cheap you'll either have to book months in advance, drop your standards or get online and trust to last-minute deals.

Money matters

When visitors moan about London prices (you know you do), their case is strongest when it comes to hotels. We reckon any decent double averaging under £120 a night is good value for this town: hence, **£** in the listings below represents a rack rate of around £100 and below. Hotels do offer special deals, though, notably at weekends; check their websites or ask when you book, and also look at discount websites such as www.lastminute.com, www.london-discount-hotel.com or www.alpharooms.com.

The South Bank

Bermondsey Square Hotel

Bermondsey Square, Tower Bridge Road, SE1 3UN (0870 111 2525, www.bespokehotels.com). Borough tube or London Bridge tube/rail. **££**.
This is a deliberately kitsch new-build on a newly developed square. Suites are named after the heroines of psychedelic rock classics (Lucy, Lily and so on), there are classic discs on the walls, and you can kick your heels from the suspended Bubble Chair at reception. But, although occupants of the Lucy suite get a multi-person jacuzzi (with a great terrace view), and anyone can get sex toys from reception, the real draw isn't the gimmicks – it's well-designed rooms for competitive prices. The Brit food restaurant-bar is a bit hit-or-miss, but the hotel's pretty and the cheerful staff are helpful.

Park Plaza County Hall

1 Addington Street, SE1 7RY (7021 1800, www.parkplaza.com). Lambeth North tube or Waterloo tube/rail. **££**.
From the tube the approach is rather grimy, but this enthusiastically – if somewhat haphazardly – run hotel is well located just behind County Hall. Each room has its own kitchenette

SHORTLIST

Best new
- 45 Park Lane (p199)
- Dorset Square (p202)
- Eccleston Square Hotel (p197)

Traditional grandeur
- Claridge's (p201)
- Connaught (p201)
- Dorchester (p202)
- Lanesborough (p198)
- St Pancras Renaissance (p204)

Modern glamour
- Soho Hotel (p206)
- Trafalgar (p197)
- W Hotel (p206)

Style on a budget
- Hoxton Hotel (p208)
- Pavilion (p210)
- Stylotel (p210)
- Sumner (p206)

Hip B&Bs
- 40 Winks (p209)
- B+B Belgravia (p197)
- Rough Luxe (p204)

Best for eating & sleeping
- Boundary (p207)
- Dean Street Townhouse & Dining Room (p202)
- St John Hotel (p204
- Town Hall Hotel (p210)

Compact rooms, low prices
- 'Tiny' rooms at Dean Street Townhouse (p202)
- Lux Pod (p198)
- 'Tiny' rooms at Shoreditch Rooms (p208)
- 'Post-supper' rooms at St John Hotel (p204)

Best hostels
- Clink78 (p201)
- YHA London Central (p207)

ESSENTIALS

(microwave, sink), room sizes aren't bad (floor-to-ceiling windows help them feel bigger) and there's a handsomely vertiginous atrium, into which you peer down on the restaurant from infrequent glass lifts. The huge new Park Plaza Westminster Bridge has now opened just across the road.

Premier Inn London County Hall

County Hall, Belvedere Road, SE1 7PB (0871 527 8648, www.premierinn. com). Waterloo tube/rail. **££**.

A position right by the London Eye (p62) and friendly, efficient staff make this refurbished chain hotel the acceptable face of budget convenience. Check-in is quick; rooms are spacious, clean and warm, with comfortable beds and decent bathrooms with good showers, although some are quite dark. Buffet-style breakfast is extra and wireless internet access costs £10 a day.

Westminster & St James's

Eccleston Square Hotel

NEW *37 Eccleston Square, SW1V 1PB (3489 1000, www.ecclestonsquare hotel.com). Pimlico tube or Victoria tube/rail.* **£££**.

This Grade II-listed Georgian house has been transformed to the tune of £6.5m into an ultra-modern boutique hotel. The focus is on high-spec technology – with 46-inch 3D flatscreens, an iPad2 to control the room environment and electronically adjustable Hastens beds in each of the 39 rooms.

Haymarket

1 Suffolk Place, SW1Y 4BP (7470 4000, www.firmdale.com). Piccadilly Circus tube. **££££**.

A terrific addition to Kit Kemp's Firmdale portfolio, this block-size building was designed by John Nash, the architect of Regency London. The public spaces are a delight, with

Kemp's trademark combination of contemporary arty surprises (a giant lightbulb over the library's chessboard, a gothic little paper-cut of layered skulls above the free afternoon canapés) and impossible-to-leave, acid green, plump, floral sofas. Wow-factors include the bling basement swimming pool and bar (shiny sofas, twinkly roof) and the couldn't-be-more central location.

Trafalgar

2 Spring Gardens, Westminster, SW1A 2TS (7870 2900, www.thetrafalgar. com). Charing Cross tube/rail. **£££**.

In an imposing building, the Trafalgar is a Hilton – but you'd hardly notice. The mood is young and dynamic at what was the chain's first 'concept' hotel. To the right of the open reception is the cocktail bar, with DJs most nights, while breakfast downstairs is accompanied by gentle live music. The good-sized rooms (a few corner suites look into Trafalgar Square) have a masculine feel, with white walls and walnut furniture.

South Kensington & Chelsea

B+B Belgravia

64-66 Ebury Street, Belgravia, SW1W 9QD (7259 8570, www.bb-belgravia. com). Victoria tube/rail. **££**.

B+B Belgravia have taken the B&B experience to a new level, although you pay a bit more for the privilege of staying somewhere with a cosy lounge that's full of white and black contemporary furnishings. It's sophisticated and fresh without being hard-edged, and there are all kinds of goodies to make you feel at home: an espresso machine for 24/7 caffeine, an open fireplace, newspapers and DVDs.

Gore

190 Queen's Gate, South Kensington, SW7 5EX (7584 6601, www.gorehotel. com). South Kensington tube. **££££**.

ESSENTIALS

Price Points

Chain hotels aren't covered in this chapter, unless they're especially well located (like the **Premier Inn London County Hall**, see p197), or unusually praiseworthy. This is simply because the internal logic of chain hotels is that one should be as similar as possible to another, with reliability one major virtue – and price the other: you can find double rooms for around £100 at **Holiday Inn** and **Holiday Inn Express** (www.ichotelsgroup.com), **Ibis** (www.ibishotel.com) and **Travelodge** (www.travelodge.co.uk).

A relatively new development has been the 'no frills' approach – very low rates, with nothing inessential included. Airline-offshoot **EasyHotel** (www.easyhotel.com) was the first to follow this road, but it now has a challenger: the first British hotel from **Tune** (www.tunehotels.com) is located not far inland from the South Bank, across the river from the Houses of Parliament. Rooms are usually around £50 a night. If you've got an awkward departure time from Gatwick or Heathrow, consider the neat and funky 'pod' rooms at a **Yotel** (www.yotel.com). A four-hour stay will cost £45.

A more traditional approach to budget accommodation can be found in London's hostels. **Clink78** (p201) sets the bar high, with an urban chic aesthetic. The smaller, quieter **Clink261** (261-265 Gray's Inn Road, 7833 9400) is nearby. And the **YHA London Central** (p207) is, to put it simply, one of the best hostels in town.

This fin-de-siècle period piece was founded by descendants of Captain Cook in two grand Victorian town houses. The lobby and staircase are close hung with old paintings, and the bedrooms all have carved oak beds, sumptuous drapes and old books. The suites are spectacular: the Tudor Room has a huge stone-faced fireplace and a minstrels' gallery; tragedy queens love the Venus room, with Judy Garland's old bed and replica ruby slippers.

Halkin

Halkin Street, Belgravia, SW1X 7DJ (7333 1000, www.halkin.como.bz). Hyde Park Corner tube. **££££**.
Gracious and discreet behind a Georgian-style façade, Christina Ong's first hotel (a sister to the more famous Metropolitan) was well ahead of the East-meets-West design trend when it opened in 1991 and its subtle marriage of European luxury and oriental serenity looks more current than hotels half its age. Off curving black corridors, each room has a touchscreen bedside console to control everything from the 'Do not disturb' sign to the air-con.

Lanesborough

1 Lanesborough Place, Knightsbridge, SW1X 7TA (7259 5599, www.lanesborough.com). Hyde Park Corner tube. **££££**.
The Lanesborough was impressively redeveloped in the 1990s. Originally an 1820s Greek Revival hospital building, its luxurious guest rooms are traditionally decorated (antique furniture, Carrera-marble bathrooms) but with electronic keypads to change the air-con or call the 24hr room service. Rates include high-speed internet, movies and calls within the EU and to the US; complimentary personalised business cards state you are resident here.

Lux Pod

38 Gloucester Road, South Kensington, SW7 4QT (7460 3171, www.theluxpod.com). Gloucester Road tube. **££**.

This little hideaway is the pride and joy of its owner, Judith Abraham, with many of the features purpose-designed. Little is the operative word: it's a tiny space that ingeniously packs in a bathroom, slide-top kitchenette and lounge, with the comfy bed high up above the bathroom and accessible only by a heavy ladder. All is shiny and modern, and the room is packed with gadgets and high-style details. The tight space is ideal for one, a little bit fiddly to get round for two, but terrific fun for any design fan, tech-geek or traveller bored of samey hotels.

Morgan House

120 Ebury Street, Belgravia, SW1W 9QQ (7730 2384, www.morganhouse. co.uk). Pimlico tube or Victoria tube/ rail. **£**.
The Morgan has the understated charm of the old family home of a posh but unpretentious English friend: a pleasing mix of nice old wooden or traditional iron beds, pretty floral curtains and coverlets in subtle hues, the odd chandelier or big gilt mirror over original mantelpieces, padded wicker chairs and sinks in every bedroom. Though there's no guest lounge, guests can sit in the little patio garden.

Number Sixteen

16 Sumner Place, South Kensington, SW7 3EG (7589 5232, www.firmdale. com). South Kensington tube. **£££**.
This may be Firmdale's most affordable hotel, but there's no slacking in style – witness the fresh flowers and origami-ed birdbook decorations in the comfy drawing room, with its inviting fireplace. Bedrooms are generously sized, bright and light, and carry the Kit Kemp trademark mix of bold and traditional. By the time you finish breakfast in the sweet and calming conservatory, which looks out on the delicious back garden with its central water feature, you'll have forgotten you're in the city.

West End

22 York Street

22 York Street, Marylebone, W1U 6PX (7224 2990, www.22yorkstreet.co.uk). Baker Street tube. **££**.
Imagine one of those bohemian French country houses you see in *Elle Decor* – all pale pink lime-washed walls, wooden floors and quirky antiques. That's the feel of this graceful, unpretentious bed and breakfast. There's no sign on the door and the sense of staying in a hospitable home continues when you're offered coffee in the spacious breakfast room-cum-kitchen with its curved communal table. Many of the rooms have en suite baths.

45 Park Lane

NEW *45 Park Lane, Mayfair, W1K 1PN (7493 4545, www.45parklane.com). Green Park or Hyde Park Corner tube.* **££££**.
A new hotel from the Dorchester Collection opened in late 2011. Situated directly across from the stately entrance of the Dorchester, 45 will feel very different from its predecessor: on a site that used to be the Playboy Club, its decor is more retro-modern and masculine than its elder sister. Of the (45, naturally) rooms, Premium and above will have fine views of Hyde Park. Star American chef Wolfgang Puck is in charge of the hotel's Cut restaurant and bar.

Academy Hotel

21 Gower Street, Bloomsbury, WC1E 6HG (7631 4115, www.theeton collection.com). Goodge Street tube. **£££**.
The Academy goes for the country intellectual look to suit Bloomsbury's studious yet decadent history. It's made up of five Georgian townhouses, and provides in all its rooms a tranquil generosity of space that's echoed in the Georgian squares sitting serenely between the arterial traffic rush of Gower Street and Tottenham Court

45 Park Lane p199

Road. There's a restrained country-house style in the summery florals and checks and sophistication in the handsome, more plainly furnished suites. The library and conservatory open on to fragrant walled gardens where drinks and breakfast are served in summer.

Charlotte Street Hotel

15-17 Charlotte Street, Fitzrovia, W1T 1RJ (7806 2000, www.firmdale.com). Goode Street or Tottenham Court Road tube. **££££**.

This gorgeous Firmdale hotel is a fine exponent of Kit Kemp's fusion of traditional and avant-garde – you won't believe it was once a dental hospital. Public rooms contain Bloomsbury Set paintings (Duncan Grant, Vanessa Bell), while the bedrooms mix English understatement with bold decorative flourishes. Huge beds and trademark polished granite bathrooms are suitably indulgent, and some rooms have incredibly high ceilings. The bar-restaurant buzzes with media types, for whom the screening room must feel like a home comfort.

Claridge's

55 Brook Street, Mayfair, W1K 4HR (7629 8860, www.claridges.co.uk). Bond Street tube. **££££**.

Claridge's is sheer class and pure atmosphere, its signature art deco redesign still dazzling. Photographs of Churchill and sundry royals grace the grand foyer, as does an absurdly over-the-top Dale Chihuly chandelier. Without departing too far from the traditional, Claridge's bars and restaurant are actively fashionable – Gordon Ramsay is the in-house restaurateur, and the A-listers can gather for champers and sashimi in the bar. The rooms divide evenly between deco and Victorian style, with period touches balanced by high-tech bedside panels.

Clink78

78 King's Cross Road, King's Cross, WC1X 9QG (7183 9400, www.clink hostels.com). King's Cross tube/rail. **£**.

In a former courthouse, the Clink sets the bar high for hosteldom. There's the setting: the original wood-panelled lobby and courtroom where the Clash stood before the beak (now filled with backpackers surfing the web). Then there's the urban chic ethos, with new graffiti-styled decor and a refurbished bar. The smaller, quieter Clink261 (261-265 Gray's Inn Road, 7833 9400), refurbished last year, is nearby.

Connaught

Carlos Place, Mayfair, W1K 2AL (7499 7070, www.the-connaught.co.uk). Bond Street tube. **££££**.

It isn't the only London hotel to provide butlers, but there can't be many that offer 'a secured gun cabinet room' for hunting season. This is traditional British hospitality for those who love 23-carat gold leaf and stern portraits in the halls, but all mod cons in their room, down to free WiFi and flatscreens in the en suite. Both of the bars – gentleman's club cosy Coburg and cruiseship deco Connaught (p108) – and the Hélène Darroze restaurant are impressive. There's also a less atmospheric new wing, wit a swish spa and 60sq m swimming pool.

Covent Garden Hotel

10 Monmouth Street, Covent Garden, WC2H 9LF (7806 1000, www. firmdale.com). Covent Garden or Leicester Square tube. **££££**.

On the ground floor, the 1920s Paris-style Brasserie Max and its retro zinc bar continues to buzz – testament to the deserved popularity of Firmdale's snug and stylish 1996 establishment. Its Covent Garden location and tucked-away screening room ensure it still attracts starry customers, and guests needing a bit of privacy can retreat upstairs to the lovely panelled private library, with honesty bar. In the individually styled guest rooms, pin-striped wallpaper and floral upholstery are mixed with bold, contemporary elements. All round, it's a stunner.

Dean Street Townhouse & Dining Room

*69-71 Dean Street, Soho, W1D 3SE
(7434 1775, www.sohohouse.com).
Leicester Square or Piccadilly Circus
tube.* **£££**.

This is the latest winning enterprise from the people behind Soho House members' club. To one side of a buzzy ground-floor restaurant are four floors of bedrooms that run from full-size rooms with early Georgian panelling and reclaimed oak floors to half-panelled 'Tiny' rooms barely bigger than their double beds – but available for from £95. The atmosphere is gentleman's club cosy (there are cookies in a cute silver Treats container in each room), but modern types are reassured by rainforest showers, 24hr service, Roberts DAB radios, free wireless internet and big flatscreen TVs.

Dorchester

*53 Park Lane, Mayfair, W1K 1QA
(7629 8888, www.thedorchester.com).
Hyde Park Corner tube.* **££££**.

A Park Lane fixture since 1931, the Dorchester's interior is opulently classical, but its attitude is cutting-edge, with a terrific level of personal service. The hotel employs no fewer than 90 chefs at the Grill Room, Alain Ducasse and China Tang. With one of the best lobbies in town, amazing park views, state-of-the-art mod cons and a magnificently refurbished spa, it's small wonder the hotel has always welcomed film stars (from the departed Liz Taylor to Tom Cruise) and political leaders (Eisenhower planned D-Day here).

Dorset Square

NEW *39-40 Dorset Square, Marylebone,
NW1 6QN (7723 7874, www.dorset
squarehotel.co.uk). Marylebone tube/rail.*
£££.

Grown-up greys are a backdrop for splashes of orange-red and midnight blue, with bold patterns completing a sophisticated modish meets traditional look – the hallmark of owners Firmdale. The Regency townhouse has 38 comfortable, spacious bedrooms, many looking on to the leafy private square; bathrooms are in granite and glass, with Miller Harris products. Downstairs is a comfortable lounge with a fireplace and the Potting Shed restaurant and bar. This property was actually Firmdale's first hotel. Sold in 2002, the company bought it again and refurbished it, opening in June 2012.

Harlingford Hotel

*61-63 Cartwright Gdns, Bloomsbury,
WC1H 9EL (7387 1551, www.
harlingfordhotel.com). Russell Square
tube or Euston tube/rail.* **££**.

An affordable hotel with bundles of charm in the heart of Bloomsbury, the Harlingford has light airy rooms with boutique aspirations. Decor is lifted from understated sleek to quirky with the help of vibrant colour splashes from the glass bathroom fittings and the mosaic tiles. The crescent it's set in has a lovely, leafy private garden.

Hazlitt's

*6 Frith Street, Soho, W1D 3JA
(7434 1771, www.hazlittshotel.com).
Tottenham Court Road tube.* **£££**.

Four Georgian townhouses comprise this charming place, named after William Hazlitt, a spirited 18th-century essayist who died here in abject poverty. With flamboyance and staggering attention to detail the rooms evoke the Georgian era, all fireplaces, heavy fabrics, free-standing tubs and exquisitely carved half-testers, yet modern luxuries – air-con, TVs in antique cupboards, free Wi-Fi and triple-glazed windows – have also been attended to. It gets creakier and more crooked the higher you go, culminating in enchanting garret single rooms.

Jenkins Hotel

*45 Cartwright Gardens, Bloomsbury,
WC1H 9EH (7387 2067, www.jenkins
hotel.demon.co.uk). Russell Square tube
or Euston tube/rail.* **£**.

Dorcherster

This well-to-do Georgian beauty has been a hotel since the 1920s. It still has an atmospheric, antique air, although the rooms have mod cons enough – TVs, mini-fridges, tea and coffee. Its looks have earned it a role in Agatha Christie's Poirot, but it's not chintzy, just quite floral in the bedspread and curtain department. The breakfast room is handsome, with snowy cotton tablecloths and Windsor chairs.

Montagu Place

2 Montagu Place, Marylebone, W1H 2ER (7467 2777, www.montagu-place.co.uk). Baker Street tube. £££.
A stylish small hotel in a pair of Grade II-listed Georgian townhouses, catering primarily for the midweek business traveller. All guestrooms have pocket-sprung beds, as well as cafetières and flatscreen TVs (DVD players are available from reception). The look here is boutique-hotel sharp, except for an uneasy overlap of bar and reception – though you can simply get a drink and retire to the graciously modern lounge.

Morgan

24 Bloomsbury Street, Bloomsbury, WC1B 3QJ (7636 3735, www.morgan hotel.co.uk). Tottenham Court Road tube. ££.
This brilliantly located, comfortable budget hotel looks better than it has for a while after recent renovations. The rooms have ditched floral for neutral, and are equipped with free wireless, voicemail, air-conditioning and flat-screen televisions with Freeview. A slap-up English breakfast is served in a good-looking room with wood panelling, decorated with London prints and blue-and-white china plates.

No.5 Maddox Street

5 Maddox Street, Mayfair, W1S 2QD (7647 0200, www.living-rooms.co.uk). Oxford Circus tube. £££.
A bit different, this: for your money, you get a chic, self-contained apartment. Shut the discreet brown front door, climb the stairs and flop into a well-furnished home from home with all mod cons, including new flatscreen TVs. Each apartment has a fully

ESSENTIALS

equipped kitchen, but room service will shop for you in addition to the usual hotel services. The East-meets-West decor is classic 1990s minimalist, but bright and clean after refurbishment.

One Aldwych

1 Aldwych, on the Strand, WC2B 4RH (7300 1000, www.onealdwych.com). Covent Garden or Temple tube, or Charing Cross tube/rail. **££££**.
You only have to push through the front door and enter the breathtaking Lobby Bar to know you're in for a treat. Despite its weighty history – the 1907 building was designed by the men behind the Ritz – One Aldwych is thoroughly modern, from Frette linen through bathroom mini-TVs to environmentally friendly loo flushes. The location is perfect for Theatreland, but the cosy screening room and swimming pool may keep you indoors.

Rough Luxe

1 Birkenhead Street, King's Cross, WC1H 8BA (7837 5338, www.rough luxe.co.uk). King's Cross tube/rail. **££**.
In a bit of King's Cross that's choked with ratty B&Bs, this Grade II-listed property has walls artfully distressed, torn wallpaper, signature works of art, old-fashioned TVs that barely work and even retains the sign for the hotel that preceded Rough Luxe: 'Number One Hotel'. Each room has free wireless internet, but otherwise have totally different characters. It's all rather hip and fun, but there is also has rather a hand-made feel – the sleeping arrangements are a classy take on on a sofa bed, pulled out by your host each night. The owners are more than happy to chat over a bottle of wine in the back courtyard where a great breakfast is served.

St John Hotel

1 Leicester Street, off Leicester Square, WC2H 7BL (7251 0848, www.stjohn hotellondon.com). Leicester Square or Piccadilly Circus tube. **£££**.

When one of London's finest restaurants, St John (p152), decides to move into the hotel trade, it's worth taking notice. Co-owner Trevor Gulliver described the 16-room hotel as 'that rare thing – a hotel where people would actually want to eat'. To which end, the first floor, ground floor and basement are given over to a bar and restaurant (p135); above them are 15 rooms and a three-bedroom rooftop suite – the bathroom's round window looks west to Big Ben. The decor is in keeping with the white, masculine, minimalist style of the original Smithfield venue.

St Pancras Renaissance

Euston Road, King's Cross, NW1 2AR (7841 3540, www.marriott.com). King's Cross tube/rail. **££££**.
A landmark hotel in every sense of the word, the St Pancras Renaissance is the born-again Midland Grand, the pioneering railway hotel designed into the station's imposing Gothic Revival frontage. It opened in 1873 but fell into disuse in the 20th century (except for appearances as a Harry Potter backdrop and in the Spice Girls' 'Wannabe' video, among other screen roles). The Renaissance group has done a beautiful and painstaking job of restoring it to its breathtaking, Grade 1-listed best while adding modern comforts. The 120 rooms and suites in the historic hotel (there's a new wing, too) have high ceilings, original features and awesome views over the station concourse or forecourt. Facilities are high-spec – Bose stereo, Nespresso machines, REN toiletries, marble baths – furniture modern classic and design sensitive to the context, re-using motifs from the original decor in the carpets, for example. Public areas (for the Ticket Office, see p124) and the gorgeous grand staircase, are similarly splendid. See also box right.

Sanderson

50 Berners Street, Fitzrovia, W1T 3NG (7300 1400, www.morganshotelgroup. com). Oxford Circus tube. **££££**.

Renaissance Review

You don't have to stay in the gorgeous St Pancras Renaissance (left) in order to appreciate its beauty (though admittedly it would be nice). In recognition of its considerable architectural and historical worth as an exponent of the Victorian Gothic style and as pioneer of the railway hotel, the Renaissance employs two historians and guides. Royden Stock and Melissa Woollard leads regular tours of the uniquely beautiful public areas of what was known as the the St Pancras Grand in its first incarnartion – and if you're lucky, he'll also let you sneak a peek into the luxury rooms and suites.

Royden has been associated with the building for 15 years, dating back to before its lavish £150 million renovation (it launched on 5 May 2011, 138 years to the day after its original opening), so he knows what he's talking about, and does so with passion, expertise and humour.

En route you'll learn how the architect, George Gilbert Scott, poured his frustrated creative energies into the project, having been overruled on his designs for the Foreign and Commonwealth Office; about the unique demands of station architecture both past and present; and how the hotel pioneered, among other developments, the revolving door, the electric lift and the women's smoking room.

To book, contact by phone on 7841 3540, or via email at royden.stock@renaissance hotels.com). Tours cost £20 per person.

ESSENTIALS

This Schrager/Starck statement creation takes clinical chic to new heights. The only touch of colour in our room was a naïve landscape painting nailed to the ceiling over the silver sleigh bed. Otherwise, it's all flowing white net drapes, glass cabinets and retractable screens. The residents-only Purple Bar sports a button-backed purple leather ceiling and fabulous cocktails; the 'billiard room' has a purple-topped pool table and weird tribal adaptations of classic dining-room furniture.

Savoy

Strand, WC2R 0EU (7836 4343, www.fairmont.com). Covent Garden or Embankment tube, or Charing Cross tube/rail. ££££.

The superluxe, Grade II-listed Savoy finally reopened in late 2010 after more than £100m of renovations – the numerous delays testimony to the difficulty of recreating a listed building, loved by generations of visitors for its discreet mix of Edwardian neo-classical and art deco, as a modern luxury hotel. Built in 1889 to put up theatregoers from Richard D'Oyly Carte's Gilbert & Sullivan shows in the attached theatre (p148), the Savoy is the hotel from which Monet painted the Thames, where Vivien Leigh met Laurence Olivier, where Londoners met the martini. There's topiary at the famous cul-de-sac entrance, a new tearoom with glass-roofed conservatory and the leather counter of the new Beaufort champagne bar is set on a former stage for big bands, but the Savoy Grill (p144) and American Bar have barely changed. Seamless service whisks you to your room almost before you notice you've arrived.

Soho Hotel

4 Richmond Mews, W1D 3DH (7559 3000, www.firmdale.com). Piccadilly Circus or Tottenham Court Road tube. ££££.

You'd hardly know you were in the heart of Soho once you're inside Firmdale's edgiest hotel: the place is wonderfully quiet, with what was once a car park now feeling like a converted loft building. The big bedrooms exhibit a contemporary edge, with modern furniture, industrial-style windows and nicely planned mod cons (digital radios as well as flatscreen TVs), although they're also classically Kit Kemp with bold stripes, traditional florals, plump sofas, oversized bedheads and upholstered tailor's dummies. The quiet drawing room and other public spaces feature groovy colours while Refuel, the loungey bar and restaurant, has an open kitchen and, yes, a car-themed mural.

Sumner

54 Upper Berkeley Street, W1H 7QR (7723 2244, www.thesumner.com). Marble Arch tube. ££.

The Sumner's cool, deluxe looks have earned it many fans – and several awards. You won't be at all surprised: from the soft dove and slatey greys of the lounge and halls, you move up to glossily spacious accommodation with brilliant walk-in showers. The breakfast room feels soft and sunny, with a lovely, delicate buttercup motif and vibrant Arne Jacobsen chairs, whereas the stylishly moody front sitting room is a cosy gem.

W London Leicester Square

10 Wardour Street, Leicester Square, W1D 6QF (7758 1000, www.wlondon. co.uk). Leicester Square tube. ££££.

The old Swiss Centre building on the edge of Leicester Square has been demolished and in its place has risen the UK's first W Hotel. The W brand has made its name with a series of hip hotels around the world that offer glamorous bars, classy food and functional but spacious rooms. The London W is no exception: Spice Market gets its first UK site within the hotel; Wyld is a large nightclub/bar space aiming to become the Met Bar for a new decade, and the W lounge aims to bring New York's cocktail lounge ethos to London. The rooms – 192 of them, across ten storeys – are well-equipped and decent-sized, and SWEAT (the hotel's state-of-the-art fitness facility) offers fine views over Soho. Also of note is the W's gob-smacking exterior: the entire hotel is veiled in translucent glass, which is lit in different colours through the day.

YHA London Central

104 Bolsover Street, Fitzrovia, W1W 5NU (0845 371 9154, www.yha.org. uk). Great Portland Street tube. **££.**
The Youth Hostel Association's newest hostel is one of its best – as well as being one of the best hostels in London. The friendly and well-informed receptionists are stationed at a counter to the left of the entrance, in a substantial café-bar area. The basement contains a well-equipped kitchen and washing area; above it five floors of clean, neatly designed rooms, many en suite. Residents have 24hr access (by individual key cards), there's free wireless internet and the quiet location is an easy walk from most of the West End.

The City

Andaz Liverpool Street

40 Liverpool Street, EC2M 7QN 7961 1234, www.london.liverpoolstreet. andaz.com). Liverpool Street tube/ rail. **£££.**
A faded railway hotel until its £70m Conran overhaul in 2000, the red-brick Great Eastern became, in 2007 the first of Hyatt's new Andaz portfolio. The new approach means out with gimmicky menus, closet-sized minibars and even the lobby reception desk, and in with down-to-earth, well-informed service and eco-friendliness. The bedrooms still wear style-magazine uniform – Eames chairs, Frette linens – but free services (local calls, wireless internet, healthy minibar) are an appreciated touch.

Apex London Wall

7-9 Copthall Avenue, EC2R 7NJ (7562 3030, www.apexhotels.co.uk). Bank tube or Moorgate tube/rail. **££.**
The mini-chain's newest London hotel shares the virtues of its predecessor (Apex City of London, 1 Seething Lane, 7702 2020). The service is obliging, the rooms are crisply designed with all mod cons, and there are comforting details – rubber duck in the impressive bathrooms, free jelly beans, free local calls. From the suites, a terrace peers into offices, but the view from the restaurant and breakfast room – of the flamboyant sculptures on the business institute next door – is as good.

Boundary

2-4 Boundary Street, E2 7DD (7729 1051, www.theboundary.co.uk). Liverpool Street tube/rail or Shoreditch High Street rail. **£££.**
In a converted warehouse, Conran's latest combines restaurant, rooftop bar, ground-floor café (Albion, p176) and excellent hotel rooms, the whole establishment clearly a labour of love. Each room has a wet room and hand-made bed, but are otherwise coolly individual, with classic furniture and original art. The five split-level suites range in style from the bright and sea-salt fresh Beach to a new take on Victoriana, while the remaining rooms are themed by design style: Mies van der Rohe, Shaker and so on. Good rates too on a Sunday.

Fox & Anchor

115 Charterhouse Street, EC1M 6AA (0845 347 0100, www.foxandanchor. com). Barbican tube or Farringdon tube/rail. **££.**
No more than a few atmospheric, well-appointed and luxurious rooms above a bustling, darkly panelled pub, this has been one of our most enjoyable stays in London. Each en suite room differs, but the high-spec facilities (big flatscreens, clawfoot bath, drench shower) and quirky attention to detail (bottles of ale in the minibar, 'Nursing

Shoreditch Rooms

hangover' signs to hang out if you want some privacy) are common throughout. Expect some clanking market noise in the early mornings.

Hoxton Hotel

81 Great Eastern Street, EC2A 3HU (7550 1000, www.hoxtonhotels.com). Old Street tube/rail. **££.**

Everything you've heard is true. First, there's the hip location. Then there are the great design values: the foyer is a sort of postmodern country lodge (with stag's head) and rooms that are small but well thought-out and full of nice touches (Frette linens, free fresh milk in the mini fridge, free mini breakfast hung on your door handle in the morning). Above all, it's the budget-airline pricing system, by which you might catch a £1-a-night ultra-bargain – but, assuming you can book far enough ahead to beat demand, ensures you get a great-value room.

Malmaison

Charterhouse Square, EC1M 6AH (7012 3700, www.malmaison.com). Barbican tube. **£££.**

It's part of a chain, but the Malmaison is a charming hotel, set in a cobblestone square near the lively restaurants and bars of Smithfield Market. The reception is stylish with its lilac-and-cream checked floor, exotic plants and petite champagne bar; purples, dove-grey and black wood dominate the rooms, where you'll find free broadband and creative lighting. The gym and a subterranean brasserie complete the picture.

Rookery

12 Peter's Lane, Cowcross Street, EC1M 6DS (7336 0931, www.rookery hotel.com). Farringdon tube/rail. **£££.**

The front door of the Rookery is satisfyingly hard to find, especially when the streets are teeming with Fabric (p158) devotees (the front rooms can be noisy on these nights). Once inside, guests enjoy a warren of creaky rooms, individually decorated in the style of a Georgian townhouse: clawfoot baths, elegant four-posters. The split-level Rook's Nest suite has views of St Paul's (p162). At the rear, a cosy honesty bar opens on to a sweet little patio.

Shoreditch Rooms

Ebor Street, E1 6AW (7739 5040, www.shoreditchhouse.com). Shoreditch High Street rail. **££.**

The most recent hotel from the Soho House members' club (see also Dean Street Townhouse, p202) might be the best, perfectly catching the local atmosphere with its unfussy, slightly retro design. The rooms feel a bit like urban beach huts, with pastel-coloured tongue-and-groove and swing doors to the en suite showers. They feel fresh and comfortable, even though they're furnished with little more than a bed, a DAB radio and old-fashioned phone, and a solid dresser (minibar, hairdryer and treats within, flatscreen TV on top). Guests get access to the eating, drinking and fitness facilities on the premises (there's an excellent rooftop pool) in the members' club next door. 'Tiny' rooms start from just £75.

Threadneedles

5 Threadneedle Street, EC2R 8AY (7657 8080, www.theeton collection.com). Bank tube/DLR. **££££**.
Threadneedles boldly slots some contemporary style into a fusty old dame of a building, formerly the grand Victorian HQ of the Midland Bank, bang next to the Bank of England and the Royal Exchange. The etched glass-domed rotunda of the lobby soars over columns over an artful array of designer furniture and shelving that looks like the dreamchild of some powerful graphics software – it's a calm space, but a stunning one. The bedrooms are individual, coherent and soothing examples of City-boy chic, in muted beige and textured tones, with limestone bathrooms. It's all well run and well thought out.

Zetter

86-88 Clerkenwell Road, EC1M 5RJ (7324 4444, www.thezetter.com). Farringdon tube/rail. **£££**.
Zetter is a fun, laid-back, modern hotel with interesting design notes, a refreshing lack of attitude, friendly staff and firm eco-credentials (such as occupancy detection systems in the bedrooms). The rooms, stacked up on five galleried storeys overlooking the intimate bar area, are smoothly functional, but cosied up with choice home comforts like hot-water bottles and old Penguin paperbacks, as well as having walk-in showers with Elemis smellies. Bistrot Bruno Loubet (p154) is thriving, and the new 13-room Townhouse – a Georgian house on the rear square – has an ace cocktail bar (p158).

Neighbourhood London

Base2Stay

25 Courtfield Gardens, Earl's Court, SW5 0PG (7244 2255, www.base 2stay.com). Earl's Court tube. **££**.
Base2Stay looks good, with its modernist limestone and taupe tones, and keeps prices low by removing inessentials: no bar, no restaurant. Instead, there's a 'kitchenette' (microwave, sink, silent mini-fridge, kettle), with all details carefully attended to (plenty of kitchenware, including corkscrew and can opener). The rooms, en suite (with power showers) and air-conditioned, are as carefully thought-out, with desks, free wireless and flatscreens, but the single/bunkbed rooms are barely wider than the beds themselves.

40 Winks

109 Mile End Road, Stepney, E1 4UJ (7790 0259, 07973 653944 mobile, www.40winks.org). Stepney Green tube. **££**. No credit cards.
Opposite a housing estate and cheap Somali diners, the flamboyantly camp and fashionable family home of an interior designer has become the B&B of choice for movie stars and fashion movers. The 'micro-boutique hotel' 40 Winks looks extraordinary (kitchen frescoes, a music room with Beatles drumkit, a lion's head tap in the bath), but each stay is made individual by owner David Carter's commitment to

ESSENTIALS

his guests. You'll feel like you're staying with an ingenious friend, rather than just renting a room.

Mayflower Hotel

26-28 Trebovir Road, Earl's Court, SW5 9NJ (7370 0991, www.mayflowergroup.co.uk). Earl's Court tube. **££.**
The Mayflower Group – the other properties are New Linden (59 Leinster Square, Bayswater, 7221 4321, www.newlinden.co.uk) and Twenty Nevern (20 Nevern Square, Earl's Court, 7565 9555, www.twentynevernsquare.co.uk) – has been leading the budget style revolution for years, but here's where the contemporary house style evolved, proving affordability can be opulently chic and perfectly equipped. Cream walls and sleek dark woods are an understated background for richly coloured fabrics and intricate wooden architectural fragments, like the lobby's imposing Jaipuri arch.

Pavilion

34-36 Sussex Gardens, Paddington, W2 1UL (7262 0905, www.pavilion hoteluk.com). Edgware Road tube or Marylebone or Paddington tube/rail. **£.**
Behind a deceptively modest façade is what could be the city's funkiest, most original hotel. A voluptuously exotic paean to excess and paint effects, the Pavilion's madly colourful themed rooms ('Highland Fling', 'Afro Honky Tonk', 'Casablanca Nights') have become a celeb-magnet and are often used for fashion shoots. Not for lovers of minimalism and 'facilities' – though it's got most of the usual necessities.

Portobello Hotel

22 Stanley Gardens, W11 2NG (7727 2777, www.portobellohotel.com). Holland Park or Notting Hill Gate tube. **£££.**
With half a century of celebrity status, the Portobello has hosted Johnny Depp, Kate Moss and Alice Cooper, who used his tub to house a boa constrictor. It remains a pleasingly unpretentious place, with a more civilised demeanour than its legend might suggest. There is now a lift to help rockers who are feeling their age up the five floors, but there's still a 24hr guest-only bar downstairs for those who don't yet feel past it. The rooms are themed – the superb basement Japanese Water Garden, for example, has an elaborate spa bath, its own private grotto and a small private garden – but all are stylishly equipped.

Stylotel

160-162 Sussex Gardens, Paddington, W2 1UD (7723 1026, www.stylotel. com). Edgware Rd tube, or Marylebone or Paddington tube/rail. **£.**
Stylotel is a retro-futurist dream: metal floors and panelling, lots of royal blue (the hall walls, the padded headboards) and pod bathrooms. But the real deal is its new bargain-priced studio and apartment (respectively, £120-£150 and £150-£200, including breakfast), designed – like the hotel – by the owner's son. These achieve real minimalist chic with sleek brushed steel or white glass wall panels and simply styled contemporary furniture upholstered in black or white.

Town Hall Hotel

Patriot Square, Bethnal Green, E2 9NF (7871 0460, www.townhallhotel.com). Bethnal Green tube. **£££.**
A Grade II-listed, early 20th-century town hall has been transformed into a classy aparthotel – despite its location beside a council estate. The decor is minimal, retaining many features (walnut panelling, marble, stained glass, fire hoses on old brass reels) that would be familiar to the departed bureaucrats, but jazzed up with art and a patterned aluminium 'veil' that covers the new top floor. The spacious apartments are well equipped for self-catering, but luxuries such as free wireless internet, TV/DVD players, a narrow basement swimming pool and the fine Viajante (p178) restaurant are also in place.

Getting Around

Airports

Gatwick Airport

0844 335 1802, www.gatwickairport.com. About 30 miles south of central London, off the M23.

The quickest rail link to London is the **Gatwick Express** (0845 850 1530, www.gatwickexpress.com) to Victoria; it runs 3.30am-12.30am daily and takes 30mins. Tickets cost £17.90 single or £30.50 open return (valid for 30 days).

Southern (0845 748 4950, www.southernrailway.com) also runs trains to Victoria, every 5-10mins (every 30mins 1am-4am). It takes about 35mins, and costs £12.50 single.

Thameslink trains (0845 748 4950; www.firstcapitalconnect.co.uk) run to St Pancras. Tickets cost £9.40 single or £17 for a 30-day open return.

A **taxi** to central London takes a bit over an hour and costs around £100.

Heathrow Airport

0844 335 1801, www.heathrowairport.com. About 15 miles west of central London, off the M4.

The **Heathrow Express** (0845 600 1515, www.heathrowexpress.co.uk) runs to Paddington every 15mins (5.10am-11.25pm daily) and takes 15-20mins. The train can be boarded from Terminals 1 and 3 (Heathrow Central tube station) or Terminal 5 (which has its own tube station); from Terminal 4, get a shuttle to Heathrow Central. Tickets are £18 single, £32 return (£1 less online, £2 more on board).

The journey by **tube** into central London is longer but cheaper. The 50-60min Piccadilly Line ride into central London costs £5 one way (less with Oyster, p213). Trains run every few minutes from about 5am to 11.57pm daily (6am-11pm Sun).

The **Heathrow Connect** (0845 678 6975, www.heathrowconnect.com) rail service offers direct access to stations including Ealing Broadway and Paddington. The trains run every half-hour, terminating at Heathrow Central; from there to Terminal 4 get the free shuttle; between Central and Terminal 5, there's free use of the Heathrow Express. A single to Paddington is £8.50, an open return £16.50.

By road, **National Express** (0871 781 8181, www.nationalexpress.com) runs coaches daily to London Victoria (90mins, 5am-9.35pm daily) from Heathrow Central bus terminal every 20-30mins. It's £5.50 for a single or £9 for a return. A **taxi** to central London costs £45-£65 and takes 30-60mins.

London City Airport

7646 0000, www.londoncityairport.com. About 9 miles east of central London.

The **Docklands Light Railway** now has a stop for London City Airport, which is often less chaotic than the city's other airports. The journey to Bank station in the City takes around 20mins, and trains run 5.30am-12.30am Mon-Sat or 7.30am-11.30pm Sun. A **taxi** costs roughly £30 to central London, but less to the City or Canary Wharf.

Luton Airport

01582 405100, www.london-luton.com. About 30 miles north of central London, J10 off the M1.

A short bus ride links the airport to Luton Airport Parkway station, from which **Thameslink** trains (0845 748 4950, www.firstcapitalconnect.co.uk) depart for stations including St Pancras and City, 35-45mins. Trains leave every 15mins (hourly through the night) and cost £12.50 single and £21.50 return.

By coach, Luton to Victoria takes 60-90mins. **Green Line** (0870 608 7261, www.greenline.co.uk) runs a 24hr service (£15 single, £22 return). A **taxi** to central London costs £70-£80.

Stansted Airport

0870 000 0303, www.stanstedairport. com. About 35 miles north-east of central London, J8 off the M11.

The **Stansted Express** (0845 748 4950, www.stanstedexpress.com) runs to Liverpool Street station, taking 40-45mins and leaving every 15mins. Tickets are £21 single, £29.80 return.

The **Airbus** (0871 781 8181, www. nationalexpress.com) is one of several coach services; it takes at least 80mins to reach Victoria, with coaches running roughly every 30mins (24hrs daily), more frequently at peak times. A single is £10.50, a return is £17.50. A **taxi** to central London costs around £100.

Arriving by coach

Coaches run by National Express (0871 781 8181, www.nationalexpress.com), the biggest coach company in the UK, arrive at **Victoria Coach Station** (164 Buckingham Palace Road, SW1W 9TP, 0843 222 1234, www.tfl.gov.uk).

Arriving by rail

Trains from mainland Europe run by Eurostar (0843 218 6186, www. eurostar.com) arrive at **St Pancras International** station (7843 7688, www.stpancras.com).

Mainline stations

For times and prices, call 0845 748 4950 or visit www.nationalrail.co.uk. All the major stations are served by the tube.

Public transport

Travel Information Centres give help with the tube, buses and Docklands Light (DLR; p216). Call 0843 222 1234 or visit www.tfl.gov.uk/ journeyplanner for more information.
Camden Direct *Camden Town Hall, Argyle Street (opposite King's Cross St Pancras).* **Open** 9am-5pm Mon-Fri.

Euston rail station Open 7.15am-9.15pm Mon-Fri; 7.15am-6.15pm Sat; 8.15am-6.15pm Sun.
Heathrow Terminals 1, 2 & 3 tube station Open 7.15am-9pm daily.
Liverpool Street tube station Open 7.15am-9.15pm Mon-Sat; 8.15am-8pm Sun.
Piccadilly Circus tube station Open 9.15am-7pm daily.
Victoria rail station Open 7.15am-9.15pm Mon-Sat; 8.15am-8.15pm Sun.

London Underground

Delays are fairly common, with lines closing most weekends for engineering works. Trains are hot and crowded in rush hour (8-9.30am, 4.30-7pm Mon-Fri). Even so, the colour-coded lines of the Underground ('the tube') are the quickest way to get about. Underground, Overground and DLR lines are shown on the **tube map** on the back flap.

Using the Underground

Tube and DLR fares are based on a system of six zones, stretching 12 miles from the central London. A flat **cash fare** of £4 per journey applies across zones 1-4 on the tube, £5 for zones 1-6; customers save up to £2.30 per journey with a pre-pay Oyster card (p213). Anyone caught with neither ticket nor Oyster will be fined £25.

To enter and exit the tube using an **Oyster card**, touch it to the yellow reader, which opens the gate. You must also touch the card to the reader when you exit, or you'll be charged a higher fare when you next use your card. On certain lines, you'll see a pink reader (the 'validator') – touch it in addition to the yellow entry/exit readers and on some routes it will reduce your fare.

To enter using a **paper ticket**, place it in the slot with the black magnetic strip facing down, then pull it out of the top to open the gates. Exit in the same way; tickets for single journeys will be retained by the gate on final exit.

Oyster cards

A pre-paid smartcard, Oyster is the cheapest way of getting round on buses, tubes and the DLR. You can get Oyster cards from www.tfl.gov.uk/oyster, Travel Information Centres (p215), tube stations, and some newsagents and rail stations. A £3 refundable deposit is payable on new cards. A tube journey in zone 1 using Oyster pay-as-you-go costs £1.90; single journeys from zones 1-6 using Oyster are £4.50 (6.30am-9.30pm Mon-Fri) or £2.70 (all other times, including public holidays).

Travelcards

If you're only taking the tube, DLR, buses and trams, using Oyster to pay as you go will always be capped at the same price as an equivalent Day Travelcard. However, if you're also using National Rail services, Oyster may not be accepted: opt instead for a Day Travelcard, a ticket that allows travel across all the London networks.

Anytime Day Travelcards can be used all day. They cost £8 for zones 1-2, up to £15 for zones 1-6. Tickets are valid for journeys started by 4.30am the next day. The **Off-Peak Day Travelcard** is only for travel after 9.30am Mon-Fri (all day for weekends and public holidays). It costs £6.60 for zones 1-2, £8 for zones 1-6.

Travelcards are also available for longer periods, in which case they can be put on to your Oyster. If you're staying in London for a week, a weekly Travelcard will probably be cheaper than pay-as-you-go.

Travelling with children

Under-5s travel free on buses and trams. Those aged **5-10** also travel free, but need to obtain a 5-10 Zip Oyster photocard if not travelling with an adult. An 11-15 Oyster photocard is needed by **under-16s** to pay as they go on the tube/DLR and to buy child-fare 7-Day, monthly or longer period Travelcards. The card allows them to travel free on buses and trams. Those aged 16-18 can get child fares with a 16+ Zip Oyster photocard. For details, see www.tfl.gov.uk/fares or call 0845 330 9876.

Visitors can apply for a **photocard** (www.tfl.gov.uk/photocard) in advance. Photocards are not required for adult rate 7-Day Travelcards, Bus Passes or for any adult rate Travelcard or Bus Pass charged on an Oyster card.

Underground timetable

Tube trains run daily from around 5am (except Sunday, when they start an hour or so later depending on the line, and Christmas Day, when there's no service). You shouldn't have to wait more than ten minutes for a train; during peak times, services should run every two or three minutes. Times of last trains vary; they're usually around 12.30am (11.30pm on Sun). The tube runs all night only on New Year's Eve; otherwise, get the night bus (right).

Docklands Light Railway

DLR trains (7363 9700, www.tfl.gov.uk/dlr) run from Bank station (on the Central tube line) or Tower Gateway, close to Tower Hill tube (Circle and District lines). At Westferry station, the line splits east and south via Island Gardens to Greenwich and Lewisham; a change at Poplar can take you north to Stratford. The easterly branch forks after Canning Town either to Beckton or, via London City Airport (p214), to Woolwich Arsenal. Trains run 5.30am-12.30am daily. With very few exceptions, adult single **fares** on the DLR are exactly the same as for the Underground (p215).

Rail & Overground

Independently run commuter services coordinated by National Rail (0845 748

4950, www.nationalrail.co.uk) leave from the city's main rail stations. Visitors heading to south London, or to more remote destinations such as Hampton Court (p188), will need to use these overground services. Travelcards are valid within the right zones, but not all routes accept Oyster pay-as-you-go.

The orbital **London Overground** line continues to open piecemeal. It already runs through north London from Stratford in the east to Richmond in the south-west, and new spurs connect Willesden Junction in the north-west to Clapham Junction in the south-west, Gospel Oak in the north to Barking in the east, and north from New Cross through Shoreditch High Street, Dalston Junction and Highbury & Islington. Trains run about every 10mins. We've listed Overground stations as 'rail', but the trains all accept Oyster and prices are, almost always, the same as the Underground (p212).

Buses

All London buses are now low-floor vehicles accessible to wheelchair-users and passengers with buggies. The only exceptions are Heritage Route 9 and 15 Routemasters. The first updated, redesigned Routemasters came into service in early 2012 (see box p78).

You must have a ticket or valid pass before boarding any bus in zone 1 and 'bendy buses' anywhere in the city. You can buy a **ticket** (or 1-Day Bus Pass) from machines at bus stops, but they're often not working; it's better to travel with an Oyster or Travelcard (p213). Using Oyster pay-as-you-go costs £1.35 a trip; your total daily payment, regardless of how many journeys you make, will be capped at £4. Paying cash costs £2.20 single. Under-16s travel for free (but must use an Oyster photocard, p213). A 7-Day Bus Pass gives unlimited bus and tram travel for £17.80. Inspectors patrol buses at random; if you don't have a ticket, you may be fined £50.

Many buses operate 24 hours a day, seven days a week. There are also some special **night buses** with an 'N' prefix, which run from about 11pm to 6am. Most night services run every 15-30mins, but busier routes run a service around every 10mins. They all feel a lot less frequent after a heavy night.

Water transport

Most river services operate every 20-60mins from 7am to 9pm, more often and later in the summer months; see the website www.tfl.gov.uk. A River Roamer day ticket with **Thames Clippers** (0870 781 5049, www. thamesclippers.com), which runs a service between Embankment Pier and Royal Arsenal Woolwich Pier, boarded at Blackfriars, Bankside, London Bridge, Canary Wharf and Greenwich, costs £12.60; there are reductions if you hold an Oyster or travelcard.

Taxis & minicabs

If a **black cab**'s orange 'For Hire' sign is lit, it can be hailed. If it stops, the cabbie must take you to your destination if it's within seven miles. It can be hard to find an empty cab, especially just after the pubs close. Fares rise after 8pm on weekdays and at weekends. You can book black cabs from the 24hr **Taxi One-Number** (0871 871 8710; a £2 booking fee applies, plus 12.5% on credit cards), **Radio Taxis** (7272 0272) and **Dial-a-Cab** (7253 5000; credit cards only, booking fee £2).

Minicabs (saloon cars) are often cheaper than black cabs, but only use licensed firms (look for a disc in the front and rear windows), and avoid anyone who illegally touts for business in the street: such drivers may be unlicensed, uninsured and dangerous. Trustworthy, fully licensed firms include **Addison Lee** (7387 8888), which will text you when the car arrives, and **Lady Cabs** (7272 3300), **Ladybirds** (8295 0101) and **Ladycars** (8558 9511), which employ only women drivers. Otherwise, text HOME to 60835 ('60tfl'; 35p plus standard call rate) for the numbers of the two nearest licensed minicab operators and the number for Taxi One-Number, which provides licensed black cabs. No matter who you choose, always ask the price when you book and confirm it with the driver.

Driving
Congestion charge

Driving into central London 7am-6pm Mon-Fri costs £10 (£9 by Auto Pay); the restricted area is shown at www.cclondon.com, but watch for signs and roads painted with a white 'C' on a red circle. Expect a fine of £60 if you fail to pay (£120 if you fail to pay within 14 days). Passes can be bought from garages, newsagents and NCP car parks; you can also pay at www.cclondon.com, on 0845 900 1234 or (after pre-registering on the website) by SMS. You can pay any time during the day or, for £2 more, until midnight on the next charging day.

Parking

Parking on a single or double yellow line, a red line or in residents' parking areas during the day is illegal, and you may be fined, clamped or towed. In the evening (from 7pm in much of central London) and at various weekend times parking on single yellow lines is legal and free. If you find a clear spot on a single yellow during the evening, look for a sign giving local regulations. During the day meters cost upwards of £1 for 15mins, limited to two hours, but they are free at certain evening and weekend times. Parking on double yellows and red routes is always illegal.

NCP 24hr **car parks** (0845 050 7080, www.ncp.co.uk) are numerous but cost £8/2hrs: try Arlington House, Arlington Street, in St James's, W1; Snowsfields in Southwark, SE1; and 4-5 Denman Street in Soho, W1.

Vehicle removal

If your car has disappeared, it's either been stolen or, if it was illegally parked, towed to a car pound. A release fee of £200 is levied for removal, plus £40 per day from the first midnight after removal. You'll also probably get a parking ticket of £60-£100 when you collect the car (£30-£50 if paid within 14 days). To find out how to retrieve your car, call 7747 4747.

Vehicle hire

Alamo (0870 400 4562, www.alamo. co.uk), **Budget** (0844 544 3439, www. budget.co.uk) and **Hertz** (0870 844 8844, www.hertz.co.uk) all have airport branches. Shop around for the best rate and always check the level of insurance.

Cycling

London isn't the friendliest town for cyclists, but the **London Cycle Network** (www.londoncyclenetwork. org.uk) and **London Cycling Campaign** (7234 9310, www.lcc.org. uk) help to keep things improving, and **Transport for London** (0843 222 1234, www.tfl.gov.uk) has been giving riders some great support, including online and printable route-finders.

Cycle hire

A City Hall-sponsored bike rental scheme launched in 2010, see box p81. South Bank's **London Bicycle Tour Company** (7928 6838, www.london bicycle.com) and **Velorution** (7637 4004, www.velorution.biz) in Fitzrovia are handy for longer rentals.

Walking

The best way to see London is on foot, but the street layout is complicated. There are street maps in the By Area chapters (pp57-192). For route advice, see www.tfl.gov.uk/gettingaround.

Resources A-Z

See http://europa.eu/travel for information on travelling to the UK from within the EU, including visa regulations and details of healthcare provision.

Accident & emergency

If you are so seriously ill or injured you need emergency care fast, call 999 or 112 free from any phone, including payphones – and ask for an ambulance, the fire service or police. For other medical emergencies, use the 24hr A&E departments at:

Chelsea & Westminster *369 Fulham Road, Chelsea, SW10 9NH (8746 8000, www.chelwest.nhs.uk). South Kensington tube.*
Royal London *Whitechapel Road, E1 1BB (7377 7000, www.bartsand thelondon.nhs.uk). Whitechapel tube.*
St Thomas's *Lambeth Palace Road, SE1 7EH (7188 7188, www.guysand stthomas.nhs.uk). Westminster tube or Waterloo tube/rail.*
University College *235 Grafton Road, Bloomsbury, NW1 2BU (0845 155 5000, www.uclh.nhs.uk). Euston Square or Warren Street tube.*

If you require treatment for an illness or injury that is not critical or life-threatening, go to a minor injury clinic or walk-in centre. No appointment is necessary. For a non-urgent police enquiry call 100.

Guy's Minor Injury Unit *Great Maze Pond, SE1 9RT (7188 7188). London Bridge tube/rail.*
St Barts Minor Injury Unit *West Smithfield, EC1A 7BE (7377 7000). St Paul's or Barbican tube.*
Soho Walk-In Centre *1 Frith Street, W1D 3HZ (7534 6500). Tottenham Court Road tube.*

Victoria Walk-In Centre *63 Buckingham Gate, SW1E 6AS (7340 1190). St James's Park tube.*

Credit card loss

American Express *01273 696933, www.americanexpress.com.*
Diners Club *0870 190 0011, www.dinersclub.co.uk.*
MasterCard/Eurocard *0800 964767, www.mastercard.com.*
Visa *7795 5777, www.visa.co.uk.*

Customs

For allowances, see www.hmrc.gov.uk.

Dental emergency

Dental care is free for the under-18s, students resident in this country and people on benefits, but all other patients must pay (NHS-eligible patients at a subsidised rate).

Disabled

London is a difficult place for disabled visitors, although legislation is slowly improving access and general facilities. The bus fleet is now low-floor for easier wheelchair access, but most tube stations still have escalator-only access; those with lifts are marked with a wheelchair symbol on tube maps. The *Tube Access Guide* booklet is free; call 0843 222 1234 for more details.

Most major attractions and hotels have good accessibility, though provisions for the hearing- or sight-disabled are patchier. The inclusive London website (www.inclusivelondon.com) gives details about the accessibility. *Access in London* is an invaluable reference book for disabled travellers, available for a £10 donation from **Access Project** (www.accessproject-phsp.org).

Electricity

The UK uses 220-240V, 50-cycle AC voltage and three-pin plugs.

Embassies & consulates

American Embassy *24 Grosvenor Square, Mayfair, W1A 2LQ (7499 9000, http://london.usembassy.gov). Bond Street or Marble Arch tube.* **Open** 8.30am-5.30pm Mon-Fri.
Australian High Commission *Australia House, Strand, Holborn, WC2B 4LA (7379 4334, www.uk. embassy.gov.au). Holborn or Temple tube.* **Open** 9am-5pm Mon-Fri.
Canadian High Commission *38 Grosvenor Street, Mayfair, W1K 4AA (7258 6600, www.canada.org.uk). Bond Street or Oxford Circus tube.* **Open** 8am-4pm Mon-Fri.
Embassy of Ireland *17 Grosvenor Place, Belgravia, SW1X 7HR (7235 2171, 7225 7700 passports & visas, www.embassyofireland.co.uk). Hyde Park Corner tube.* **Open** 9.30am-5.30pm Mon-Fri.
New Zealand High Commission *New Zealand House, 80 Haymarket, St James's, SW1Y 4TQ (7930 8422, www.nzembassy.com). Piccadilly Circus tube.* **Open** 9am-5pm Mon-Fri.

Internet

Most hotels have broadband and/or wireless access, and many cafés now offer wireless surfing.

Insurance

There's access to free or reduced-cost healthcare for residents in the European Economic Area and Switzerland (bring a valid European Health Insurance Card, www.ehic.org. uk), as well as some countries with bilateral agreements with the UK. We still recommend you take out appropriate travel insurance – it's essential for all visitors from any other country.

Left luggage

Bus and rail stations have left-luggage desks rather than lockers; call 0845 748 4950 for details.

Gatwick Airport *01293 502014 South Terminal, 01293 569900 North Terminal.*
Heathrow Airport *8745 5301 Terminal 1, 8759 3344 Terminal 3, 8897 6874 Terminal 4, 8759 3344 Terminal 5.*
London City Airport *7646 0162.*
Stansted Airport *01279 663213.*

Opening hours

Banks 9am-4.30pm (some close at 3.30pm, some 5.30pm) Mon-Fri; sometimes also Saturday mornings.
Businesses 9am-5pm Mon-Fri.
Post offices 9am-5.30pm Mon-Fri; 9am-noon Sat.
Pubs & bars 11am-11pm Mon-Sat; noon-10.30pm Sun.
Shops 10am-6pm Mon-Sat; many also open noon-6pm Sun.

Pharmacies

For advice on over-the-counter medication, sometimes including emergency contraception and sexual health advice, visit a pharmacist. Text 'pharmacy' to 64746 to find your nearest). Most pharmacies open 9am-6pm Mon-Sat.

Police

Look up 'Police' in the phone book or call 118 118, 118 500 or 118 888 if none of these police stations are convenient.

Charing Cross *Agar Street, Covent Garden, WC2N 4JP (0300 123 1212). Charing Cross tube/rail.*
Chelsea *2 Lucan Place, SW3 3PB (0300 123 1212). South Kensington tube.*
West End Central *27 Savile Row, Mayfair, W1S 2EX (0300 123 1212). Piccadilly Circus tube.*

Post

For general enquiries, call 0845 722 3344 or consult www.royalmail.com. Post offices are usually open 9am-6pm Mon-Fri and 9am-noon Sat, although the **Trafalgar Square Post Office** (24-28 William IV Street, WC2N 4DL, 0845 722 3344) opens 8.30am-6.30pm Mon-Fri and 9am-5.30pm Sat.

Smoking

Smoking is banned in enclosed public spaces, such as clubs, hotel foyers, shops, restaurants and public transport.

Telephones

London's dialling code is 020; standard landlines have eight digits after that. If you're calling from outside the UK, dial your international access code, then the UK code, 44, then the full London number, omitting the first 0 (Australia 61, Canada 1, New Zealand 64, Republic of Ireland 353, South Africa 27, USA 1). **US cellphone users** need a tri- or quad-band handset.

Public payphones take coins and/or credit cards. International calling cards are widely available.

Tickets

It's usually worth booking ahead – even obscure acts sell out, while major gigs and sport events do so in seconds. Agencies include **Ticketmaster** (0844 844 0444, www.ticketmaster.co.uk) and **See Tickets** (0871 220 0260, www.seetickets.com); they charge booking fees, so it's usually cheaper to go direct to the venue's box office. For West End tickets use **tkts** (p139).

Time

Greenwich Mean Time (GMT) is five hours ahead of US Eastern Standard time. In autumn (28 Oct 2012, 27 Oct 2013) clocks go back an hour to GMT; they go forward one hour to British Summer Time in spring (31 Mar 2013).

Tipping

Tip in taxis, minicabs, restaurants, hotels, hairdressers and some bars (but not pubs). Ten per cent is normal, with some restaurants adding a service charge of as much as 15%. Always check whether service has already been included in your bill - if it has there's no need to add a tip.

Tourist information

Britain & London Visitor Centre *1 Lower Regent Street, SW1 4XT (7808 3800, www.visitbritain.com). Piccadilly Circus tube.* **Open** 9.30am-6pm Mon; 9am-6pm Tue-Fri; 9am-5pm Sat; 10am-4pm Sun.
City of London Information Centre *St Paul's Churchyard, EC4M 8BX (7332 1456, www.cityoflondon. gov.uk). St Paul's tube.* **Open** 9.30am-5.30pm Mon-Sat; 10am-4pm Sun. Also offers tours with specialist City-trained guides.
Greenwich Tourist Information Centre *Discover Greenwich, Pepys House, 2 Cutty Sark Gardens, SE10 9LW (0870 608 2000, www.greenwich whs.org.uk). Cutty Sark DLR.* **Open** 10am-5pm daily.

Visas

Citizens of the EU don't require a visa to visit the UK; for limited tourist visits, citizens of the USA, Canada, Australia, New Zealand and South Africa can also enter the UK with only a passport. But *always* check the current situation at www.ukvisas.gov.uk well before you travel.

What's on

Time Out remains London's only quality listings magazine. It gives listings for the week from Thursday.

ESSENTIALS

Index

ESSENTIALS

ESSENTIALS